LB159
HENRY P. TRAWICK JR

FORTS WITHIN A FORT

NIAGARA'S REDOUBTS

BY
BRIAN LEIGH DUNNIGAN

OLD FORT NIAGARA ASSOCIATION, INC.
YOUNGSTOWN, NEW YORK
©1989

ISBN: 0-941967-08-5

This publication is made possible, in part, with public funds
from the New York State Council on the Arts

TABLE OF CONTENTS

**For Doris, Connie, Cordelia,
Sister Felicity Clare, Candi Sue,
and other characters as yet unrevealed.**

REDOUBTS, BLOCKHOUSES OR TOWERS?

AN INTRODUCTION TO A REDOUBTABLE TOPIC

Standing today in Old Fort Niagara are a pair of square stone towers, graying and long stripped of the whitewash which once covered and protected their walls. Although not as old nor as well known as the "French Castle" which faces them across the parade ground, these two buildings were constructed with similar purposes in mind and followed roughly parallel courses of development, use and reuse by Fort Niagara's British and United States garrisons. The two structures, termed variously throughout their histories "redoubts", "blockhouses" or "towers", were an integral part of the defenses of Fort Niagara from the 1770's until the end of the Civil War. As such, and like most of the surviving architecture of Old Fort Niagara, they long outlived their original designed purpose and survived only because of their massive construction and the fact that later tenants found new uses for the historic buildings.

Old Fort Niagara's stone towers were originally and most properly called "redoubts", and so they are known today. The term is generally an unfamiliar one, being rather specific to the technical aspects of fortification. Some will be familiar with the similar word, "redoubtable" ("formidable"), which is still a part of the language, although not often heard. Redoubtable, however, has an entirely different etymology than "redoubt". The latter word has made its way to us from the Medieval Latin for a "secret place". Although the original usage hardly describes the stone buildings at Old Fort Niagara, the relationship between a "secret place" and the strong, stone towers is apparent.

The pair of redoubts situated in Old Fort Niagara provide rare and virtually unique North American examples of a particular form of military architecture. A near-bewildering array of small fortifications known as "redoubts" guarded locations of strategic or tactical importance in seventeenth through nineteenth century America. These took a variety of shapes, forms of construction and appearances, and the term redoubt may be considered, functionally, to include almost any small, self-contained fortification without flanking devices such as bastions. A variety of military structures may be included under this definition,

An aerial view of Old Fort Niagara, 1960, showing the locations of the redoubts in the bastions. *Courtesy, New York Power Authority.*

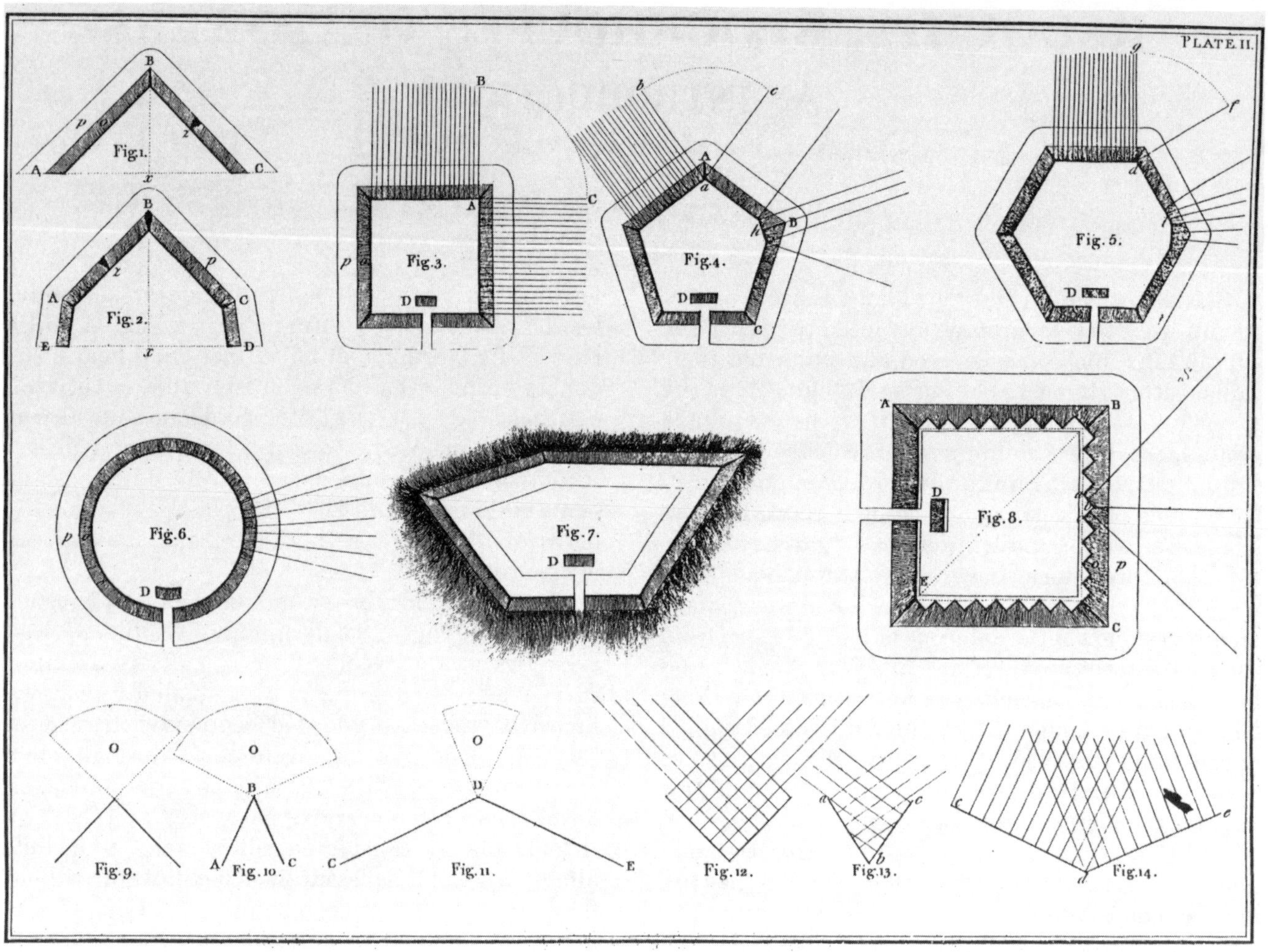

Lewis Lochée illustrated a variety of forms for redoubts in his 1780 *Elements of Field Fortification*. These would be employed in the sense of John Muller's third definition for a redoubt.

The South Redoubt. *OFN 5231/28C.*

from small, square, round or polygonal forts to the familiar log blockhouse of the American frontier when the latter stood alone and was not part of a larger fort.

The Old Fort Niagara redoubts differ from most such fortifications on this continent in that, like blockhouses, they were roofed and could be used to shelter men and supplies. The only other similar redoubt is a brick building at Fort Pitt (Pittsburgh, Pennsylvania), one of five erected in 1764. Although coming from the same tradition of military architecture, the Fort Pitt redoubts were designed to serve a different purpose than those at Fort Niagara. Aside from the single surviving Fort Pitt redoubt, only a few fortified towers or "keeps" situated in larger forts are related to the Fort Niagara redoubts. A number of "Martello towers" erected in Canada and the United States between 1796 and 1850 bear a superficial resemblance and perhaps a distant architectural relationship but were actually constructed for a very different purpose.

In order to properly appreciate the design of the Fort Niagara redoubts, it is necessary to first understand the term and the several ways in which it was applied by military engineers of the late eighteenth century. Early treatises, such as M. Le Blond's *The Military Engineer,* define redoubts primarily in relationship to a larger fortress. These ancillary fortifications might be located in the bastions or the outer works to serve as strong points or citadels.[1] By the 1770's, the time during which Fort Niagara's redoubts were constructed, the term had broadened somewhat to include small fortifications located at a distance from the main fortress. John Muller's *A Treatise Containing the Elementary Part of Fortification, Regular and Irregular* clearly describes three major forms of redoubt:

> Redoubt, *is a kind of work placed beyond the glacis, of various forms.*
>
> Redoubt, *is also the name of a small work made in a ravelin, of the same form.*
>
> Redoubt, *is likewise a square work without any bastions, placed at some distance from a fortification, to guard a pass, or to prevent the enemy from approaching that way.*[2]

The three definitions describe small fortifications serving very different purposes. The first type was a structure placed beyond the "glacis" or outer slope of a fortress. There it could serve as an advance post and strong point from which to annoy besiegers before they reached the outermost defenses. The second form of redoubt was located within the outer defenses themselves, specifically within a "ravelin" - a work, usually triangular or pentagonal in form, placed before the "curtain" or main wall of the fortress to cover it from enemy fire. The third and final definition described a small outpost placed "at some distance" from the main fortress to guard a spot deemed important to its approaches or some other strategic purpose.

The fortifications required to serve the functions noted by Muller did not need to be particularly sophisticated. Redoubts associated with fortresses did not require flanking structures since they would be covered from the main defenses, and those used in the field were not expected to hold out against a formal attack. The ability to "flank" all angles of the walls of a fortress was particularly important. It allowed defenders an unobstructed field of fire for muskets and cannon directed along all sections of the walls and assured that attackers would find no blind spots where they might take shelter from the hail of shot directed against them. According to Captain George Smith's *An Universal Military Dictionary*, "any fortification, which has no defence but right forward, is faulty, and to make it complete, one part ought to flank the other."[3]

"Bastions" (projections from the corners of a fort) were the most typical flanking structures. True bastions consisted of two "faces" and two "flanks". The latter stood at right angles to the main walls or "curtains." This allowed the fire of defenders in the bastions to enfilade the curtains. The goal was to leave no "dead ground" where attackers could find shelter. The primary rule in designing a bastion was that "every part of it must be seen and defended from some other part," and, according to Smith and others, "on them the defence chiefly depends".[4] Redoubts, by definition, *lacked* bastions. Those associated with fortresses had no need of them, while the absence of bastions was prescribed for redoubts placed at a distance from major fortifications. While not as defensible as bastioned forts because, in the words of a nineteenth century military engineer, "there is a sector without fire in front of each salient [corner]," their simplicity made redoubts well-suited for temporary field fortifications.[5]

The North Redoubt. *OFN 803/30C.*

The materials used to construct redoubts varied greatly. European examples were built primarily of stone, brick or earth. The ready availability of timber in North America made wood an inexpensive and practical alternative. Many redoubts of American wars were constructed with horizontal log, log and earth or vertical stockade walls. The selection of construction materials depended upon the degree of permanence desired. Most field or frontier works were erected using either earth or timber or a combination of the two, and few lasted longer than the duration of a campaign or a winter encampment.

The availability of large timber led to the development of perhaps the best known type of fortification in the history of North America - the "blockhouse". The term is rife with connotations of the developing fron-

A decrepit South Redoubt on the eve of restoration, 1929. *OFN 4454/28A.*

The North Redoubt was still in basically sound condition in 1929. *OFN 4446/30A.*

tier where the easily-constructed blockhouses frequently sheltered embattled pioneers from the Native American occupants of the new land. Blockhouses were also used by the military, often as part of a larger fort. Strangely, the term "blockhouse" does not appear in the major eighteenth century works on military engineering nor in Smith's 1779 dictionary, despite the fact that the blockhouse had been in widespread use in North America for a century. The name probably derives from the German "*blochaus*" meaning "a house which blocks a pass." It is likely that the horizontal log North American blockhouse had its origins on the early New England frontier and spread from there to the rest of the continent. Originally, the term seems to have referred simply to a defensive structure and not to a particular form of construction. By the eighteenth century, however, the classic American blockhouse was well-developed. Whether intended for civilian or military use, the structure usually included the elements of horizontal log or masonry construction, a "machicolated" or overhanging upper story permitting downward flanking fire through openings in the floor and narrow loopholes or ports for musket and cannon fire.[6]

Blockhouses took many forms. They could be square, rectangular or polygonal in plan. Some were of only one story, while other two-story designs lacked the overhanging upper floor. Blockhouses were often used, as were those constructed at Fort Mackinac in 1798, to replace and serve the function of bastions in frontier military posts. Their totally enclosed and roofed construction allowed such buildings to serve the additional purposes of barracks and storehouses.[7] Blockhouses were often constructed within redoubts or even complete forts to strengthen their interior defense and provide shelter. They might also stand alone without additional fortifications as did a number of such buildings constructed in Canada during the eighteenth and nineteenth centuries.[8] Thus, while a blockhouse was not necessarily a redoubt, it could serve the purposes of one.

Fort Niagara's redoubts were most frequently referred to as "blockhouses" following renovation of the earthworks in the 1770's. While this is a misnomer in terms of the original purpose of the buildings, many late eighteenth and nineteenth century observers viewed the redoubts as potential strong points *within* Fort Niagara. D.H. Mahan described this role for blockhouses in his 1836 treatise. Mahan noted that they could be useful in "positions covered by extensive earthen works" where "they might serve, in case of the main works being forced, as rallying points under cover of which the main body of troops may retreat with safety."[9]

The Old Fort Niagara redoubts are also frequently described as "towers", especially during the War of 1812 when their roofs had been removed and the top floors converted to elevated gun platforms. They had certainly assumed the appearance of towers. The use of the term was undoubtedly influenced by the contemporary popularity of a type of structure known commonly as a "Martello tower". Large numbers of these were built along the coasts of the British Isles during the Napoleonic Wars. Round towers had been constructed in Halifax as early as the 1790's, and the design enjoyed some popularity in Canada and the United States until the 1850's. The true Martello tower was a circular masonry structure of two stories with a bombproof arch above the second story. The top of the building supported from one to four cannon, and the interior provided space for quarters, storerooms and powder magazines. Access to the building was by means of a doorway on the exterior of the second floor reached by a moveable drawbridge or ladder. These buildings, like blockhouses, are sometimes found alone or sometimes surrounded by simple outer works.[10] A

Martello tower, although not technically a redoubt, could also serve the purpose of one.

Contemporary comparisons between the Fort Niagara redoubts and Martello towers is understandable. The Niagara buildings had always mounted light artillery on their top floors. Their resemblance to towers increased greatly in the autumn of 1812 when the roofs were removed to allow a better field of fire for the guns. In his work on Martello towers, Ivan J. Saunders notes that the earliest Canadian examples were constructed before the 1794 incident which gave Martello towers their name and that the origins of their design were unclear. Similar structures were being built on the British Channel Islands by the late 1770's, and British engineers were familiar with defensible towers from the Mediterranean, notably the island of Minorca which they had occupied during the eighteenth century.[11] Perhaps the design of the Fort Niagara redoubts was influenced by similar but earlier Mediterranean contacts. It seems likely that the brick tower begun in 1814 in Fort Mississauga, at the mouth of the Niagara River, owes some of its design elements to the older buildings in Fort Niagara as well as to contemporary Martello towers.[12] These possibilities will be discussed later.

Having described the various types of structures with which the Fort Niagara buildings have been confused or associated, we should return to the design and use of redoubts in the eighteenth century. All three types of Muller's redoubts are to be found in North America. Some examples will serve to further describe their purposes. Muller's third form of redoubt was very common. This was the "square" work without bastions located to guard an important pass. Many such fortifications were employed in the campaigns of the French and Indian War and the American Revolution to protect camps, bridges and roads. They were certainly not all square, and later military engineering manuals describe a variety of shapes to be determined "by the spot of ground on which it is raised and the purposes for which it is constructed."[13] Redoubts played an important part in the battles around Saratoga in 1777 and in other actions of the American Revolution.

Redoubts of various descriptions had been used by military forces at Niagara well before construction of the stone buildings. The earliest fortification on the site was a small protected storehouse erected by the explorer René-Robert Cavelier, Sieur de La Salle in 1679. Descriptions of Fort Conti are scanty, the best being from La Salle's own account:

> ... *I contented myself with making there two redoubts 40 feet square, upon a point easy of defense, made of great timbers, one upon another, musket proof, and joined by a palisade ...*[14]

These redoubts were placed to protect the storehouse which was presumably located within the stockade connecting the two horizontal log structures.[15] Muller does not describe a redoubt in this context, but a function similar to that intended by La Salle appears in the earlier treatise by Le Blond. The latter work is more relevant to redoubts constructed in the late seventeenth century. Le Blond's second definition roughly fits La Salle's fortification:

> Redoubt, *a bastion which strengthens the gorge of the side of the place, and serves the same use as a citadel.*[16]

La Salle's redoubts, therefore, probably served the same function as bastions.

The West Blockhouse at Fort Mackinac, Michigan, one of three constructed by United States troops in 1798. The first story and basement are masonry. The second story is made of squared timbers covered with weatherboards. The building displays most features of the classic American blockhouse, notably the "machicolated" or overhung second floor. *Courtesy, Mackinac Island State Park Commission.*

A redoubt of Muller's third definition had also been constructed at Niagara prior to 1770. The "French Castle" of 1726, earliest building of Fort Niagara, was based on a plan for a "machicolated redoubt" prepared by Gaspard-Joseph Chaussegros de Léry, in 1714. De Léry's original proposal was intended as a practical and relatively inexpensive design for guarding passes and bridges in Europe.[17] His stone towers were machicolated, that is the uppermost story overhung the facades to allow vertical flanking fire through openings in the floor. The design of the stone house erected at Niagara in 1726 was modified to give it a less warlike appearance, but a machicolated redoubt constructed by de Léry at Fort St. Frédéric (Crown

Sir William Johnson constructed a pair of stone blockhouses in 1764 to flank his Mohawk River mansion. The vestigial machicolations of their second floors were not functional. *Courtesy, New York State Office of Parks, Recreation and Historic Preservation, Johnson Hall State Historic Site.*

Point on Lake Champlain) in 1737 was truer to his original plan.[18] Although both buildings were major pieces of construction enclosed by outer works, de Léry considered them redoubts by virtue of the fact that they were far from formal fortresses and guarded passes of vital importance to the colony of New France. A year after the establishment of the stone house at Niagara, the British erected a similar building at Oswego. De Léry, who observed the rival post, described it as a "machicolated redoubt". The structure displayed a strong resemblance to his 1714 design and also incorporated elements of the traditional American blockhouse.[19]

Another and perhaps better application of Muller's third definition may also be found at Niagara. During the summer of 1763 the Indian tribes of the Great Lakes rose against the British. Most of the small forts of the region quickly fell to stratagem or assault. Only Detroit, Fort Pitt and Niagara were able to maintain themselves. Detroit's position was tenuous and totally dependent upon the arrival of supplies and reinforcements from Niagara. These had to transit an exposed, eight-mile overland route around Niagara Falls. The security of this portage was found sadly wanting on September 13, 1763, when a large party of Seneca Indians ambushed and obliterated a column of empty wagons and the relief force which attempted to rescue it.[20] Three days after the disaster Fort Niagara's commandant, Lieutenant Colonel William Browning, predicted that the British could expect "Constant insults of this sort untill Posts can be made at Different distances on the Waggon Road."[21]

The following year's campaign was aimed at putting down the uprising and reestablishing British control of the lakes. Colonel John Bradstreet was ordered to lead an army to Detroit, and his force required a secure supply line. For the Niagara Portage, Bradstreet specified "small & Secure Redoubts at about Eight hundred yards distant from each other across the Carrying Place." Each was garrisoned by eight to ten men during the campaign.[22] Construction was accomplished during June and early July of 1764 under the supervision of Lieutenant John Montresor. Eight stockaded redoubts and one of horizontal log construction were erected along the road.[23] A plan prepared by Lieutenant Bernard Ratzer, one of Montresor's assistant engineers, illustrates the simplicity of these structures. A square enclosure made of vertical wooden pickets was backed by an earthen firing step or "banquette" to allow defenders to fire through raised loopholes in the walls. One side was pierced by a gate and the side opposite by a cannon port.[24] Presumably, the single horizontal log redoubt followed the same plan. These tiny structures served their purpose and were abandoned at the end of the Indian war.

Examples of Muller's first definition of redoubt, "a kind of work placed beyond the glacis of various forms," are also to be found with frequency in America. These were associated with some of the larger colonial fortresses, notably Ticonderoga and the huge British fort at Crown Point on Lake Champlain. The latter post included three outposts, the "Grenadier's", "Light Infantry" and "Gage's" redoubts. All were polygonal in form and constructed of double horizontal log walls filled with earth, the same technique used in the fortress itself. They were placed across the Crown Point peninsula to serve as advance posts and to cover the approaches to the fort.[25]

Redoubts of the second definition, "a small work made in a ravelin, of the same form," were also associated with fortresses. This type is found less frequently in a North American context. The surviving redoubt at Fort Pitt falls broadly within this definition, although it might also be taken as a structure of Muller's first definition since it was located at the edge of the ruined glacis. While the Fort Pitt redoubt was not actually within a ravelin, it had the general shape, location and orientation of one. It was placed where a ravelin would have been sited to cover the "Lower Town" (northwest) Curtain of Fort Pitt which had been severely undermined by rampaging flood waters in 1762 and 1763. The damaged fortress had been held against the Indians during the summer of 1763, but future security would have required costly repairs to the main walls. The Fort Pitt redoubt was constructed by order of Colonel Henry Bouquet with two others to cover the equally damaged "Ohio" and "Monongahela" Curtains. It seems likely that all three were of the same general design. Two more redoubts later constructed beyond the outer works of Fort Pitt appear to have more clearly been intended to serve the purposes of Muller's first definition.[26]

The Fort Pitt redoubt is an amazing survival of eighteenth century military construction. Architecturally, it bears the closest resemblance to the Old Fort Niagara redoubts of any North American examples. Fort Pitt's redoubt also bears the closest functional resemblance to the Fort Niagara buildings. Like the latter structures, it was originally intended to strengthen deteriorated regular fortifications against Indian attack. The Fort Pitt building is pentagonal in plan, two stories high and constructed of brick on a tall stone foundation. It is loopholed for musketry on both floors but has no cannon ports. Like the Fort Niagara redoubts, it is roofed, although there seems to have been no provision for quartering in the relatively small building since it lacks fireplaces. The single entrance is on the side which faced the "Lower Town" Curtain where friendly access to the redoubt would have been protected by fire from the fort. Anyone advancing against the curtain would have encountered heavy musket fire directed against their flanks and rear until the redoubt had been captured. Undoubtedly because of its appearance, the building today is known popularly as "The Blockhouse".[27]

The "Murney Tower" in Kingston, Ontario is typical of the sophisticated Martellos constructed in Canada in the 1840's. *Courtesy, Environment Canada, Canadian Park Service.*

A square tower with rounded corners is the central feature of Fort Mississauga, begun in 1814 across the river from Fort Niagara. The brick structure appears to combine elements of the Martello tower and the square redoubts in Fort Niagara. The roof shown here dates to the late nineteenth century. *OFN 4632 / 132.*

The Niagara redoubts do not neatly fit into any of the three definitions provided by Muller in 1774. A few years later, however, Smith's *An Universal Military Dictionary* broadened the second definition somewhat to note that a redoubt could be "made sometimes in a bastion" as well as within a ravelin.[28] Here the definition finally applies to the situation of Fort Niagara's redoubts. Each is located within one of

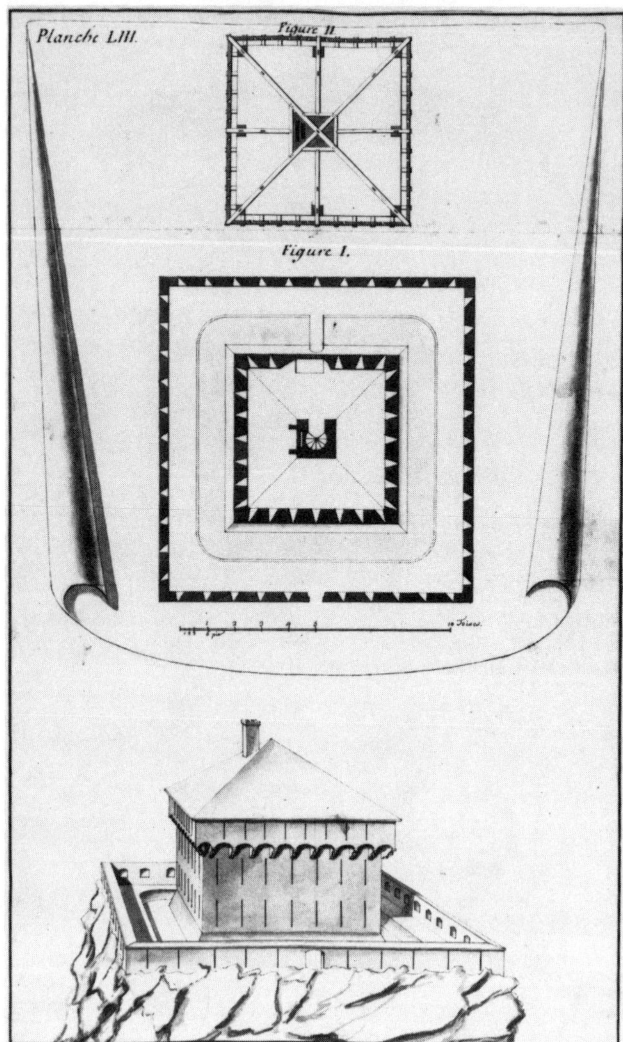

This "machicolated redoubt" was proposed, in Gaspard-Joseph Chaussegros de Léry's 1714 treatise of fortification, as an economical way to block narrow passes. *Courtesy, National Archives of Canada, C105265.*

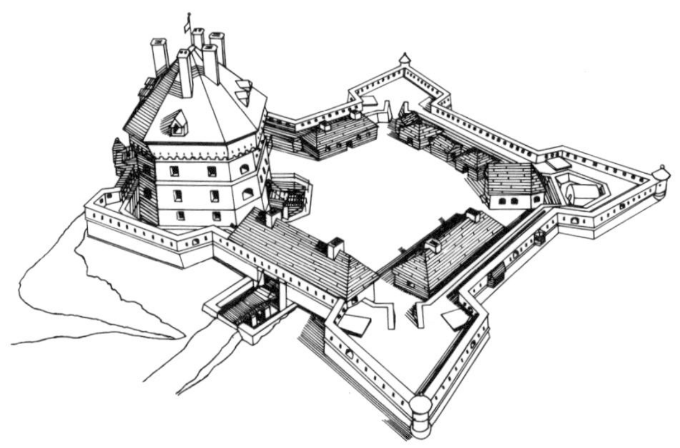

The machicolated redoubt constructed by de Léry in 1737 at Crown Point served the same function as Fort Niagara's "French Castle" but bore a closer resemblance to the engineer's proposed building of 1714. *Courtesy, New York State Office of Parks, Recreation and Historic Preservation, Crown Point State Historic Site.*

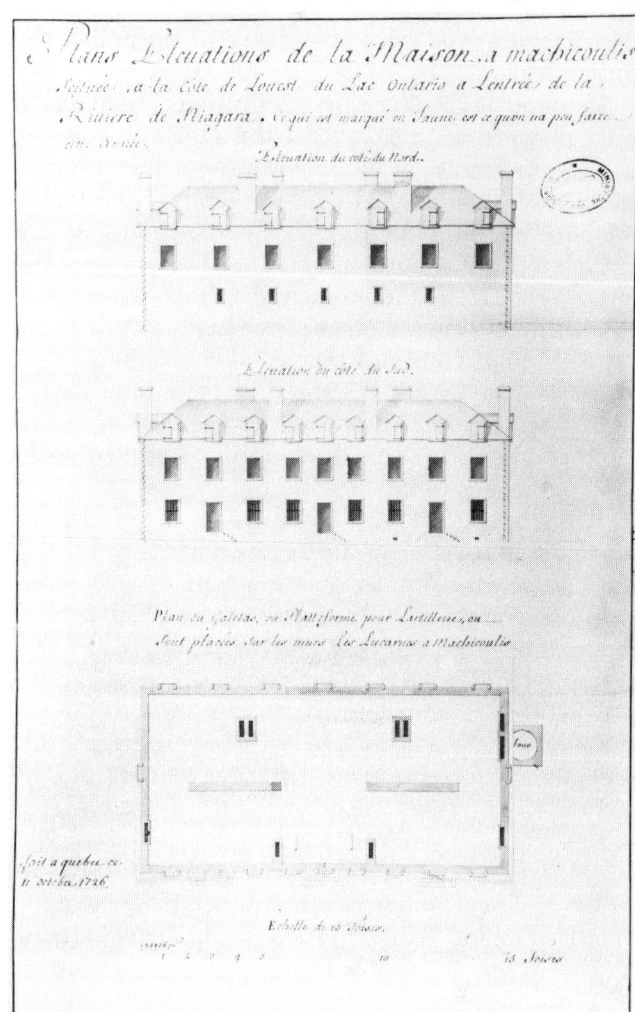

Fort Niagara's "Maison à machicoulis" of 1726 was a variation of de Léry's 1714 design for a machicolated redoubt. *Courtesy, National Archives of Canada, C16289.*

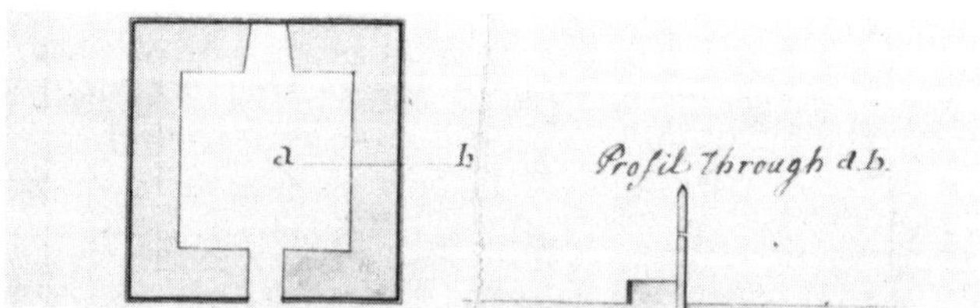

Plan, by Lt. Bernard Ratzer, for the stockaded redoubts constructed on the Niagara Portage in 1764. *Courtesy, William L. Clements Library.*

the fort's land-side bastions (technically "half" or "demi-bastions") where, as in the case of a redoubt located in a ravelin, it could serve as a citadel and place of refuge for the defenders.

The pair of stone redoubts in Old Fort Niagara have their roots in a clearly defined tradition of eighteenth century military architecture. The terminology used to describe them varies with the time period, the orientation of their observers and the condition of the outer defenses. In a sense, the structures are at once redoubts, blockhouses and towers -

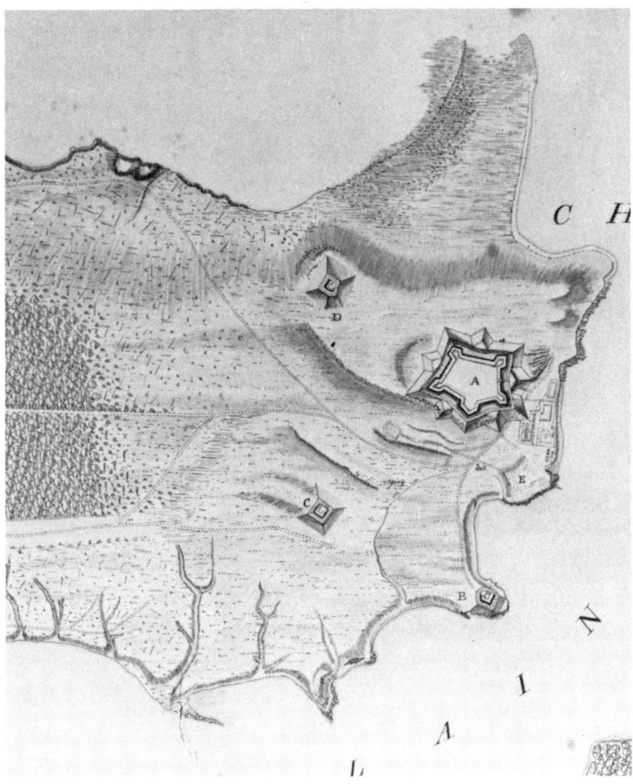

Three redoubts of Muller's first definition served as advance posts for the huge British fort begun at Crown Point in 1759. *Courtesy, New York State Office of Parks, Recreation and Historic Preservation, Crown Point State Historic Site.*

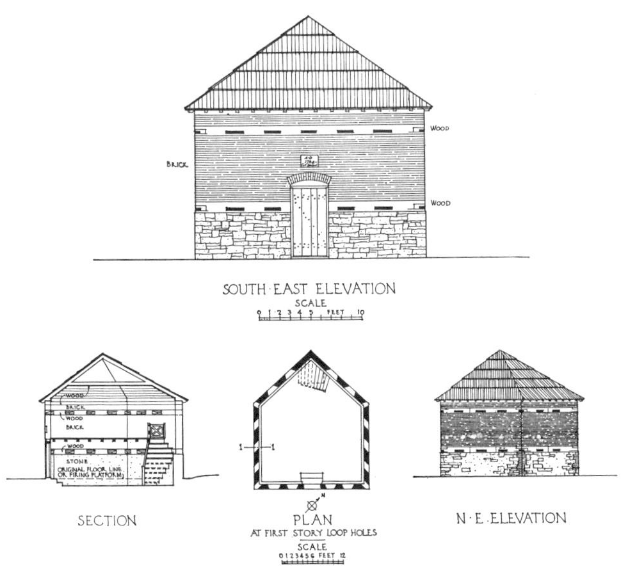

The pentagonal Fort Pitt redoubt of 1764 strongly resembles a blockhouse. It lacked a fireplace or any facilities for accommodating a permanent garrison. *Drawing by Charles M. Stotz in "Defense in the Wilderness".*

towers by virtue of their architectural design, blockhouses because of their function as strong points within the fort and at the main gate, and redoubts due to their location within the total eighteenth century plan of Fort Niagara. To their designer and builder, however, the buildings were clearly redoubts, placed

The overgrown ruins of "Gage's Redoubt" at Crown Point. The walls were constructed of horizontal logs and earth. *Courtesy, New York State Office of Parks, Recreation and Historic Preservation, Crown Point State Historic Site.*

Like Fort Niagara's buildings, the Fort Pitt redoubt was roofed, giving it the appearance of a blockhouse. *Courtesy, Pennsylvania Historical and Museum Commission, Fort Pitt Museum.*

within the bastions of the fortress at a time when the outer defenses of Niagara, like those of Fort Pitt, were crumbling and in need of a relatively inexpensive and effective means of repelling Indian attack. Despite the specific circumstances and needs surrounding their construction, however, the buildings were laid out so that they would be useful to the overall plan of the fortress. In later years, after the main walls had been substantially renovated, the redoubts would thus continue to play an active and important role in the land-side defense of Fort Niagara.

"TWO REDOUBTS FOR THE BETTER DEFENCE OF THAT PLACE"

1766 - 1775

The history of the Fort Niagara redoubts cannot be told out of context of the land-side defenses which they strengthened and supported. They were erected at a time when the walls of Fort Niagara were virtually in ruins, and the stone buildings were intended as an economical solution to the problem of defending a rambling fortress with the smallest possible number of troops. In later years, after the earthworks had been reconstructed along their original lines, the redoubts were positioned to continue an effective role in the defense of the post - initially to provide defensive fire into the ditches from cannon mounted on their upper stories and later as elevated gun platforms from which enemy positions across the river could be bombarded. The buildings were useful adjuncts to Niagara's fortifications from their construction until at least the 1860's. The nature of their utility changed during this time, however, with the shifting requirements of the defense of the position at the mouth of the Niagara River.

The story of Niagara's fortifications is one of constant change. The earliest posts on the site were simple log stockades erected in 1679, 1687 and 1726. The first two, Forts Conti and Denonville respectively, each stood for only a year. Permanent establishment of "Fort Niagara" came in 1726 with construction of the machicolated stone house, known popularly today as the "French Castle". The building had been enclosed by a wooden stockade with four bastions by 1727. This type of fortification would protect the post until 1755. None of the earliest enclosures utilized more area than the extreme tip of the peninsula jutting into the Niagara River, and all were simple wilderness forts defensible against Indians or British raiders equipped only with small arms.[29]

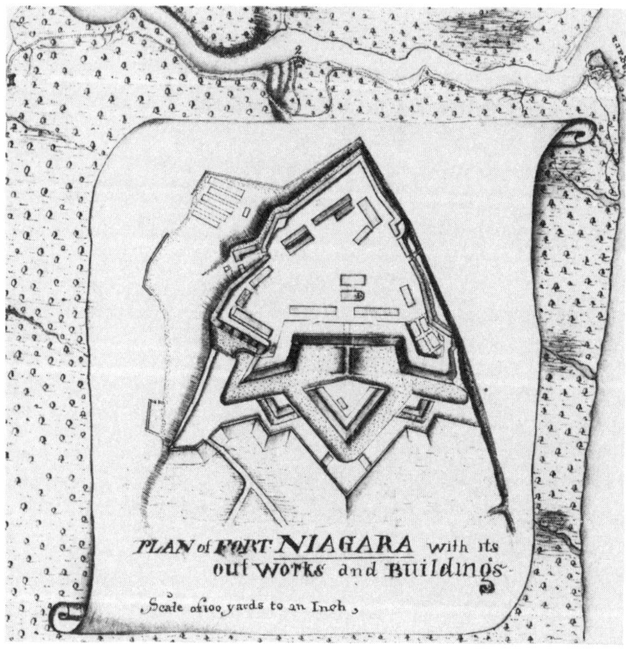

The French earthworks had not been altered by the time Lt. George Demler prepared this plan of Fort Niagara in 1762. *Courtesy, British Library, Crown Maps, cxxi, 73.*

In less than thirty years the changing military situation along the Great Lakes and the boundaries between French and British North America would render the simple wooden walls of Fort Niagara terribly obsolete. The outbreak of the French and Indian War in 1754 was quickly followed by the introduction to both colonies of large numbers of trained European regular soldiers. For the first time, Fort Niagara was exposed to the possibility of assault by forces armed with artillery. Even cannon of light caliber would have found the tottering stockades little challenge. The Governor of New France pessimistically reported, in the summer of 1755, that not only was Fort Niagara inadequate, but it was so dilapidated that it would have been "impossible to put a peg in it without causing it to crumble."[30]

These nearly worthless walls were about to be threatened. During the summer and early fall of 1755, British troops assembled at Oswego for a stroke against Niagara. Under the leadership of General William Shirley, they were to have cooperated in a multi-pronged attack upon the frontiers of New France by capturing Niagara and severing French communications with the West. Fortunately for Niagara's few defenders, Shirley proved incapable of moving his army along Lake Ontario to his goal. By autumn the expedition had been postponed.[31] The French reacted rapidly. In September Governor Vaudreuil ordered the regular army battalion of *Guienne* to Niagara to provide labor for rebuilding the defenses. Direction of this work was placed in the capable hands of Captain Pierre Pouchot, an infantry officer of the battalion of *Béarn* who was acknowledged to be "in possession of engineering talents." Pouchot and the soldiers were to place Niagara "in the best posture of defense" and render the position tenable against a regular siege.[32]

Although much was accomplished that first winter, it was two full years before Pouchot could report that "Fort Niagara and its buildings were finished, and its covered ways stockaded."[33]

The alterations made to Niagara between 1755 and 1757 were the most significant in its history and define the shape of the fort to this day. The small wooden stockade around the French Castle was abandoned, and the post was expanded to encompass most of the point. The new walls were laid out in the formal military engineering tradition of eighteenth century Europe following the system developed by Sebastien le Prestre de Vauban. Great economy was employed in designing the fortress. Because of its situation, Fort Niagara was most likely to be attacked from the east. Pouchot's fortifications reflected this. Across the neck of the peninsula he placed a curtain wall with two half-bastions. In advance of this line was a ditch, outworks, a covered way, glacis and other basic elements of a fortress intended to resist artillery fire. The sides toward the Niagara River and Lake Ontario were not as heavily fortified because the threat against them was less. Access to the interior was over a drawbridge and through an entrance, dubbed the "Gate of the Five Nations", located on the river side of the south or river half-bastion. Additional barracks and storehouses were constructed within the fort to accommodate a greatly enlarged garrison.[34]

Pouchot's work totally changed the nature of the defenses of Niagara. After 1755 the walls were intended to resist a European enemy armed with siege artillery. The increased area of the fort required a much larger force of soldiers to properly defend its walls. Wartime expediency made it necessary for Pouchot and his men to construct the new defenses simply, using a relatively impermanent technique. Earth excavated from the ditches was thrown up to form the walls. These were faced with sod pinned securely in place with wooden pegs. The sod would grow into a mass of vegetation to impede erosion, but it was no substitute over time for masonry construction. While the sophisticated defenses, large garrison and hasty construction methods were necessary during the height of the French and Indian War, all would present difficulties to an economy-minded British administration during the peace that followed 1763.

Two years after Pouchot completed his alterations to Fort Niagara, he was called upon to defend the post against a besieging force. The long-awaited British arrived on July 6, 1759. They found a strong fort and proceeded to approach it in the same fashion as they might a similar fortification in Europe. Pouchot and his garrison resisted for nineteen days, but on July 25 they were forced to yield to fatigue, overwhelming artillery fire and the relentless approach of the British siege lines.[35] The French garrison had no sooner been marched off as prisoners-of-war when British work parties began repairing the battered fortress. By August 26 Niagara's commandant could report that he had "put the place on as respectable a footing as it was when wee first broke ground," but nothing more had been done than to repair the French

Maj. Gen. Thomas Gage, Commander-in-Chief in North America, found himself responsible for numerous, rapidly decaying forts. *Courtesy, William L. Clements Library.*

Lt. Col. John Vaughan, 46th Regiment of Foot, was one of many British commandants who complained about the condition of Fort Niagara. *Courtesy, William L. Clements Library.*

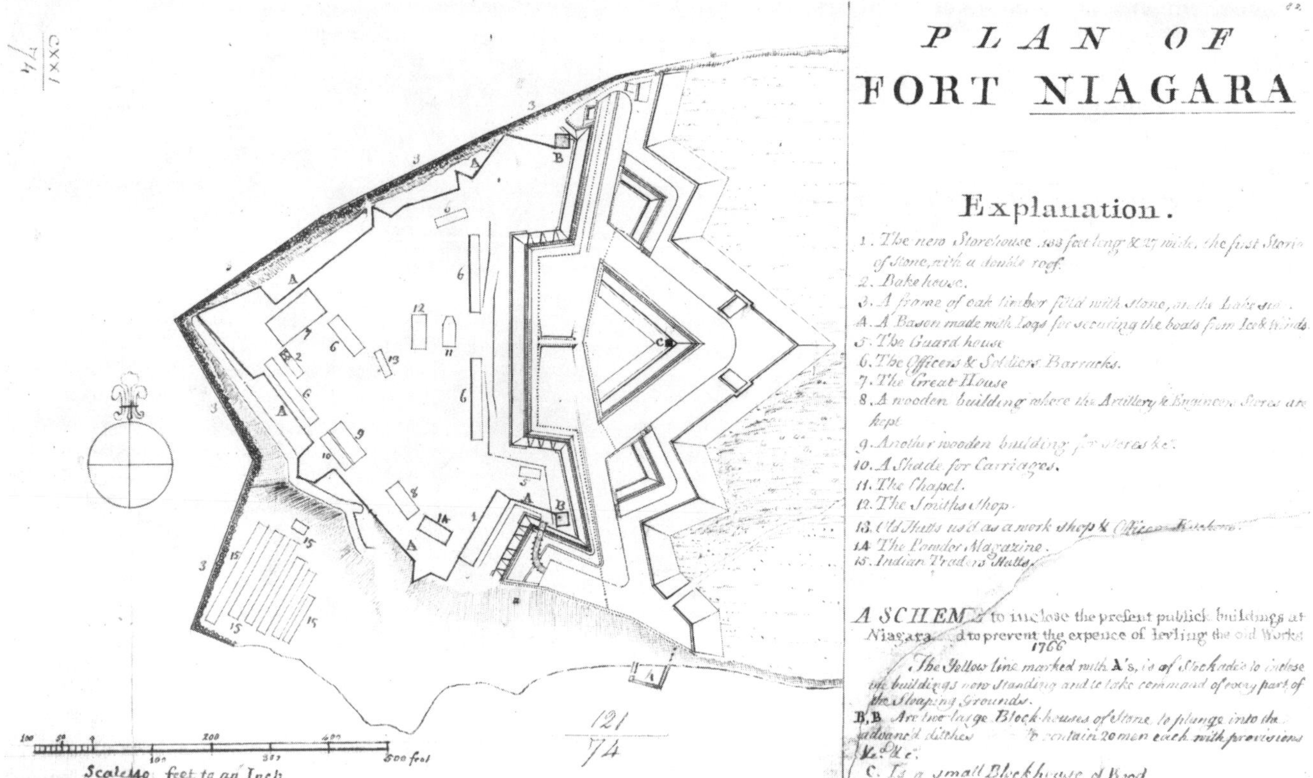

The 1766 plan to enclose Fort Niagara with stockades was the first to project "two large Block-houses of Stone to plunge into the advanc'd ditches." They are marked "B". *Courtesy, British Library, Crown Maps, cxxi, 74.*

fortifications.[36] From this time on, Fort Niagara's British commandants would battle the ravages of climate in a largely futile attempt to preserve the sodworks in defensible condition. They were under no illusions. By September,1759, Lieutenant Colonel William Farquhar had summarized the problem of maintaining Fort Niagara's earthen walls:

> *... This Fortification, I am now too well convinc'd, will be constant work for any Garrison wee can afford to leave in it. The nature of the Earth is such that rain, much more frost and snow, will tumble it, and spring and autumn must be employ'd in repairs, till revettd with stone, and Brick, as our Enemys for certain intended ...*[37]

Expensive masonry retaining walls were out of the question, however, and Farquhar's comments presaged a litany of complaints directed to superior officers by Fort Niagara's commandants over the next decade. Lieutenant Colonel John Vaughan, early in 1765, aptly compared Fort Niagara and its extensive walls to "a ruinous old house which must always be attended with a constant expense and which must be the case always."[38] Such opinions were not welcome news to British commanders-in-chief charged with maintaining secure defenses in the colonies.

Almost any type of fortification was a perishable affair in the severe climate of North America. Wooden stockades soon rotted while even good masonry was susceptible to frost and water damage. Fortifications could be maintained, at a price, but there had to be reason for doing so. Justification for repairing the extensive earthen walls of Fort Niagara began to fade soon after its capture by the British. New France was surrendered to Britain in September, 1760, and the only hostile regular troops within striking distance of Fort Niagara laid down their arms. The worldwide conflict between France and Britain was not yet over, however, and Spain would join the fray in 1761. The soldiers of the garrison therefore continued to repair, resod and improve the walls. Their labor was supplemented by that of three hundred New Jersey provincials during the summer of 1762. The land-side defenses were still not brought under control. [39] When a general peace was concluded in 1763, however, all likelihood of a formal attack on Fort Niagara disappeared.

The same year saw a new threat materialize - one which would seriously affect the nature of Fort Niagara's defenses and eventually result in the construction of its redoubts. With the French military threat effectively removed from North America, the British concentrated on establishing control of former enemy possessions in Canada, the Ohio Valley and the Great Lakes. This activity was suddenly halted in the early summer of 1763 when the western Indians rose against the British. Their fury was directed against the small military posts scattered throughout the region. Most fell within a few weeks. The larger forts at Pittsburgh, Detroit and Niagara were preserved, and they served as bases for counterattacks after adequate numbers of troops had been assembled. Fort Niagara was not attacked, although a considerable amount of raiding activity was directed at the nearby portage. The post was unprepared for this sort of threat, despite the considerable amount of labor expended on its fortifications during the preceding four years. Additional defenses, chiefly stockades and blockhouses, were quickly cobbled together to secure the garrison against "Sculking parties & c." of Indians. The great earthworks were of little use in this type of war.[40] During a peace council held with the Indians at Niagara in the summer of 1764, many warriors were, in fact, able to slip in and out of the fort's defenses at will.[41]

The Indian uprising carried into 1764 and occasioned a great deal of effort on the part of British military forces in North America before it was finally put down. The events of 1763-64 had a sobering effect on the British colonial administration and would influence official policy toward the interior posts and relations with the Indians until the American Revolution. Because of their isolation and the way in which they scattered troop strengths, many of the small forts were not reoccupied after the conclusion of the Indian war. The primary posts of the Great Lakes - Oswego, Niagara, Detroit, and Michilimackinac - were regarrisoned, however, since they provided at least a modicum of control over the area. Major General Thomas Gage realized their importance and summarized the reasons for their existence:

> *The Forts upon the Lakes, kept up for the Purposes of being some Check over the Indians, by having a Force with Military Stores lodged in their Country, Serving as Places of Rendezvous in Case of a war with them, and according to late Regulations, being the only Marts for the Trade; are as few as can be maintained for the Purposes Mentiond.*[42]

Security was particularly important in these circumstances. Post commandants were cautioned to be on their guard not to be surprised by the Indians. After 1764, troops were concentrated in the major forts to allow larger bodies of them to be assembled in the event of another Indian war, but garrisons overall were reduced "to such numbers as shall be merely necessary for their Defense."[43] The smaller numbers of soldiers complicated efforts to keep the posts in repair. Michilimackinac, Detroit and Fort Erie (located at the head of the portage above Niagara Falls) were stockades. Although their wooden pickets rotted quickly, they could be replaced with a minimum of labor. Fort Ontario at Oswego was a large regular fortification constructed of "logwork" - a double horizontal log wall with the space between filled with earth. The problems of its maintenance were solved when the post was abandoned in 1769. Niagara, another regular fortification with its rambling sodded earthworks, was a particular problem, and yet the post was by far the most important of those in the interior of the continent by virtue of its control of the Niagara Portage.

Preoccupied with defense against Indians and the need to keep up the posts, General Gage suggested that those of the Great Lakes and the rest of the interior be replaced as they deteriorated with smaller but more durable construction. He recommended, in 1766, that:

> ... *As the Forts in general decay very fast, and are falling into Ruins, I would take the liberty to propose instead of repairing them, at a great expence, and keeping them on the extensive plan they now are, that as they fall in ruin, they should be rebuilt in a much smaller Compass of Stone or Brick, It's not proposed to erect strong works to resist Artillery, a Wall of about two feet thick, and about Eighteen feet high with Loop-holes, Some small peices of Ordnance, and a Stage of Wood erected withinside, for the Defendants to stand upon, and for Platforms for the Artillery will be the best security against Indians. These kinds of Forts will be more durable and lasting than those we have made with Loggs and Earth, which require a great number of hands, and which we find by experience perish in a very few Years.*[44]

These small works were to be constructed with bastions for the artillery.[45] In their general tone, however, Gage's comments suggest the substantial effort that would soon be invested in constructing the redoubts at Niagara.

While General Gage's idea of gradual replacement of the interior posts with smaller but more durable works was excellent in theory, it was not carried out. Most fortifications were maintained in their original state, being rebuilt or repicketed as necessary. Various expedients were found for the more troublesome large, regular forts such as Niagara. From the end of 1764 until the early 1770's, a number of projects would be undertaken to keep Niagara in a defensible state. These relied, for the most part, on the use of

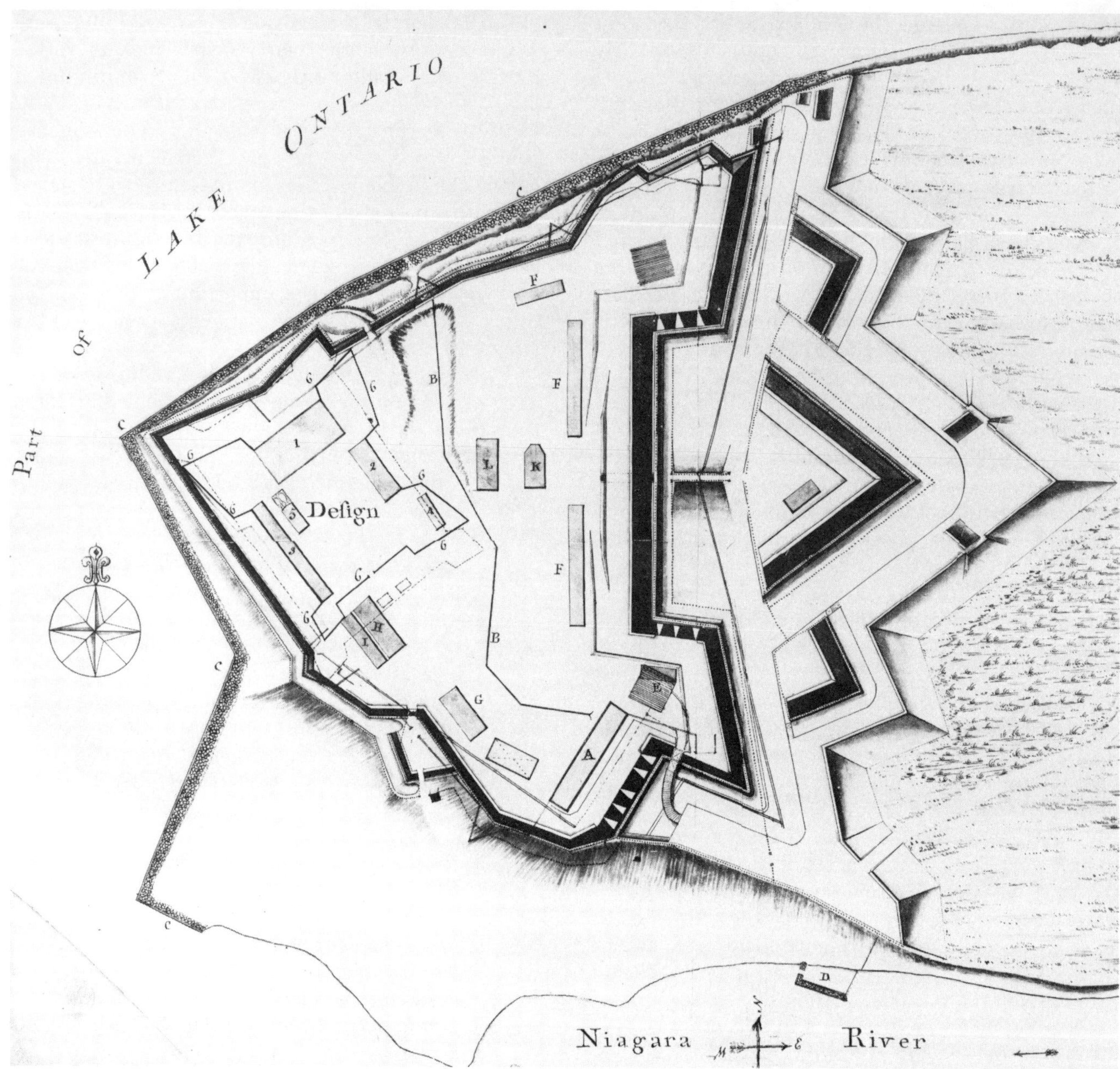

Alterations in the plan to secure Fort Niagara were proposed by Capt. John Montresor and forwarded to Capts. Sowers and Brown in June, 1768. The redoubts were later sketched into the bastions on this plan. *Courtesy, British Library, Crown Maps, cxxi, 75.*

wooden stockades to close up the lake and river sides of the fort and to secure the crumbling earthworks. Eventually, an acceptable solution would be found. The stone redoubts would prove to be the final phase of the effort to make Fort Niagara defensible against Indians.

A wooden stockade had provided the chief defense of the river and lake sides of Fort Niagara since shortly after the British capture of the post. These two fronts had been covered by light earthworks when the fort was expanded in 1755-1757, but by 1763 they had been replaced with vertical wooden pickets.[46] By 1765, Fort Niagara's stockades and earthworks were reported to be in terrible condition although an attempt was being made to maintain the latter in their original state. Wooden pickets had, in fact, been a secondary feature of the sodworks from the beginning. They were placed along the walls and in the bottom of the ditch to impede attackers. To the commandant's pleas Gage ordered that, where the earthworks "have tumbled down, the Fort must be shut in by Pickets" and noted that more substantial work would have to await orders from England.[47] Engineer Captain Harry Gordon was sent to Niagara that summer with a number of workmen. Although he concentrated chiefly on repairing buildings, he also erected or reset two lines of palisades in the ditch and along the berm of the earthworks. The upper part of the earthworks

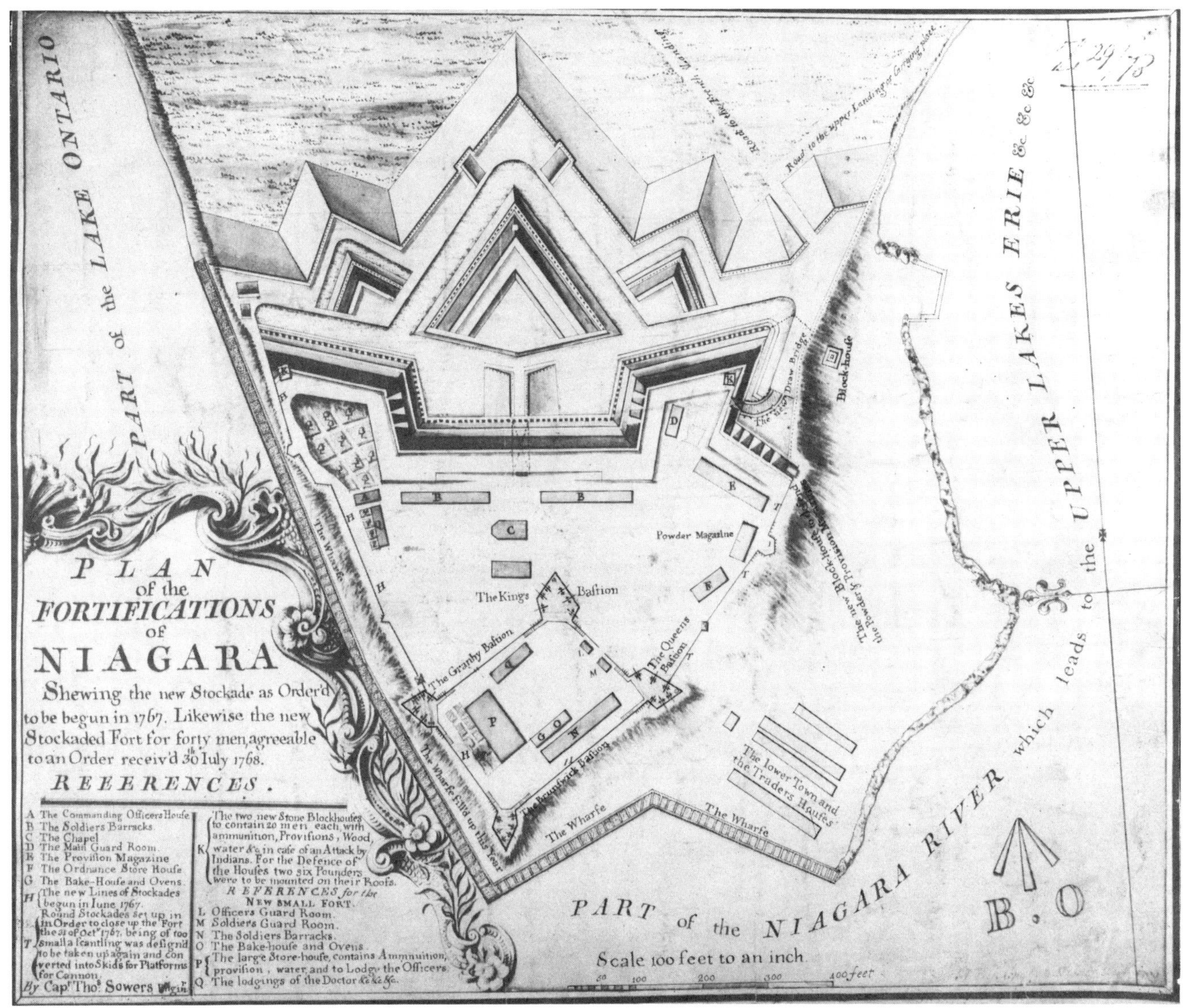

Construction of the inner stockade was documented by Capt. Thomas Sowers during the winter of 1768-69. He continued to project the blockhouses, "K", at the salients of the bastions. *Plan in the British War Office, Caxton House, London in 1929 and now believed lost.*

were again sodded, thereby preserving the original design for another year.[48]

Gordon's work was not sufficient to alleviate all the ills of Fort Niagara's defenses. A new commandant, Captain John Brown, arrived at the post in September, 1766. He promptly dashed off a complaint to Gage that "every part of the Works is in the greatest ruin" and that "with the Garrison here ... I am not able to keep out the Hogs." Brown recommended repairing the pickets once again "which would at best oblidge any stragling Indian that may Incline to come into the Fort to pass at the Gate." Gage expressed surprise that Niagara was in such a miserable state considering the work accomplished in 1765 and the fact that Captain Thomas Sowers had been ordered up the lakes in the spring of 1766 to attend to further repairs. Gage referred Captain Brown to Sowers and reassured him that "it will be necessary to put in Such Pickets as shall be wanting, as well to Keep out the Indians as the Hogs."[49]

Plans to properly secure Fort Niagara were, in fact, well advanced by the time of Captain Brown's complaint. When Captain Sowers passed through Fort Niagara on his way to Detroit, he left with Lieutenant Francis Pfister, garrison engineer, a carefully drafted plan and instructions to begin work.[50] The design had been prepared in the Engineer's office in New York, based on an earlier survey of Fort Niagara. In addition to showing the existing buildings, it included three elements for properly enclosing the post and preserving the original outline of its walls. The first and most extensive part of the project was a stockade along the lake and river sides. This was described as a "Scheme to inclose the present publick buildings at Niagara, and to prevent the expence of leveling the old Works." The stockade commenced just inside the

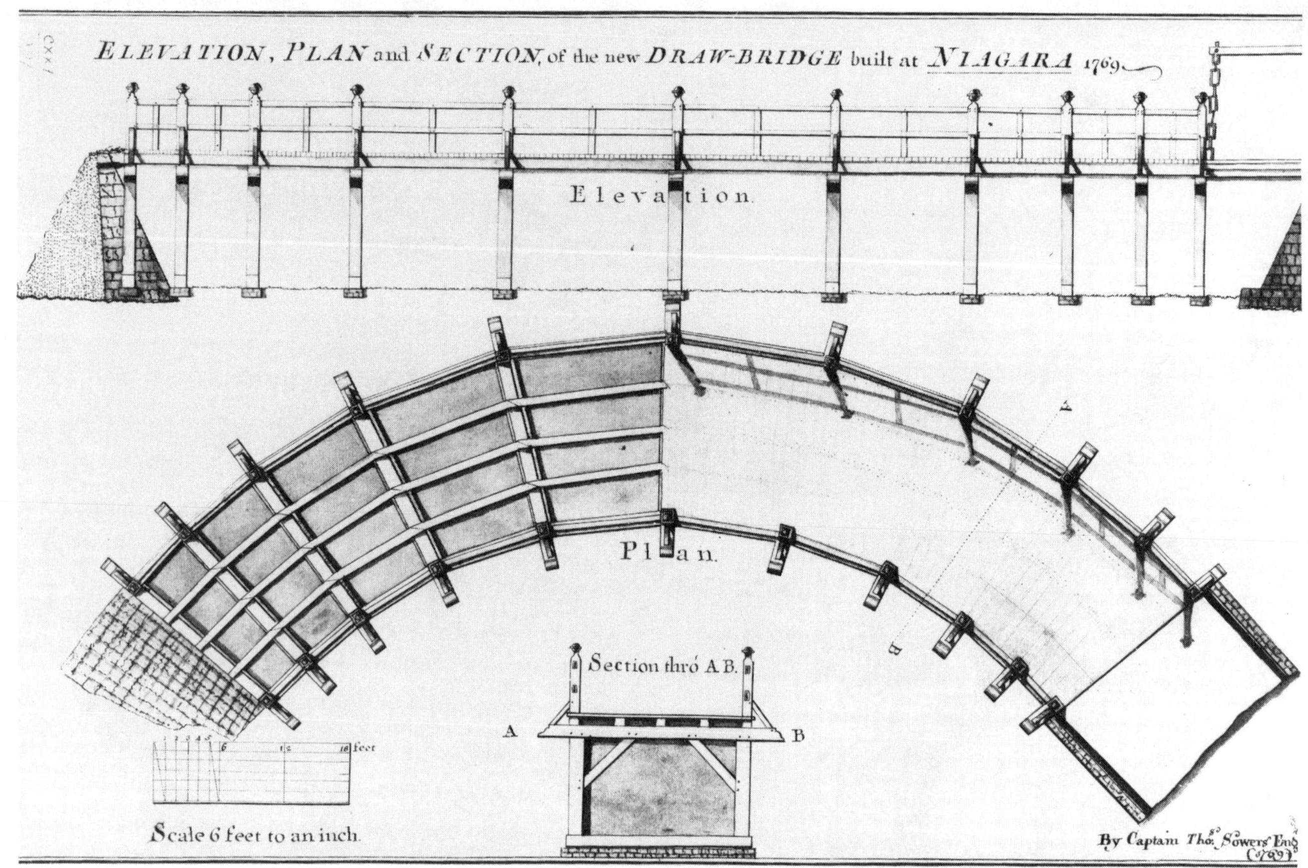

Capt. Thomas Sowers' 1769 plans of the new drawbridge constructed at Fort Niagara in the summer of 1768. *Courtesy, British Library, Crown Maps, cxxi, 77.*

Gate of the Five Nations at the southeast corner of the fort and followed the river and lake sides to a terminus at the salient angle of the lake bastion. A number of small bastions were placed along the length of the stockade to provide positions for flanking fire.

The other elements of this plan were several "blockhouses" covering parts of the land side defenses. One, a small wooden structure perched at the salient angle of the ravelin, overlooked the glacis and parts of the covered way. The other two were larger and placed in the salient angles of Fort Niagara's two bastions. They were sited immediately behind the earthen parapets and described in the key to the plan as "two large Block-houses of Stone, to plunge into the advanc'd ditches ... to contain 20 men each with provisions &c &c." These buildings included most of the features later incorporated into the redoubts and must therefore be considered their antecedents both in design and purpose. Each blockhouse anchored one end of the new stockade line and connected it to the sodworks and pickets of the land front. Fire from the blockhouses could be directed into the ditch against anyone approaching the crumbling earthworks. The two buildings were alternately described in a construction estimate as "towers" from which fire could "plunge into the Ditches and Flank the Land Front."[51]

Plans for Niagara's two stone blockhouses were probably prepared during the winter of 1765-66, but their completion was not expected during the latter year. The engineer recommended repicketing Fort Niagara and preparing materials for construction of the blockhouses in 1767. It was estimated that they would cost about £300 apiece.[52] Given the poor condition of the walls, it is understandable that Captain Brown gave priority to repairing the pickets and closing up his fort. More than six hundred logs had been cut by the end of September, but a shortage of workmen kept Brown from erecting them.[53] Clearly, the picketing would not be completed until the following year. By November, the blockhouse project had definitely been pushed into 1767, and the cost, including quarrying and carting the stone, burning lime for mortar and constructing the walls was estimated at £700.[54]

In reality, the project to enclose Niagara was barely begun in 1766. By the end of the year General Gage was projecting the picketing for the spring and indicating that the stockade would protect the buildings while the two stone blockhouses would be perched on the ruins of the two earthen bastions. From there, the fire of their defenders would "plunge into all the outworks which are decayed and command every thing without and within the pickets."[55] Gage had given up any hopes of maintaining the earthworks in defensible condition. The land side of Fort Niagara would thereafter be covered by the lines of pickets and by fire from the proposed blockhouses while the sod-works would be allowed to fall into complete ruin. By the spring of 1767, Fort Niagara's garrison was busily cutting logs for the stockade, and Captain Thomas Sowers had again been ordered up from New York to direct the work.[56] The small garrison labored throughout the summer and fall beside hired carpenters taken up by Sowers, but the work was still not completed. Bad weather, the constant deterioration of wooden elements and erosion of the earthworks all conspired to slow progress. By the time Sowers returned to New York in October, Captain Brown had to report that "much is still wanting", and that, although most of the picketing was erected, it still needed to be finished along with the necessary platforms, embrasures, gates, and a new drawbridge at the Gate of the Five Nations.[57]

Gage, by this time no doubt heartily sick of the demands of Fort Niagara, resigned himself to another year of expensive labor there and hoped that the work could be completed by the end of 1768. Sowers was again ordered to Niagara to complete the post according to the plan of 1766. Gage "earnestly" recommended that everything be finished by the end of the season.[58] In this he would again be disappointed, not by any failing of Sowers, Brown or their workmen but because of further changes in British policy toward the posts. In June, Gage received a letter from the Earl of Hillsborough pointing out the necessity of relieving the Kingdom "from every Expence that is not of absolute necessity." Hillsborough called for further reductions in the posts of the interior of North America, although he recommended that Niagara, Detroit and Michilimackinac be maintained along with the naval vessels used for communication on the Great Lakes.[59] Gage replied at length, detailing needs and plans for reducing troops, garrisons and the expense of supplying those that were to be retained. He acknowledged that, if foodstuffs could be grown at Detroit for the garrisons in the upper country, the troops at Niagara would no longer be needed to help move provisions across the portage and could therefore be reduced.[60]

Gage's next concern was to redirect the ongoing work at Niagara. Five days after his reply to Hillsborough, the general penned letters to Brown and Sowers informing them that the fortifications must be altered to be defended by forty men, a reduction in the garrison of at least two-thirds! Although he solicited their opinions as to the best course of action, Gage expected that the earthworks would be totally demolished and a smaller fort constructed to protect the tiny garrison. Demolition of the earthworks would have required the removal of any part of the stone blockhouses already begun. In his letter to Sowers, Gage pointed out that "having begun them must be no Obstacle to changing the first design." He further suggested that "Perhaps the Blockhouses brought further back [their fire] might notwithstanding be made to plunge into the Ditches." Enclosed with Gage's letter to Sowers was a plan prepared by Captain-Lieutenant John Montresor illustrating "two or three projects" which could be followed to contract the works. Gage expected that this eleventh hour change would be effected "in the best manner You can" and that Brown and Sowers, familiar with the site, would be the best judges of the proper course and act accordingly.[61]

Montresor's plan has survived, and it provides an excellent idea of the concept that would finally bring about construction of the stone redoubts at Fort Niagara. His "Plan of Fort Niagara with a design for Contracting the same", is superimposed on the 1766 design for repicketing the fort. Montresor showed two outlines of four-bastioned stockades around the "Great House" or "French Castle". Their perimeters enclosed the garrison bakehouse, a barracks and one officers' quarters. Other buildings situated between this inner fort and the old earthworks were to be left standing for the time being, but the earthworks themselves were to be demolished and all defense centered on the small fort. The surviving copy of Montresor's plan includes a square sketched in each bastion at the locations of the redoubts. These are rendered rather crudely and in a different hand than the rest of the plan. They were very likely added later, perhaps after the final configuration of the two buildings had been determined or following their completion in 1770-71. Their locations correspond to Gage's suggestion that the earlier projected blockhouses could be "brought further back" and still be effective. These would be the final sites for the stone buildings first proposed in 1766.[62]

The sudden change in plans for the defense of Fort Niagara does not seem to have upset either Sowers or Brown. Apparently, the stone blockhouses had not been commenced, and the only major new construction had been a drawbridge at the Gate of the Five Nations. The old bridge had literally fallen down in July, and its replacement had just been completed when Gage's orders arrived at Niagara. Brown and Sowers immediately set about selecting one of Montresor's options and erecting a stockade. Work was underway in August with but little alteration from Montresor's suggestions. The two officers did believe that demolition of the old earthworks would be impossible with the number of men available to do the work. Brown and Sowers recommended that the earthworks be left standing for the time being as they would command more respect from the Indians in

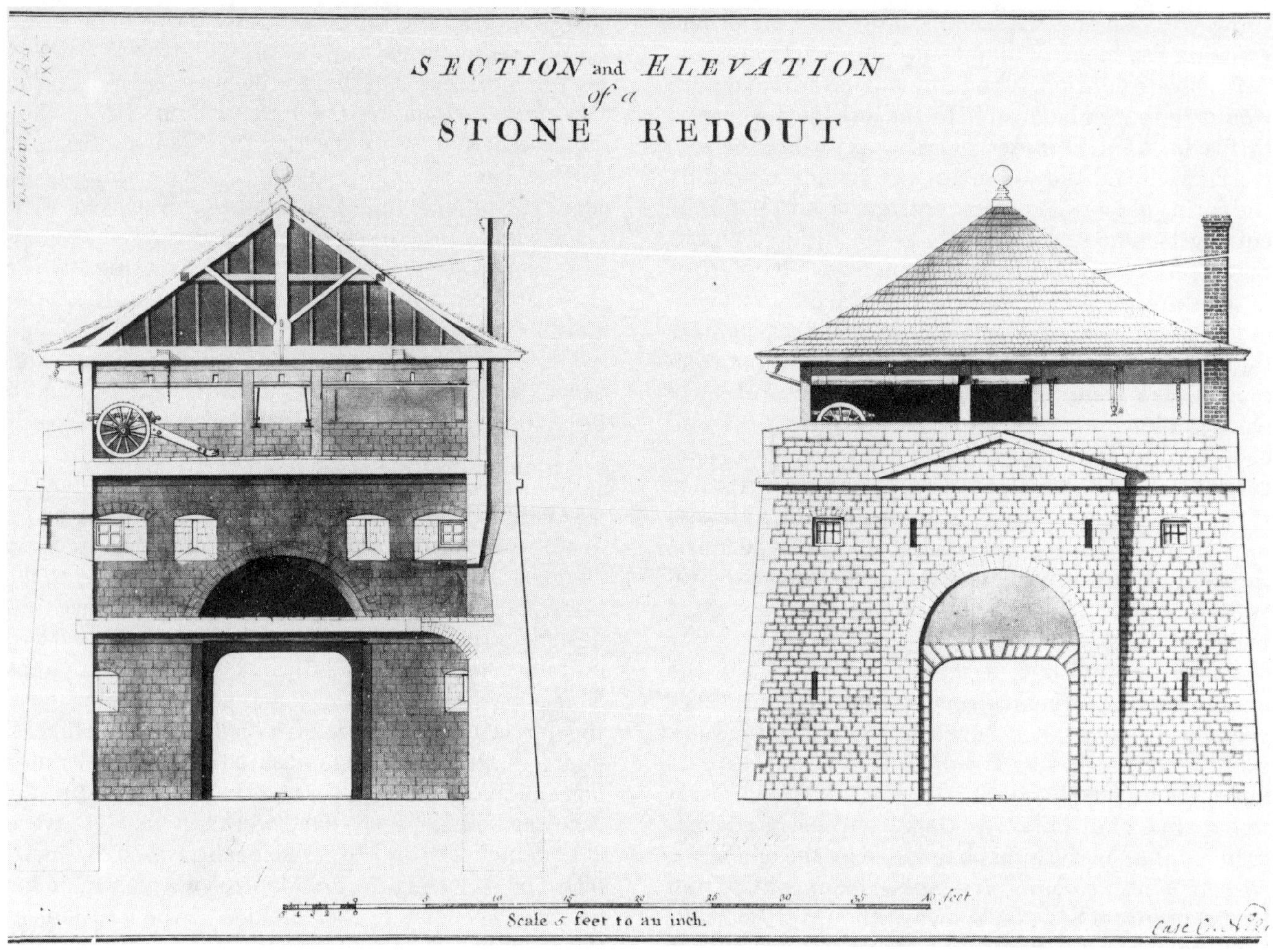

This "Section and Elevation of a Stone Redout" is the design used for the South Redoubt of Fort Niagara. The original was probably prepared at New York in 1769 or 1770. The design has been attributed to Capt. John Montresor. *Courtesy, British Library, Crown Maps, cxxi, 78.1.*

their current condition than if partially destroyed. Gage deferred to their opinion that the old walls be left "in Statu Quo" for the winter in the confidence that whatever they did would be "conducive to the good of the Service."[63]

The new construction was begun promptly. By November 6, Brown was able to report that a stockade had been erected around the French Castle and a number of nearby buildings and that the enclosure was available whenever the garrison might be reduced. The inner fort was a slightly irregular rectangle with four bastions of varying sizes. The stockade had been finished, although much of the detail work such as completion of the platforms, cutting of loopholes and finishing of gunports had yet to be done.[64] Sowers returned to New York and reported similar progress to Gage. The engineer also drew a plan showing what had been accomplished.[65] The new stockade was carefully rendered with its gate on the southeast side and a pair of newly constructed guardhouses flanking the entrance.

Sowers' plan also shows the "two new stone Blockhouses" located exactly where they had been on the plans of 1766 and 1768. His reference to them as "new" would seem to imply that they had been completed. There is no evidence to support this, however, and such expensive construction would surely have been reported by Captain Brown. It seems likely that the long range design for Fort Niagara still included the stone blockhouses, and that Sowers, expecting them to be built in 1769, merely added them to ensure that his plan would remain current. He further noted that the blockhouses were to contain twenty men each with "ammunition, Provisions, Wood, water & c. in case of an Attack by Indians." Two six-pounder cannon were to be mounted on the roof of each. A pair of stone blockhouses to cover the land side therefore remained a part of the plan to secure Fort Niagara, even after its alteration to accommodate a smaller garrison. No work was recorded during 1769, however. Gage's papers are sparse for that year with little or nothing in the way of correspondence from or about Niagara. This is particularly frustrating since it must have been during 1769 that the decision was made to enlarge the proposed buildings and move them from the top of the earthworks to the interior of the bastions. From this point they may properly be called redoubts by virtue of their locations within the bastions, and so they would be known during construction.

Completion of the long process of making Fort Niagara tenable against Indians would finally come in 1770-71 with construction of the redoubts. No major reductions in the garrison followed Gage's orders of 1768, despite the alterations of the defenses to facilitate this eventuality. The post retained its complement of three companies of troops. Defense against Indians remained the highest priority, with Fort Niagara considered to be the interior post of greatest importance. "Niagara may be called the key to the upper Lakes, on the [west] side of Lake Ontario, securing a Pass which can't be avoided," Gage wrote to Lord Barrington in 1769.[66] His feelings were shared in England. Gage was again cautioned by Lord Hillsborough, in the winter of 1770, that intelligence of the "Views and Designs of the Savages" indicated that the security of Niagara and the other interior posts was "an Object that merits Attention."[67]

Orders to commence construction of the two stone redoubts must have been received at Niagara sometime during 1769. Instructions were probably communicated directly to Captain Brown when he visited New York that summer. Brown returned to his post on November 30. On February 4, 1770, he made his first mention of progress on the "stone Redoubts proposed", noting that his men had been quarrying rock for the new buildings since his arrival at the post. They were working at the "Lower Landing", eight miles up the Niagara RIver from the fort. The quarry had previously yielded large quantities of limestone for Fort Niagara during construction of the bakehouse and provisions storehouse in 1762. Brown noted that the new buildings would consume immense quantities of stone and that additional skilled laborers - masons, carpenters and blacksmiths - would be required if the work was to be completed during the summer of 1770. Unskilled laborers were needed as well since the garrison was small in proportion to the amount of work proposed. Brown suggested that if Captain Sowers was sent to supervise the construction he could hire and bring craftsmen with him. If Sowers was not available, Brown recommended that Lieutenant Francis Pfister be given direction of the work. Quarrying of stone continued for the rest of the winter, and large quantities had been stockpiled by the end of February.[68]

General Thomas Gage heeded Captain Brown's suggestions and ordered Sowers to hire artificers in New York and send them to Niagara with appropriate materials. Masons and carpenters were on their way up the Hudson and Mohawk Rivers by late April.[69]

Capt. John Montresor, painted in New York by John Singleton Copley in 1771. *Courtesy, the Detroit Institute of Arts, Gibbs-Williams Fund, Acc. No. 41.37.*

Captain Sowers was not assigned to Niagara for the summer of 1770, however, and direction of the construction fell to the officer recommended by Brown. Francis Pfister was then a lieutenant in the 2nd Battalion, 60th (Royal American) Regiment of Foot and had already enjoyed a long and profitable association with Niagara. German by birth, he was one of a number of European Protestants with engineering skills who had received commissions when the Royal American Regiment was raised in 1757-58. Pfister began his British service as an ensign on September 15, 1758, rising to lieutenant on September 18, 1760. He served in the campaigns of the French and Indian War and was well-known to Sowers, having worked as his assistant engineer during the construction of Fort Ontario at Oswego in 1759-61. Pfister first came to Niagara in the fall of 1763 when he was sent from Fort Stanwix to relieve the ailing garrison engineer, Lieutenant George Demler.[70]

Pfister soon proved his usefulness. During the summer of 1764 he worked with Lieutenants John Montresor and Bernard Ratzer to fortify the Niagara Portage. Pfister supervised construction of Fort Erie at the head of the Niagara River while Montresor continued to Detroit with Bradstreet. Reductions in the army at the conclusion of the Indian war placed Pfister on the half-pay (inactive) list where he re-

The redoubts stood high enough above the walls for their guns to fire over the earthen parapets. The taller, reshaped walls of 1863-72 today obstruct the view of the ditch from the second floor loopholes. *OFN 5073/30C.*

mained until granted a full-pay commission in the 2nd Battalion, Royal Americans on October 9, 1767. Pfister had remained at Niagara throughout his time on half-pay. By the summer of 1765, he had obtained a highly lucrative contract to operate the Niagara Portage and had taken up residence above Niagara Falls near the abandoned Fort Schlosser. Upon his recommissioning in the Royal Americans in 1767, Pfister was the eldest foreign lieutenant in the regiment.[71]

Lieutenant Pfister's background made him the logical choice to direct construction of the redoubts. He had never entirely given up his engineering duties. During his time on half-pay, Pfister apparently continued to serve as Niagara's garrison engineer whenever a regular engineer from New York was not present. The portage contract also gave Pfister the opportunity to direct improvements to his buildings at Fort Schlosser, and he continued his business activities even after returning to full-pay in the army. In 1768 he built a sawmill above Niagara Falls where he sawed plank for the garrison, including that for the redoubt project.[72] To Pfister would fall the responsibility for ensuring that the two stone redoubts were constructed according to plan.

It was not necessary for Lieutenant Pfister to design the new buildings. This task had been accomplished in the engineer's office in New York during 1769. A set of plans was sent to Pfister, and the basic construction document has survived.[73] This unsigned "Section and Elevation of a Stone Redout [sic]" has long been attributed to Captain-Lieutenant John Montresor. No reason for the attribution is known other than that Montresor was then serving as chief engineer in North America. Plans for a very similar structure prepared in 1774 have also been credited to Montresor, but they too are unsigned.[74] Montresor's otherwise copious journals unfortunately shed no light on his connection with the Niagara redoubts or that proposed for Boston in 1774, so his responsibility for the projects must remain conjectural.[75] Considering Thomas Sowers' long association with Niagara, one might argue for his participation in the design of the redoubts. However, although he was in New York when the Niagara plans were drawn, Sowers had left America by 1774 which makes it more likely that Montresor or one of his assistants drew both sets of plans.

John Montresor had come from an engineering background, and his family history might provide some clues to the origin of the design for the Fort Niagara redoubts. Son of another engineer, James Montresor, John was born at Gibraltar in 1736 where he spent much of his youth. He came to America with his father, who had been named chief engineer for General Edward Braddock, and entered the army as an ensign in the 48th Regiment of Foot in 1755. Montresor saw extensive service during the French and Indian War, chiefly in engineering capacities. He came to Niagara during both campaign seasons of the Indian uprising of 1763-64. In the latter year he supervised the construction of fortifications along the portage and continued to Detroit as chief engineer of Colonel John Bradstreet's army. Promoted to Captain-Lieutenant in 1766, Montresor was, by 1770, responsible for Gage's engineering department.[76]

Given the apparent dearth of antecedents for the design of the Fort Niagara redoubts, one is drawn to the rough similarities of these buildings to the Martello towers constructed in England during the first decade of the nineteenth century. It seems likely that the latter fortifications were influenced by existing towers in the western Mediterranean, notably those on Minorca.[77] British troops had occupied that island for much of the century, and the closest friendly post was, of course, Gibraltar. Perhaps Montresor or his father were familiar with Minorca's stone towers from their time at Gibraltar, and the Mediterranean structures might have influenced John Montresor's 1770 and 1774 designs for very specialized redoubts for North American use.

Both of Montresor's redoubt plans show structures with gateways piercing the ground floors. The Niagara design is for the building which would become the South Redoubt. It was placed in the South or River Bastion where it could serve as a second entrance to the fort by backing up the Gate of the Five Nations. The North Redoubt was somewhat different, chiefly on its ground floor, which lacked the gateway, and in the facade which had a much smaller classical front over the doorway. Fortunately, several plans have survived which allow us to reconstruct the appearance of the Fort Niagara redoubts as built. Montresor's plan of 1770 and that proposed in 1774 for the

Beacon Hill redoubt provide much information on the South Redoubt as well as for the second and third stories of both buildings. A general plan of Fort Niagara prepared by Francis Pfister in 1773 shows ground floor plans for both buildings and another elevation of the South Redoubt. A plan of the ground floor of the North Redoubt was prepared by United States Major John Jacob Ulrich Rivardi in 1798. This almost certainly represents its configuration as built in 1771 with some minor alterations to loopholes.[78] Various views of Fort Niagara from the late eighteenth century shed additional light on the general appearance of roofs, facades and other details.

As constructed, each of the redoubts was a thirty-six foot square limestone masonry tower of two full stories with a roughly three foot high parapet extending above the third floor. The buildings stood twenty-seven feet high. Their walls were battered or tapered inward slightly from bottom to top so that, at parapet level, each building was thirty-four feet square. The stone walls were nearly five feet thick at the base and four feet thick at parapet level. The top floor was intended to support cannon and was covered by a tall wooden roof raised well above the parapet by square posts. The open space thereby created between the top of the parapet and the eaves allowed the guns to be fired in all directions. These openings were closed by thick wooden shutters which could be raised and lowered with ropes and pulleys to provide protection from the weather and, during military action, small arms fire. The roofs were topped with round finials and weather vanes. Each redoubt also had a tall brick chimney to ventilate a single fireplace on the second floor. The walls of the two buildings were pierced with loopholes for musketry. Most tapered from inside the structure to a narrow slit on the exterior, although the loopholes of the northwest facade of the North Redoubt appear to have been wider on the outside. Four small windows were placed in the second story of each building to provide light to the guard rooms.

The two redoubts were essentially identical in plan on the second and third floors. The latter were intended to support light artillery and serve as fighting platforms. They were therefore designed simply as open space, unencumbered by anything other than stairway openings. The locations of the stairways between the second and third floors are unknown, but they were probably placed directly above the lower stairs. The second floor of each redoubt was intended as a guard room for twenty men and was equipped with a single fireplace for heating and cooking. The fireplace in the South Redoubt was on the southwest side of the building. That in the North Redoubt was above the ground floor doorway, also on the southwest side. No specific information has been discovered about furnishings for the guard rooms, but the shelf bunks, tables and stools reproduced during restoration probably duplicate the original furniture with fair accuracy. The chief problem with the restoration furnishings is that the locations of the shelf bunks against the walls would probably have interfered with use of the loopholes. By 1798, the second floors were considered commodious enough to house forty to fifty men when equipped as a barracks.[79] The second and third floors were constructed of heavy timbers covered with plank.

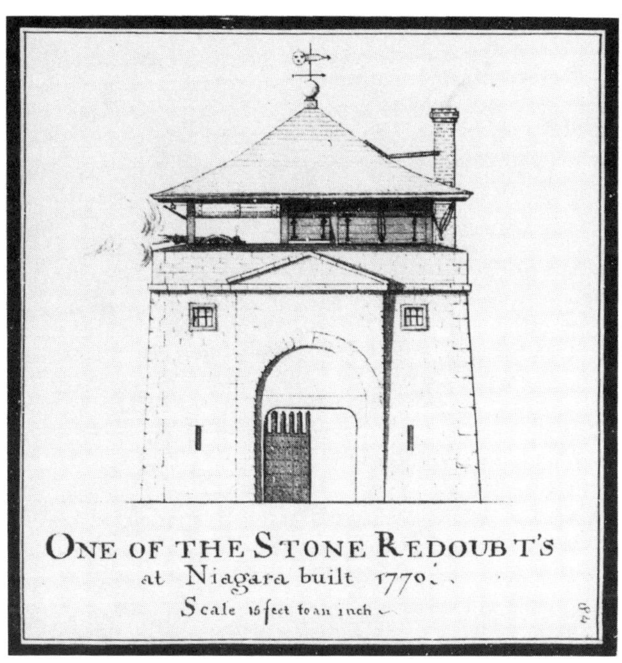

Lt. Francis Pfister drew the northwest facade of the South Redoubt in 1773. It varies from the 1770 elevation in that it lacks loopholes above the gateway. Pfister provided excellent details of the gates and gun deck shutters and depicted an ornate weather vane which also appears on other early views of the building. *Courtesy, British Library, Crown Maps, cxxi, 76.*

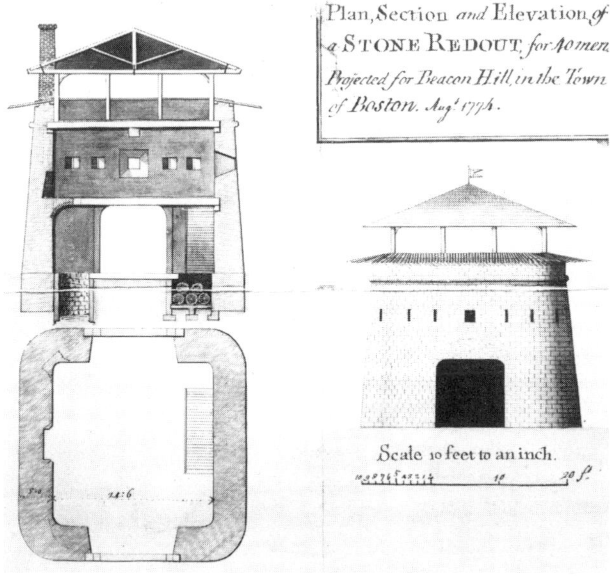

A version of Fort Niagara's South redoubt, minus the classical and oriental detailing, was projected for Boston's Beacon Hill in 1774. The building was never erected. *Courtesy, William L. Clements Library.*

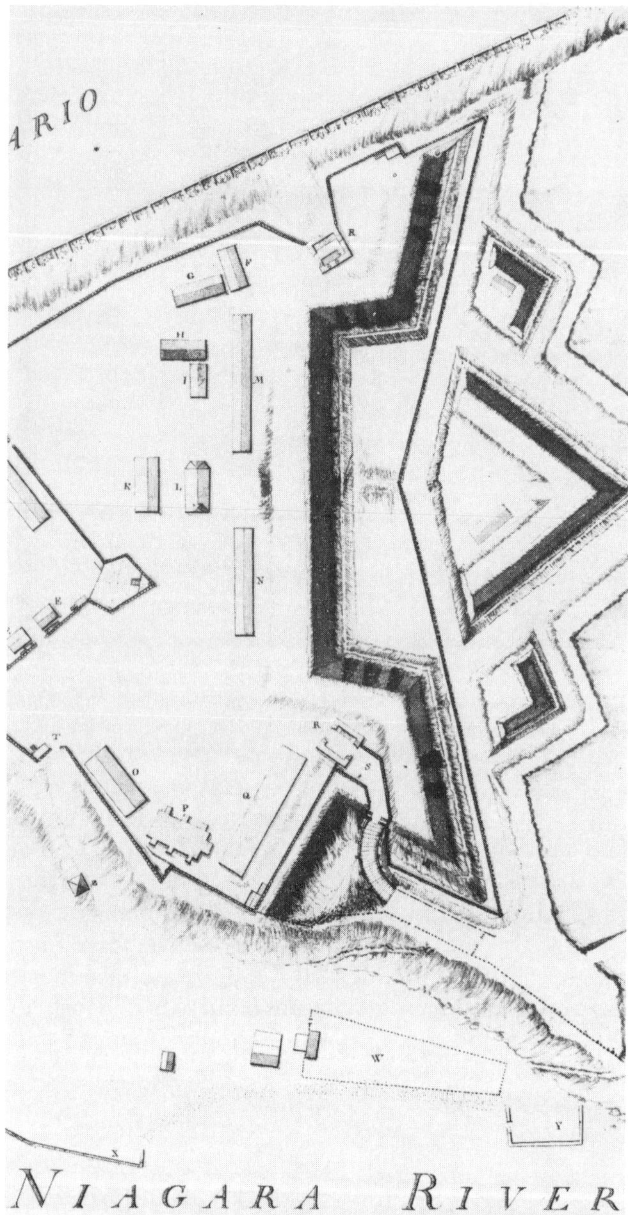

The ground floor interiors of both redoubts are shown in Lt. Francis Pfister's "Plan of Niagara with an Explanation of its present State", prepared in 1773. Pfister represented the ruinous state of the earthworks and showed the Gate of the Five Nations (bottom) in detail. *Courtesy, British Library, Crown Maps, cxxi, 76.*

The ground floor layouts of the redoubts differed greatly, reflecting peculiarities of their locations and functions within the fort. These factors also affected the appearances of the facades (see Appendix A). The North Redoubt was far from any gateway and a good distance from the main powder magazine. It therefore had only a small entrance on the southwest side, and much of the ground floor was taken up by a powder magazine, apparently of masonry construction. These features are clearly shown on the plan of September 28, 1773 and the June 10, 1798 "Plan of the Northern Blockhouse". The same drawings depict the stairway to the second floor located along the inside of the northwest wall. The North Redoubt was further distinguished by narrow powder magazine ventilator slits on the southwest and southeast facades. These were baffled to prevent sparks from being drawn into the magazine.

There were minor differences in defensive features as well. Neither building was constructed with many loopholes on their ground floors. The 1773 plan shows only a single gunslit in the first story on the northwest side of the North Redoubt. By 1798, however, two are depicted. Both plans also indicate that the ground floor loopholes on the northwest side were wider on the exterior, tapering to narrow slits on the inside. As originally placed, the northwest face of the building covered an area of the lake bank that had been badly eroded, and fire from loopholes on that facade would have covered the washout and part of the seawall below the bank. The wider loopholes provided a better field of fire in this situation, and there was less chance of return fire against the wider, more exposed slits. It seems likely that the second loophole was a later addition, installed sometime before 1798.

The ground floor of the South Redoubt had an entirely different function. It was intended as a secondary entrance to Fort Niagara. The building was placed in the South Bastion, close behind the Gate of the Five Nations. Primary access to Fort Niagara was across the stationary wooden bridge and drawbridge rebuilt by Sowers in 1768 and through two sets of gates in the earthworks. The path from the interior side of the gate was flanked by stockade lines of stout pickets terminating on either side of a large arched entrance on the southeast side of the South Redoubt. This doorway was equipped with its own set of gates. The complex entrance to Fort Niagara continued through the redoubt and out a corresponding gateway on its northwest side. All traffic was thus directed through the building and under the second floor guardroom. It is interesting to note that, even though the earthworks were to be abandoned, the South Redoubt was placed with them in mind. The wide gateways of the South Redoubt made for entrance facades completely different than that of the North Redoubt. The classical Georgian temple front that surrounded the South Redoubt gateways extended to the parapet level, while that of the North Redoubt was much shorter and narrower, terminating just below the second floor.

The 1774 plan of the redoubt for Beacon Hill shows at least one further detail which seems to have also been a feature of Fort Niagara's South Redoubt. The stairway to the second floor of the Beacon Hill redoubt is located to the right of the main entrance, opposite the second floor fireplace, just as it was in the South Redoubt. The section of the Beacon Hill redoubt shows a cellar filled with provisions barrels directly below the stairway. On the opposite side of the gateway is what appears to be a well. There is good evidence that the South Redoubt also had a cellar as part of its original design. In 1798 the building was described as having a "place under the Stair, which is used as a black hole." [80]

These severely functional buildings were not without aesthetic touches. Both were indelibly marked with elements of two styles popular in eighteenth century Europe. The masonry towers were given a number of classical Georgian features such as temple fronts and pediments over doors and gateways, rounded arches above second floor windows and entrances, and a belt course surrounding each building at the level of the third floor. Most of these details survived later alterations and are still in place. Despite the classical elements, however, the redoubts have a very oriental appearance. The batter or receding slope of the stone walls from ground to parapet level and the the noticeable flare of the eaves reflect the Chinese styles so popular in decorative arts of the time. Although the oriental roofs were removed during the War of 1812, they were reconstructed in the twentieth century based on the original section and elevation of the South Redoubt. The combination of the two styles is surprisingly appealing, and Fort Niagara's "Chinese Chippendale" redoubts have an architectural uniqueness that sets them apart from other Georgian military buildings. Most of these details were deleted from the redoubt designed four years later for Boston. Perhaps they were considered frivolous during a time of increased tension or had added so much to the expense of the Niagara redoubts that they were not repeated.

The artificers hired by Captain Sowers probably reached Fort Niagara sometime in May and immediately began construction using the stone and plank stockpiled by the garrison. By July 20 "one of the Stone buildings" (the South Redoubt) was well advanced. Work on the North Redoubt had also begun, but Pfister seems to have given priority to the other structure. The only real difficulty came from the huge quantities of limestone needed for the thick walls and the necessity of bringing it as well as all the timber from a considerable distance.[81] The foundations had to be quite deep in order to be secure, and they were laid roughly level with the bottom of the main ditch. This greatly increased the amount of stone required. All of it was quarried at the Lower Landing (modern Lewiston) and barged to Fort Niagara.[82]

This steady progress was about to be disrupted by a dispute between Fort Niagara's commandant and its engineer. As September approached, Captain Brown turned his thoughts to the seasonal needs of his garrison. Niagara's harsh winters required huge quantities of firewood to warm the troops. Repairs to barracks and chimneys were also necessary to keep the occupants snug until spring. These chores would require considerable amounts of labor from the soldiers, most of whom were still working to maintain the flow of materials needed for construction of the redoubts and continued picketing of the fort. On August 20 Brown sent a note to Lieutenant Pfister informing him that the need to begin cutting firewood would cause him to reduce the engineer's work parties by one half in the middle of September. With this in mind, Brown asked Pfister to present his opinion as to whether he would then be able to finish enclosing the fort with stockades *and* complete the second redoubt. Brown believed that General Gage expected the stockades to be in good order by the end of the season. The captain made his own feelings quite clear. "I look upon it to be more Essential for the Security of this Fort to have it well Stockaded," he wrote, "than to have another Stone Building, and the Stockades neglected."[83]

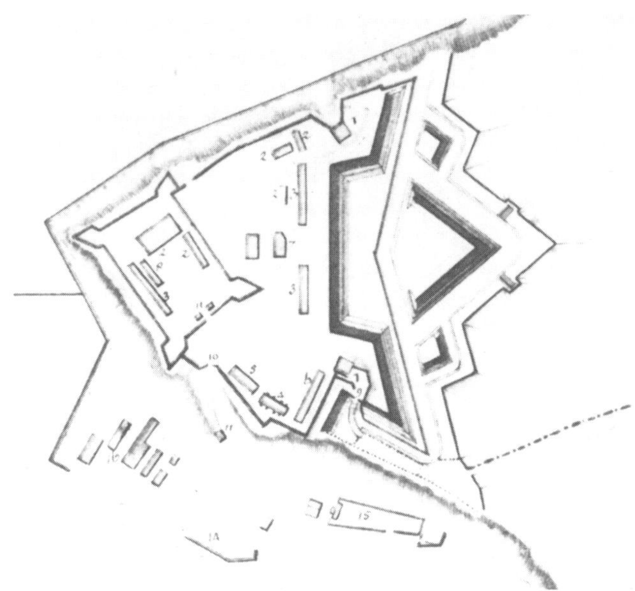

Lt. Francis Pfister's 1771 "Plan of Niagara" was probably prepared to mark the completion of the redoubts. *Courtesy, William L. Clements Library.*

Pfister replied the same afternoon and set in motion an exchange that would eventually reach General Gage. The lieutenant consulted with the master mason who believed that, with the number of men attending his workers and favorable weather, he would be able to finish the North Redoubt by the end of the season. Since sufficient manpower would not be available to also erect palisades in the fort ditch, however, Pfister admitted that he would be unable to finish both the redoubt and the stockade. Completion of the second stone building was obviously the lieutenant's priority. A week after Pfister's reply, Brown decided to put the question to the other officers of his garrison. Would it, "in case of an Indian War next Spring," he asked, "be more for the Security of the Garrison to

The relationship of the redoubts to the Castle and earthworks is clear in this photograph. Gen. Gage was convinced that "no Body of Indians would ever venture between the Fire of two Redoubts." *OFN 715/28C.*

have the Same properly Picketted in, than to have the other Stone Building (now begun) finished, and the garrison left open?" Brown admitted that Fort Niagara had little to apprehend from a direct assault, but he feared surprise and noted that every year of the four he had commanded the post had brought rumors of the Indians "breaking out in mischief." Lieutenants Poynton and Polson and Ensign MacDonald of the 60th Regiment and Lieutenant Dysart of the Royal Artillery agreed that the stockading was more important than the redoubt. Brown reported this to Gage and ordered Pfister to "Employ a party in Setting up Stockades." As for the North Redoubt, he suggested that Pfister "continue to Employ the Masons to the best advantage" in forwarding work on the building.[84]

Superintendent of Indian Affairs Sir William Johnson approved of Capt. John Brown's Indian diplomacy. *Courtesy, New York State Office of Parks, Recreation and Historic Preservation, Johnson Hall State Historic Site.*

Lieutenant Pfister presumably complied with his orders, but September brought further tension between the commandant and the engineer. On the 21st, Captain Brown noted to Gage some problems concerning Pfister's submission of vouchers for the work at Niagara.[85] Then, five days later, Brown learned that Pfister was about to discharge the masons who had been sent up from New York to build the redoubts. Brown wanted them to undertake repairs to the garrison bake oven, the guard house and the barracks chimneys. Pfister replied that such work was the responsibility of the Barracks Master General's Department, not the Engineer's Department, and that the masons had requested their discharge because they were getting no assistance from the garrison. The troops were busy cutting firewood and setting pickets, and work on the North Redoubt had apparently come to a standstill. Brown, in return, grumbled that if the masons did not make the needed repairs he would have to lay the matter before General Gage.[86] On September 27 Captain Brown wrote Gage and complained bitterly about the "jealousy" between the Barracks and Engineer Departments. He was disgusted that he had been unable to rehire the masons to work on the other buildings. To add insult to injury, little of the five hundred cords of firewood needed for the winter had yet been cut.[87]

Brown's complaints would not find a receptive audience in General Thomas Gage. By the time the captain's latest letter left Fort Niagara on September 27, Gage was already upset about Brown's actions in August and angry that "the Engineer has been interrupted in the Execution of the Works ordered to be compleated at Niagara." Gage, who might charitably be described as thrifty, was unhappy that "Artificers are to be kept on Pay and Provisions without being able to do a Day's Work during the Winter." He disagreed with Brown about the relative priority of stockades and redoubts and wrote chidingly:

> *... I am much of Opinion, that no Body of Indians would ever venture between the Fire of two Redoubts, tho' the Ditch was not Stockaded, more particularly as they would soon be exposed to the Fire of the interior Works* [inner stockade], *of the Fort, which have been Stockaded and secured last year* [actually 1768]. *Stockades may be sett up by the Garrison at any time, when the Ground is not actually froze, where as Mason's Work must be finished sometime before the frost setts in, that there may be time for the Mortar to dry.*

Then, more ominously, he noted that he would be "much displeased if obliged to retain or send up Artificers next year; to finish what might have been compleated this year.[88] Gage's response to Brown's report of September 27 was surprisingly mild considering this implied threat. He pointed out that Pfister was only following orders in discharging the masons and that proposed repairs must first be submitted for approval. He called for harmony in the garrison and resigned himself to the expense of sending masons to Niagara in 1771 to finish the North Redoubt.[89]

There the matter would rest for the winter. The South Redoubt had been completed, but the northern building would remain unfinished until masons could be sent up again in the spring of 1771. The stockading was completed, however, and Captain Brown must have felt vindicated in his decision when, on October 12, he finally had some Indian trouble on his hands. On that day a pair of traders were plundered by a party of Seneca on the upper Niagara River. The victims reported their predicament to a passing boat-

This was a visitor's first sight upon entering the Gate of the Five Nations between 1770 and 1810. *OFN 726/28C.*

load of soldiers from the Fort Niagara garrison who stepped in to recover their goods. During the incident the Indians fired into the soldiers' boat, wounding one of them. The man died at Fort Niagara three weeks later.[90] Brown promptly apprehended suspects and confined them in the "black hole" of the "French Castle". Concerned with possible repercussions, he sent messages to the Seneca villages of the Genesee River asking to speak with their chiefs. After holding a council with them on October 30, Brown released his suspects on the Senecas' promise to turn the real culprits over to Indian Superintendent Sir William Johnson. The chiefs repeated their promise after the soldier died, and the incident blew over with both Gage's and Johnson's approval of Brown's diplomacy.[91]

The incident nonetheless underscored the continuing British preoccupation with the possibility of another Indian war and the need to keep the posts secure. Isabella Graham, wife of Fort Niagara's sur-

This view of the northwest facade of the South Redoubt emphasizes the mixture of classical and Chinese elements. *OFN 712/28C.*

Wooden bunks, a table and benches were reproduced for the guardrooms in 1933-34. The second floor of the South Redoubt is pictured. *OFN 758/28C.*

geon, wrote to her mother in February, 1771, that there had recently been "several threatenings of an Indian war," but that, "thank God, it seems to be quite hushed again." Mrs. Graham, who had watched construction of the redoubts, probably expressed the fears of most of Fort Niagara's occupants when she wrote that "War with civilized nations is nothing to war with Indians. They have no mercy, nor give any quarter to man, woman or child."[92] Mrs. Graham and the others were surely glad that Fort Niagara was secure against assaults of the kind seen in 1763.

A detail from James Peachey's watercolor of circa 1783 shows Fort Niagara dominated by the "French Castle" (left) and the redoubts. *Courtesy, National Archives of Canada, C2035.*

While the latest Indian tension had been put to rest, the North Redoubt still remained unfinished. There was little for Gage to do but send up masons from New York once again. By November, 1770, Captain Brown had received confirmation that this would occur.[93] He was still justifying his conduct of the previous summer and fall to Gage and maintaining that it had been impossible to finish both buildings before the end of the season. By early April the masons and carpenters had set out under the direction of Lieutenant Pfister who had spent the winter in New York. Gage communicated this to Captain Brown and pointedly noted that they were being sent, "I hope for the last time."[94] Gage at least had the satisfaction of reporting to the Earl of Hillsborough that the Great Lakes posts were finally "in general in a very defensible state," and that very little remained to be done that year other than complete the redoubt at Fort Niagara.[95]

The 1771 work went smoothly and without conflict. On August 11 Brown wrote that every available man in the garrison was at work on the "Second Stone Building", and that progress was rapid. By the end of the month he could report that the redoubt would soon be finished.[96] The last cash was disbursed for the project at the end of the year. Total cost of the two buildings, including transportation of the masons and carpenters, amounted to £5564-3-7. Although this figure probably includes part of the cost of erecting stockades in 1770 and 1771, it was still a far cry from the £700 estimated for the two smaller stone blockhouses in 1767. Nearly £2159 of this expense had been incurred during the second season of work.[97] Fort Niagara was finally secure against Indian attack.

The new redoubts were indeed impressive structures. They were equipped with artillery immediately upon completion although, as late as 1774, the gun deck shutters could not be raised for want of rope! At that time, each building was reported to mount two six-pounders on traveling carriages, exactly the armament projected as early as 1766 and similar to that shown on the section and elevation of 1770.[98] Philadelphian Jabez Fisher visited Fort Niagara in the summer of 1773 and was duly impressed by the two structures. He noted that:

> *... there are 2 large Redoubts, built of Stone the Walls of which are 5 feet thick and Impervious to every attack in the Lower part of each there is a Large Magazine of Ammunition & the upper Part which overlooks the River Niagara the Lake Ontario & back of the Fort for several Miles which is all clear'd ground are several brass cannon which may be fir'd on the Enemy to great advantage as the Men are totally secure from any assault.*[99]

Fort Niagara had been converted from a regular fortification into one which could be effectively defended against Indians. And yet, the job had not been completed. The old earthworks remained in place although in a terribly deteriorated condition. The picketing along the ruined earthen curtain and bastions still had to be maintained, and the Gate of the Five Nations continued to be the primary entrance to Fort Niagara. These residual fortifications would have been of no use against a regular army. Ironically, partial abandonment of the formal defenses came only a few years before Niagara's commandants would again be concerned with just such a threat. The outbreak of the American Revolution would make Fort Niagara a potential target for armies equipped with siege artillery. On the eve of that conflict, Lieutenant Colonel John Caldwell, newly arrived at the post, complained of the "decaying state of the Long Curtain, Bastions their Guns and Carriages" but noted that he supposed "it was meant they should all go to ruin from the time the two Blockhouses were built."[100] Indeed it had been, but the possibility of an attack by Continental Army troops would see the restoration of the earthworks and a revised role for the two stone redoubts.

The North Redoubt with its shutters lowered. It is unlikely that the shutters, which kept out the weather, were opened with any frequency during the eighteenth century. *OFN 780/30C.*

"THE STONE BUILDINGS WHICH CONSTITUTE ITS CHIEF DEFENCE"

1775 - 1815

By the time British troops clashed with Massachusetts militia at Lexington and Concord, Niagara was a vastly different fortification than it had been during the previous North American war. In 1775, a garrison of three companies guarded the Niagara Portage and British interests among the Indians from a wooden stockade, perched on a point of land behind ruined earthworks. A rough line of pickets followed the nearly worthless land-side defenses. These were overshadowed by the two new redoubts which served as guardhouses and provided the advance defenses of the post. The two stone towers covered a powder magazine and other buildings, including the commandant's house, which had been left standing between the earthworks and the inner stockade.[101] The garrison had little to fear from Indian attack. As colonial unrest turned into armed conflict, however, the poor condition of Fort Niagara and the small size of its garrison would be of more concern, especially after the loss of Ticonderoga and other derelict fortresses of the 1750's. The garrison was gradually bolstered after 1776. Little was done to once again make the old earthen walls tenable against artillery, however. Fort Niagara was still not in any state for a regular defense as late as September, 1778, when Lieutenant Colonel Mason Bolton described his rambling post:

> *This Fort measures about 1100 yards in Circumference, there are five Bastions & two Blockhouses to be defended & many other parts necessary to be manned ... with a Garrison of five hundred Men or a less Number, it is impregnable against all the Savages in America but if a Strong body of Troops with Artillery Should move this way I believe no Engineer who has ever seen those Works will say it can hold out any considerable time.*[102]

The next few years would see this problem remedied, spurred by American incursions into the country of the Six Nations of the Iroquois. During the summer and fall of 1779 General John Sullivan led a large force of Continental regulars against the homeland of the Seneca. Advance elements of his army approached to within about eighty miles of Fort Niagara, but Sullivan lacked siege artillery, adequate provisions and enough time to make an attempt on Fort Niagara.[103] This threat provided the spur for the British to renovate the old earthworks. By the autumn of 1779 the walls, parts of which had been almost leveled by the neglect of the past fifteen years, had been largely restored. The sodworks were rebuilt and fitted with new palisades and fraising - a sort of horizontal palisade which slanted downward from the top of the wall to impede assault. Only the two triangular "lunettes" which had once flanked the ravelin were not restored having been completely leveled by the garrison sometime between 1774 and 1776.[104] By September, 1779, Lieutenant Colonel Bolton could confidently report that "Our Works are almost finished, and I have no doubt will be defended with spirit."[105]

Labor on the fortifications would be more or less continuous for the remainder of the American War for Independence. Biannual engineer returns for 1781 through 1784 indicate the nature of work on walls and buildings.[106] Little seems to have been done to the stout and relatively new stone redoubts, and they do not appear in the reports. Major changes were made to the configuration of the fort itself, however, and these would affect the way in which the redoubts were used. With restoration of the walls, the inner stockade around the "French Castle" became quite useless. It remained standing at least through the summer of 1779, but a plan believed to be of 1780 and another from 1781 or 1782 show that this citadel against Indian attack had been removed by that time.[107] The stockade along the lake and river banks remained intact. So too did the relationship of the two redoubts to the land side fortifications and the Gate of the Five Nations. Although they had been constructed at a time when it was anticipated that the old walls would be demolished, the towers had been placed so that fire from artillery on their upper floors could sweep the ditches and outworks. The redoubts therefore remained useful components of the land-side defenses when the old walls were restored. While they would surely have proven exposed and dangerous positions during a formal siege, they had resumed the function described in Muller's third definition of a redoubt.

It was also during this period that the redoubts took on outer defenses of their own. A few years after the end of the American Revolution, Captain John Enys described the square "towers" in each bastion and noted that they were "divided from the inside of

A rare view of Fort Niagara from the east riverbank, about 1785, shows minor details of the upper floors and classical elements of the redoubts. Both appear to have weather vanes. *Courtesy, William L. Clements Library.*

the fort by high strong Pickets."[108] It is unclear when these stockades were erected, but it was probably after 1780 since they do not show on the plan supposed to be of that year. While engineer returns from 1781 through 1783 record the cutting of many oak and cedar pickets, they lack specific mention of the construction of stockades around the redoubts.[109] Plans of the 1790's show exactly what had been done. The North Redoubt was surrounded by a square enclosure with simple flanking projections at the center of each side. This stockade was pierced by a gate at a point opposite the doorway of the redoubt. The pickets were backed by a wooden scaffolding or banquette, three feet high. This provided a firing step for men standing behind the stockade and raised the loopholes beyond the reach of anyone on the outside. No height is given for the pickets, but they probably stood between twelve and fourteen feet above ground level. The enclosure around the South Redoubt was larger and more complex due to the building's function as a gatehouse. Double gates on two sides of the stockade permitted access to the archway through the redoubt. The proximity of the earthworks to several sides of the South Redoubt prevented construction of a simple square stockade like that around the North Redoubt. It was thus more elongated and not as well flanked. This structure was also backed by a firing step.[110]

From the time of the American Revolution, the stone redoubts were increasingly viewed as citadels for the garrison. The stockades which separated them from the rest of Fort Niagara were restored in 1794 during a period of particular tension between Great Britain and the United States. American military action against the Indians that year caused the British posts of the Great Lakes to be put on alert. Lieutenant Governor John Graves Simcoe, charged with the defense of Upper Canada, gave special attention to the works at Fort Niagara. He planned to further close off the interiors of both bastions with stockades and convert the two redoubts to defensible barracks. The drawbridge gate was to be abandoned as useless, permitting the South Redoubt to be more securely enclosed. Simcoe compared the redoubts to "caveliers" (buildings within a fort intended to mount guns on their roofs to fire over the walls) so this original function was maintained.[111] It does not appear that Simcoe's recommendations were followed. The Hamilton plan of circa 1795 and the earliest American plans of 1798 probably represent the redoubt stockades as rebuilt at Simcoe's orders in 1794, but the old drawbridge Gate of the Five Nations remained in use. Each redoubt continued to mount a pair of cannon on its top floor throughout this time.[112] Use of the stone redoubts as strong points would continue well into the period of United States occupation.

The years immediately following the American Revolution also saw a change in the way in which the two buildings were described. Use of the term "redoubt" disappears entirely. Most visitors referred, as did Lieutenant Thomas Hughes in 1786, to the "stone blockhouses in the bastions."[113] When Captain John Enys visited Fort Niagara the following year he noted that in each bastion was "a Square stone Tower with a Block house on the top of it."[114] Enys no doubt observed the masonry towers topped by their imposing Chinese roofs and heavy wooden shutters. He confused these features with a wooden blockhouse of the kind so common on the American and Canadian frontiers by the 1780's. Enys and his contemporaries probably described the buildings as blockhouses because of their defensive function within the interior of Fort Niagara. This impression was reinforced by the fact that, although Fort Niagara possessed many elements of regular fortification, it was still perceived by most European officers as a frontier fortress. In 1795 the French traveler Rochefoucault, Duc de Liancourt, mentioned the "blockhouses" mounted with cannon but noted that "this fort, in common with all such small fortified places, cannot long withstand a

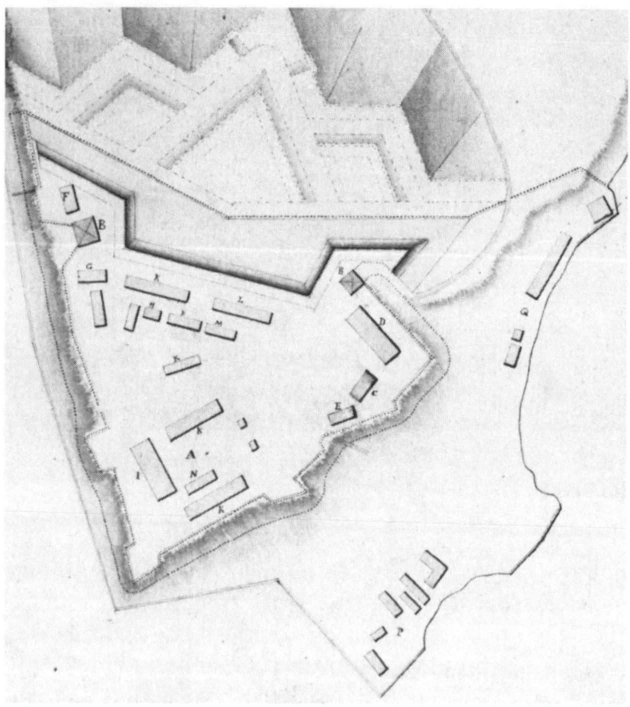

This undated plan is believed to have been made about 1780. The inner fort has been dismantled, but stockades have not yet been erected around the redoubts. *Courtesy, Public Record Office, MPH 275.*

regular attack, yet the besiegers cannot take it without a considerable loss."[115] Here was perhaps the most important consideration in the purpose of the redoubts during the last quarter of the eighteenth century. Although they might have been of relatively little use in a formal siege employing heavy artillery, the two buildings greatly strengthened Fort Niagara's land defenses and interior against attack by infantry, whether they be Native American warriors or European regulars.

There was a real possibility that Fort Niagara might once again face besiegers during the 1790's. The Treaty of Paris had ended the American War for Independence in 1783, but many points remained unresolved between Great Britain and the United States of America. Further tension was created by the fact that troops of the new republic clashed repeatedly with the Indian tribes of Ohio and Indiana during the 1780's and 1790's. Many of these native groups had been allies of the British during the War for Independence, and Americans firmly believed that the Indians continued to receive covert support in their efforts to stop white encroachment. Particularly galling to the United States was the fact that the five major Great Lakes posts - Carleton Island, Oswego, Niagara, Detroit, and Michilimackinac - remained in British hands, even though they had been ceded by the 1783 treaty. British charges of non-compliance with certain terms of that document provided a rationale to retain the posts. The small size of the United States Army precluded military action to seize them. The two countries came perilously close to open conflict in 1794 when the Indians were defeated by United States forces on the Maumee River in Ohio, but additional negotiations were even then being concluded. Jay's Treaty of 1794 settled the disagreements and guaranteed withdrawal of British garrisons from the Great Lakes posts. On August 10, 1796, a small detachment of United States regulars took possession of Fort Niagara.[116]

The weak military situation of Fort Niagara's new occupants gave renewed importance to the redoubts. In 1796, Fort Niagara's British garrison, which had recently numbered as many as four hundred men, was replaced by a mere fifty United States artillerymen.[117] The British withdrew across the Niagara River and began construction of a new post which would become Fort George. Potential enemies were therefore close at hand, and the tiny American garrison had no friendly post nearer than Oswego, 150 miles to the east. The new situation also totally changed the utility of Fort Niagara's defenses. The great walls constructed in the 1750's and restored during the American Revolution had anticipated a land attack from the east. With the Niagara River now an international boundary and hostile guns mounted on the opposite shore, the old defenses suddenly faced the wrong direction! The new threat to the west and southwest was opposed by only the poorly fortified river side of the post. Even worse, the new British fort stood on slightly higher ground than Fort Niagara, and artillery mounted there could command the American garrison. The problems of inadequate garrisons, isolation, obsolescence of the defenses, and exposure to enemy fire were all recognized by American and British officers.[118] They would be demonstrated with painful clarity during the War of 1812.

Although Fort Niagara's deficiencies were recognized, it was quite another matter to do something about them. The number of soldiers in the garrison was so small that even proper maintenance of the numerous and aging buildings was difficult. English traveler Isaac Weld noted, rather contemptuously, in 1796 that "every part of the fort now exhibits a picture of slovenliness and neglect."[119] Stopgap measures would be taken during the first decade of the nineteenth century to minimize the danger and improve the security of Fort Niagara, but the expense of reorienting the defenses and providing an adequate garrison would prove to be prohibitive. Likewise, the possibility of establishing a new, smaller and less exposed post would be explored and eventually discarded.[120] The tiny United States garrison of Fort Niagara would thus be saddled with the challenge of defending a post that was too large, poorly placed and commanded by enemy guns.

The first United States troops found the land-side earthworks to again be in deplorable condition. These had been faced with heavy plank by 1795 in a continuing effort to slow erosion.[121] Judging from comments by Niagara's second American commandant, Major John Jacob Ulrich Rivardi, this had not solved the old problem. Rivardi had little good to say about the walls or the British engineers who had repaired them over the past two decades. To Major General Alexander Hamilton he wrote in 1799:

> *... This place affords an other instance of the dispositions of British Engineers who in this Part of the World at least take care to build their works in Such a Manner & of Such materials that they are Sure To be in constant employment as the repairs are constantly wanting - The Parapets are composed of loose earth intertwined with branches of trees not even divested of their leaves - The whole is kept together by a revetment of boards, The branches decaying, excavations ensue, of course; the earth is washed to the bottom of the revetment which gives way & must be made New ...*

Ironically, Rivardi suggested that "At half the expense good works of Solid clay well sodded could have been constructed." This was, of course, the very construction that the plank revetting was intended to improve. Rivardi sadly noted that, in the event of war with Great Britain, it was "a certainty" that Niagara, "in its present State, could not be kept fourty eight hours if Seriously attacked."[122]

Given the condition of the defenses, it is not surprising that the stone redoubts were immediately pressed into service as strong points, and so they would remain during the first years of American occupation. It is clear from the earliest known United States plan of the post that the stockades surrounding each building were maintained until at least the end of the century. The South Redoubt served as the post guard house, and the powder magazine in the northern building remained in use.[123] Estimates and proposals were prepared in 1798 for reconstruction of the firing step behind the stockades around the two buildings, and it seems likely that this work was accomplished.[124]

From the time of his arrival in 1797, Major Rivardi had looked to the two stone towers and the large "Stone house" (French Castle) as the "three only points capable of resistance" within Fort Niagara. Shortly after the appointment of Alexander Hamilton as Major General commanding the northern posts of the United States, Rivardi wrote him with ideas for making Fort Niagara tenable against attack. He recommended erecting or maintaining stockades

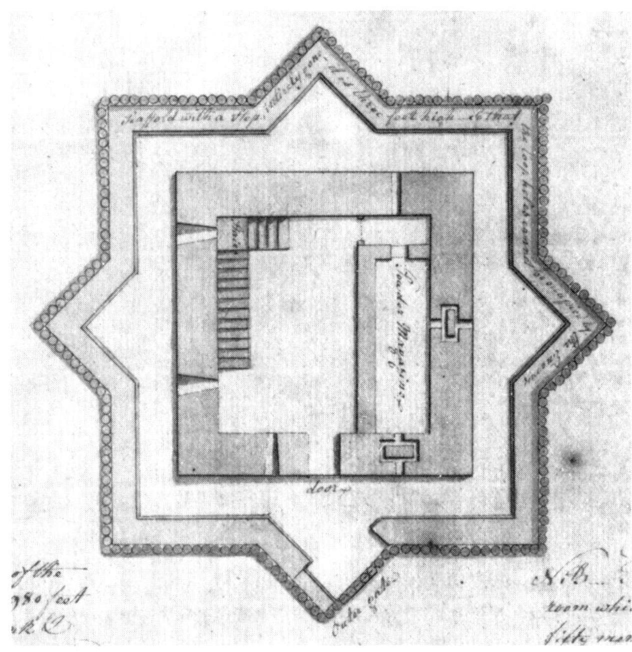
Maj. John J.U. Rivardi's 1798 ground plan of the North Redoubt and its stockade depicts loopholes only on the lake side (left) and near the entrance. The building appears to have been only slightly altered since 1771, but the number of powder magazine ventilators disagrees with plans of 1773 and 1842. *Courtesy, National Archives and Records Administration, RG 77, Dr. 3, Sht. 13.*

around the two stone redoubts and the stone house, then in use as officers' quarters. The three strong points were to be connected by stockades serving as covered lines of communication. This plan would, in effect, have placed a large triangular stockade within the enclosure of Fort Niagara. Rivardi's lines were not intended to replace the main walls but rather to strengthen the internal defense of the place which he believed to be sadly deficient, especially with the small garrison available to hold it. These particular measures had apparently been on Rivardi's mind for at least a year since they were shown on a plan prepared by him as early as June, 1798. Following Hamilton's appointment, Rivardi sent the general a similar plan with a description of his proposed alterations.[125]

In order to make this plan work, however, it would be necessary to dismantle many of the old barracks and storehouses which virtually filled the interior of Fort Niagara. Few of these structures were needed by the small American garrison, and many of them were aging encumbrances dating to the British and even the French occupations. Their demolition was advisable to clear fields of fire for the three strong points and to deny cover to attackers who might gain entrance to the post. Rivardi asked Hamilton's permission to "remove a number of buildings which not only would afford Shelter to an enemy, but Supply him with Materials ready placed & prepared to reduce the garrison into ashes." The streets ran in several direc-

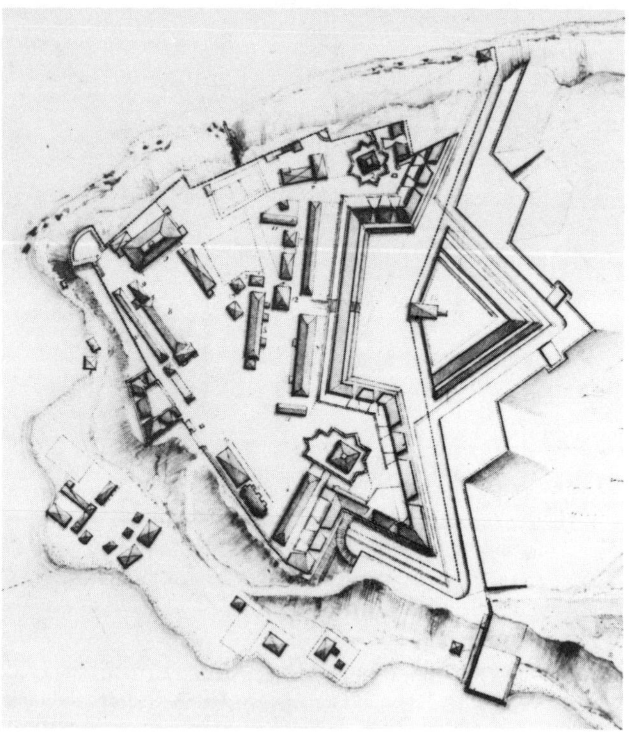

Fort Niagara in 1798. The redoubts had been stockaded since the 1780's. *Courtesy, National Archives and Records Administration, RG 77, Dr. 3, Sht. 2.*

tions and were not commanded by the strong points. Bodies of enemy troops might therefore safely form in them, the major felt. The presence of the old wooden buildings made it impossible for the three citadels to "afford each other mutual protection." Rivardi also argued that these useless structures were "a receptacle of filth & render the garrison unhealthy." In addition to his suggestions for increasing the security of Fort Niagara when held by a small garrison, Rivardi also recommended construction of new fortifications on the river side of the post to strengthen it against fire from the Canadian shore.[126]

Major Rivardi's comments received careful attention, but it was not deemed advisable to make such drastic modifications to the internal arrangement of Fort Niagara without further consultation. In the fall of 1799, Rivardi was informed that it had been suggested that Fort Niagara be abandoned and a better location selected along the Niagara River. Hamilton noted that this would receive due consideration, and that, in the meantime, the possibility of moving the post was "a reason for avoiding all expence except such as may be absolutely necessary to preserve valuable things from falling into ruin."[127] During 1800 the question of alterations to Fort Niagara was revived when Senator Uriah Tracy inspected the Great Lakes posts. In his report, Tracy reemphasized Fort Niagara's many shortcomings but admitted that a post of some kind was necessary at the mouth of the river. He had discussed the situation at length with Major Rivardi and "earnestly" recommended removal of many of the old buildings because of the danger of fire and the possibility that they might shelter enemy troops who had forced their way into the works.[128] Tracy's findings appear to have been heavily influenced by Rivardi, but the major left Fort Niagara without seeing substantial demolition of the older structures. Many of these would succumb to age and neglect during the first decade of the nineteenth century, but Rivardi's plan to clear the interior and greatly strengthen the stone house and two redoubts does not seem to have been realized.

The decade prior to the War of 1812 was characterized by maintenance of the most useful parts of Fort Niagara and a gradual deterioration and removal of those old buildings for which the garrison had little or no need. The redoubts certainly fell within the former category. They, in fact, presented less of a problem than most structures of the post. The two stone buildings were noted as being in good repair at the turn of the century. They were probably reshingled during general work on the garrison structures carried out between 1801 and 1803.[129] Although Fort Niagara itself was described by DeWitt Clinton as being "in a ruinous condition" in 1810, the "two blockhouses at the east and west end" of the fortifications do not seem to have been included in that sweeping and gloomy comment.[130]

Throughout this time, the appearance of the two buildings was altered very little. The stockades were removed sometime early in the first decade of the century, but the Chinese-style roofs were still intact in 1806 and remained so as late as the first months of the War of 1812.[131] It seems that the uses of the towers also remained relatively unchanged during this time. The North Redoubt was described in 1798 as having a powder magazine on the ground floor, a large room on the second which could serve as quarters for forty to fifty men and a covered platform at the top fit to support light artillery. The South Redoubt was almost identical except for the ground floor which had no powder magazine and was "reserved for the guard". Under the stairs was a place used as a "black hole" or solitary confinement cell.[132] The South Redoubt was the logical location for the guard room because of its proximity to the main gate. Although there is no specific mention of the gateway passing through the building, plans of Fort Niagara from as late as about 1805 show this to have been the case. The ground floor must have been much less comfortable for the guard than the room above with its fireplace. Perhaps the ground floor location was more convenient to the gate and sentry posts or the second floor, like that of the North Redoubt, was reserved for use as a barracks.

It was during the first decade of the nineteenth century that the black hole in the South Redoubt held a particularly talented inmate. Fifer John Carroll served at Fort Niagara between 1800 and 1812. He was a fine musician, according to Samuel De Veaux, then a contractor for the garrison and later author of a short history and guide to the Niagara area. De Veaux speculated that Carroll might have been a relative of a famous Irish harpist by the same name. He noted that, like the harpist, Fort Niagara's musician was "of all things devoted to music and whiskey." Carroll had a number of scrapes with army discipline brought on by his drinking habits and his tendency to speak freely while under the influence, even to post commandant Major Moses Porter. On one occasion Carroll was discovered drunk on parade. He was reprimanded and threatened with confinement. Carroll, according to De Veaux, "was not then in so beggarly a state as to bear censure patiently." His tongue got the better of him:

> *... He first retaliated in words, but shortly became so furious and ungovernable, as to make it necessary to confine him; and, what was very unusual, he was conveyed and locked up in the black hole. In the middle of the night, the most dismal sounds were heard from the place of his confinement; and orders were given that he should be looked to. He was found in a piteous condition; declaring that he had been visited by all the hobgoblins, and all the devils in existence; that they came to him immediately at his entrance, and had haunted him all the while he had been confined. He begged that he might be allowed a light, his fife, and pen, ink and paper; that, by employing himself in some way, he might be able to drive away the horrid thoughts and phantoms that assailed him. In the morning, when he was released, and met the other musicians, he produced them a tune which he said he had composed during the latter hours of his confinement. He called it "Carroll's thoughts on eternity."*[133]

De Veaux reported that Carroll produced a number of other musical pieces, all of them unpublished, and that he perished in 1812 in an epidemic then sweeping the army. His music, however, survives. A manuscript copybook begun at Fort Niagara in October, 1804, and bequeathed to none other than "S. DeVeaux" in November, 1812, is in the collections of the Newberry Library in Chicago. The book contains more than six hundred pieces of music, including thirteen written by Carroll himself. Among them is "Carroll's Thoughts on Eternity".[134] If Carroll and De Veaux are to be believed, this tune was composed in a cramped cell below the stairs of the South Redoubt.

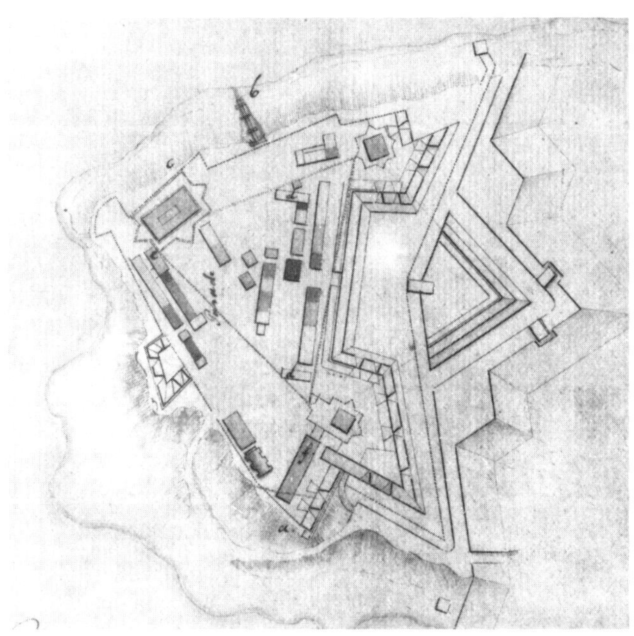

Maj. Rivardi's 1798 plan for strengthening the interior of Fort Niagara recommended stockading the redoubts and the French Castle and connecting those three structures with lines of communication. The numerous old buildings within the fort presented a fire hazard and masked the three strong points. *Courtesy, National Archives and Records Administration, RG 77, Dr. 3, Sht. 13.*

Sometime during the first decade of the nineteenth century an important change was made to the walls of Fort Niagara which would have an immediate effect on the function and an eventual impact on the appearance of the South Redoubt. Although the Gate of the Five Nations is shown in use on plans of the post as late as 1805, it had been abandoned and filled in by 1810. Thereafter, the entrance to Fort Niagara would be on the river side of the post. The new access road led from the garrison common, through the glacis and down the bank to the large patch of land at water level between the fort and the river. From there the road climbed the bank to pass through a gate situated midway along the river side wall, roughly on the site of the extant Postern Gate.[135] The reason for this alteration is unknown but may be surmised. British Lieutenant Governor John Graves Simcoe had recommended abandonment of the old drawbridge gate as early as 1794. His advice was not heeded. Simcoe believed the "land Post-Gate" was useless. This fact, combined with the difficulty and expense of maintaining a wooden bridge, probably sealed the fate of the structure sometime before 1810.[136] The new entrance was shielded from the land side by the walls of Fort Niagara but was curiously exposed to observation from the Canadian shore. Relocation of Fort Niagara's main entrance made the gateway through the South Redoubt a useless anachronism. The building does not seem to have been altered at this time, but its function as the post's main guardhouse ended. Refer-

Maj. Moses Porter confined Fifer John Carroll in the black hole of the South Redoubt. From *Historical Collections of the Danvers Historical Society*, Vol. 15 (1927).

ences from the first year of the War of 1812 indicate that the guardhouse was located elsewhere.[137] A river-side gate would provide the main access to Fort Niagara until reconstruction of the Gate of the Five Nations in 1930-31.

Sixteen years after United States troops first marched into the post, Fort Niagara faced its second and most challenging test of fire. The outbreak of the War of 1812 found military forces on both sides of the Niagara River quite unprepared for a major conflict. Fort Niagara had changed a great deal since its last British garrison had crossed over the river. By the summer of 1812, many of the old wooden buildings of the post had finally been removed. Most had not been replaced. DeWitt Clinton noted the deterioration of the place in 1810 and sadly remarked that "The only pleasant thing to the feelings of an American are the new barracks which are building."[138] The tiny garrison needed only a few structures. Fort Niagara had been occupied by a single company since about 1805, and, as late as April, 1812, the post was held by only three officers and seventy enlisted men of Captain Nathaniel Leonard's company of the 1st Regiment of Artillery.[139] The garrison occupied a number of wooden and masonry buildings. The former numbered at least three barracks and some storehouses. The stone structures all dated to the French and British periods and included a powder magazine, bakehouse, provisions storehouse, the "Mess House" or French Castle which served as officers' quarters, and the two stone redoubts.[140] The latter were most commonly termed "blockhouses" or "towers" by this time. Fort Niagara's land-side defense was provided by the old earthworks, still faced with plank, but the walls were nothing to boast of. Less than a week after the United States declared war on Great Britain, New York Governor Daniel D. Tompkins was informed that the works of Fort Niagara were "in a miserable and decayed situation and can make but a feeble defence."[141]

Large numbers of New York militia were marching to the Niagara Frontier even before the declaration of war. Most of these men assembled in Lewiston, six miles up the river, while Fort Niagara was held by soldiers of the regular United States Army. The perilously small garrison began receiving reinforcements early in July. By the middle of that month it had been augmented by newly arrived regulars to somewhere between 400 and 450 men.[142] A garrison of this size was quite adequate for the defense of Fort Niagara. The post commandant had worries other than troop strength, however. Open hostilities would inevitably involve an exchange of artillery fire between Fort Niagara and Fort George. The American post was woefully short of artillery. Its heaviest guns were mere six-pounders, supplemented by a number of howitzers and a pair of large brass mortars. By July 6 only six of the six-pounders were mounted. The howitzers and mortars were still not emplaced, but they would have been useless in any event since there were no shells on hand for them![143] Fort Niagara's deficiency of heavy garrison artillery would not be corrected until early September.[144]

Of even greater concern to the United States garrison was the exposed position of Fort Niagara and the poor state of its fortifications. The fact that the American fort was commanded from the higher ground of Fort George had been known for many years, and it was commonly believed that Fort Niagara might have to be abandoned in time of war.[145] No such hasty move was made. Rather, New York militia engineer Nicholas Gray began making recommendations to Captain Nathaniel Leonard of ways in which he might improve the defense of his post. Gray selected the two "towers" and the Mess House to anchor a new battery and fortifications on the river side of Fort Niagara. Even Gray's proposals contained an element of doubt, however, as to whether the position could be held. He described his contingency plans to Governor Tompkins late in July:

> ... *I have recommended him* [Captain Leonard] *to throw up a new bastion in the west* [river side] *so as to command the British fort and the town of New-*

Fort Niagara from Navy Hall, 1804, by Surgeon Edward Walsh. The stockade along the weakly fortified river side is clearly visible. *Courtesy, William L. Clements Library.*

> *ark, which will contain seven guns of a large calibre (when he gets them,) the stone tower* [South Redoubt] *forming one of the angles, and will be protected on the north and north-east by the messhouse* [Castle] *and another stone tower to the east* [North Redoubt]. *I propose to throw up a breastwork from the last mentioned tower to the skirt of the wood, a distance of about three hundred yards, sufficiently high to protect a retreat in case such were necessary.*[146]

Gray's proposal was an attempt to reorient the fortifications to face the primary threat. The towers, almost certainly mounting one or more six-pounder cannon each, were again to be strong points - this time facing attack from the rear.

It is uncertain how much of this work was accomplished during the summer of 1812. Some of the urgency disappeared when a truce was arranged for the Niagara River front. This would continue into early October. The truce allowed time for United States forces to strengthen their positions, obtain heavy artillery and gather reinforcements. The destination of many newly recruited regular troops was Fort Niagara. Early in September, Lieutenant Colonel John Fenwick of the Regiment of Light Artillery arrived and assumed command of the post. Fenwick was not impressed by what had been done to improve Fort Niagara. "The defence of this place is precarious outside of the stonehouse [Mess House]", he reported to Major General Stephen Van Renssalaer.[147] The fort was still not tenable, and measures were being taken to bury military stores and artillery in the event the place had to be abandoned. Work nonetheless continued on additional batteries to oppose British guns.[148] Captain Leonard had apparently done little to implement Colonel Gray's plans to strengthen Fort Niagara. Superior officers charged that the new commandant was no more energetic. When Fenwick was slow following orders to strip the roof from the Mess House and convert it to an elevated battery, Colonel Solomon Van Renssalaer charged that "unfortunately Col. Fenwick and Capt. Leonard are too much addicted to liquor to attend to this duty as they should."[149]

The decision to utilize the Mess House as a gun platform anticipated major changes in the appearance of the redoubts. Guns placed on the Mess House could command Fort George and several batteries across the river. Its roof was removed in September, and three cannon were mounted on the third floor. Not surprisingly, this treatment was extended to the two stone towers which had originally been designed to carry fieldpieces on their upper floors. It is uncertain when their roofs were removed, however. In his letter reporting the conversion of the Mess House, Colonel Van Renssalaer noted that each of the "blockhouses" mounted six-pounders but did not say whether their roofs remained intact.[150] The lone source which mentions removal of the lovely Chinese roofs of the North and South Redoubts seems to indicate that the alterations were accomplished between November 14, when Lieutenant Colonel George McFeely arrived at the post, and the 21st when Forts Niagara and George again exchanged fire. During this period McFeely recorded in his journal that:

> *...The roofs were taken off the Block-houses to prevent the enemy from fire-ing them with shot, all hands were set to work day and night in building sod Battries on the tops of the Block houses and mounting guns ...*[151]

The removal of the roofs and construction of earthen or sod breastworks atop the masonry parapets was very similar to what had been done to the Mess House in September.[152] McFeely's fear that the British might burn the redoubt roofs with heated shot also suggests that they were removed sometime after the October 13 Battle of Queenston Heights. At that time the enemy guns in Fort George were not as effective as they might have been because the British had no furnaces for heating shot.[153] McFeely probably believed that their oversight would be corrected next time. Removal of the roofs also improved the field of fire of the guns mounted on the tops of the stone towers and lessened the danger of casualties caused by wood splinters.

The redoubts did not receive their true baptism of fire until October, 1812. The buildings had not yet been constructed when Fort Niagara last faced bombardment by heavy guns during the siege of 1759, and the summer's truce along the river had delayed an exchange of shot and shell between the opposing forts. With the expiration of the truce, however, war along the Niagara Frontier finally began in earnest. Early on the morning of October 13, United States forces began crossing the river from Lewiston to invade Upper Canada at the village of Queenston. The issue hung in the balance for most of the day, but the British prevailed. The defenders lost Major General Isaac Brock, while the American attack was repulsed and large numbers of prisoners taken.[154]

Although Fort Niagara was located six miles down river from the scene of the action, its artillerymen were heavily engaged throughout the morning of October 13. British guns in Fort George opened fire at 5:30 and were immediately answered from Fort Niagara. The exchange continued for seven hours. Several buildings in the village of Newark were destroyed by heated shot from Fort Niagara. Fort George's powder magazine was set afire and only extinguished through the quick action and "heroic presence of mind" of Captain Henry Vigoureux and a number of volunteers. The British guns, some of them firing explosive shell, eventually silenced the batteries of Fort Niagara and drove the American artillerymen from their guns. Captain Leonard ordered the post abandoned and led a retreat to the woods - the same refuge suggested by Lieutenant Colonel Gray earlier that summer. Once the garrison had reached safety, however, there was concern that the British would cross the river and occupy Fort Niagara. At this point, Captain James McKeon led a guard of twenty volunteers back to the fort. They watched over the place until the following morning when the rest of the garrison returned.[155]

McKeon, who commanded a company of the 3rd Regiment of Artillery, served with distinction throughout the day-long battle. His original post had been on the upper floor of the South Redoubt where he commanded a single six-pounder gun. Both stone towers were used as elevated gun platforms that day, and their fire seems to have been the most effective of any directed against the opposite shore. McKeon's six-pounder discharged a large number of red-hot shot against Fort George and the village of Newark. One of McKeon's gunners claimed that his six-pounder ignited the Newark court house, a brewery and a tan house. The latter two structures were totally consumed. The South Redoubt drew its share of return fire, however, and the defenses (and perhaps the roof) were "shivered almost into splinters." The matter was decided when the British guns began firing "bomb-shells" (actually "spherical case", a new and effective anti-personnel ammunition) at the building. Miraculously, none of the gunners on the South Redoubt had been injured and the six-pounder was still in service by the time Captain Leonard ordered Fort Niagara abandoned.[156]

The situation was not so fortunate atop the North Redoubt. That building was armed with a single twelve-pounder which fired away through most of the action, crewed by men from Captain Leonard's company of the 1st Regiment of Artillery. They too must have suffered when the British began directing shell at Fort Niagara. At this critical moment, the gunners became careless and failed to properly ram home the heavy powder charge. The cast iron twelve-pounder burst, sending jagged chunks of metal richocheting around the confined gun deck. Private Shaw was killed outright, and Private Todd lost both legs, surviving the accident by only a few hours. Despite the intensity of the seven hour action, however, the two unfortunate artillerymen seem to have been the only fatalities in the United States garrison.[157]

Fort Niagara had clearly received the worst of its first exchange with Fort George. The commanding position of the British guns, the skill of their gunners and their access to effective explosive shell all had a demoralizing effect on the American garrison. One wonders, however, if Captain Leonard did not retreat too precipitously from his post, especially when casualties had been so light after a seven hour action. Leonard was fortunate that the British did not have the troops available to cross the river and enter Fort Niagara since its recapture by United States forces from the land side would have required a full-scale siege.

Work on Fort Niagara resumed as soon as the guns had fallen silent. For the rest of October and into November, parties of soldiers labored to strengthen the main fortifications and construct detached batteries facing Fort George.[158] The American post received a new commandant on November 14 when Lieutenant Colonel George McFeely of the 22nd Regiment of Infantry relieved Colonel William Winder of the 14th. McFeely set his men to work "day and night" further preparing the defenses for the next clash. It seems to have been at this time that the wooden roofs were removed from the redoubts and sod stacked atop the parapets to provide additional cover for the gun crews.[159] The armament of the towers was also rearranged in the wake of the disastrous bursting of the twelve-pounder on October 13. The ruined gun on the North Redoubt was replaced with a six-pounder, perhaps that from the south tower, and an iron twelve-pounder was hoisted to the top of the South Redoubt. Each weapon was served by twelve men drawn equally from the artillery and infantry detachments in the garrison. Captain McKeon remained in command of the "south tower" while a Captain Jacks of the 7th Regiment, New York Militia Artillery was given responsibility for the "north tower".[160]

McFeely's preparations were completed with no time to spare. Around noon on November 20 Fort Niagara's sentries noticed frantic activity in Newark where residents of the town were observed moving furniture out of their homes. At sundown a courier arrived from headquarters in Buffalo. He carried a message from Brigadier General Alexander Smyth informing McFeely that an armistice then in effect would end at 1:00 a.m. on the 21st. Smyth would himself lead another invasion of Upper Canada from Buffalo to Fort Erie. The British garrison of Fort George and the citizens of Newark had received the news hours earlier thanks to a system of beacons or "combustible telegraphs" which lined the Canadian side of the river. Fort Niagara's garrison immediately lit the shot furnaces and prepared their batteries for action. By midnight all was in readiness, but McFeely would not give permission to open fire because he feared that "12 hours cannonading would exhaust all the ammunition in the fort." The men stood to their guns and waited for dawn.[161]

The British artillerymen in Fort George opened fire at 6:00 on the morning of November 21, 1812. Fort Niagara was soon enduring a rain of heated shot and spherical case, estimated by McFeely as 2,000 of the former and 180 of the latter. The American post was far better prepared than on the previous occasion, however, and better armed. Nor was Lieutenant Colonel McFeely of a temperament to abandon his position. His gunners had in the fort and in the "Salt Battery", located in Youngstown about a mile upriver,

The North Redoubt retains its Chinese roof in this 1806 view by Sempronious Stretton. Fort Niagara's flagstaff had traditionally been located in the North or Lake Bastion. Late in the War of 1812, the pole would briefly stand on the North Redoubt itself. *Courtesy, National Archives of Canada, C18775.*

three eighteen-pounders, two twelve-pounders and two six-pounders. The two heavier calibers of gun fired red-hot shot, and these again played with effect on the wooden buildings of Newark and Fort George.[162] The British, for their part, considered the enemy fire "sharp but ill-directed" and claimed their own share of hits on the American positions, including the destruction of several buildings situated between Fort Niagara and the river. On the British side, Lieutenant Colonel Christopher Myers admitted damage in Fort George and the village as well as the complete destruction of the old barracks at Navy Hall. The firing continued for about eleven hours before it finally died out around 5:00 p.m.[163]

Fort Niagara's redoubts again figured prominently in the action. For a second time they also proved to be badly exposed and likely to endure substantial casualties because of their open but confined upper decks. Captain Jacks and his militia gunners stood by their six-pounder on the North Redoubt even though, according to McFeely, they were in "a situation most exposed to the fire of the enemy." The militia artillerymen nonetheless "maintained their position like veterans."[164] Their steadiness cost them dearly. British Colonel Myers watched as a "well directed shell" from one of his guns "burst upon the enemy's north blockhouse". He claimed that the gun there was dismounted

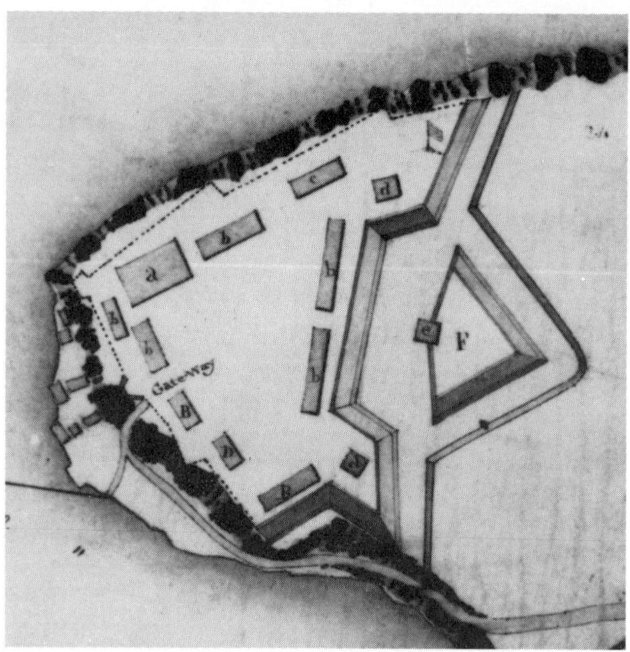

By the time A. Gray drew this plan in November, 1810, the drawbridge entrance had been replaced by a new gateway on the river side of the fort. *Courtesy, National Archives of Canada, H2/440/Niagara/1810, NMC19551.*

and abandoned. McFeely reported no damage to his guns but noted that one British shell "did injury to our men." This was probably on the North Redoubt, and it is likely that two men were killed by the explosion and flying shrapnel.[165]

Atop the South Redoubt, Captain McKeon again "distinguished himself by his usual gallantry and skill," and the hot shot from his twelve-pounder must have caused some of the damage on the opposite shore. This effective service was ended by yet another loading accident, however. In using hot shot, the solid, cast iron balls were heated in a furnace, carried to the gun, rammed home, and promptly fired. The tremendous amount of heat stored in the shot easily set fire to any wooden structure. There were hazards to the men using hot shot as well. The ball had to be separated from the powder charge by soaking wet wadding. The gun was rapidly loaded and fired to avoid premature ignition by the heated shot. As one of McKeon's gunners rammed a hot shot down the barrel of the twelve-pounder, the ball, which had expanded because of the heat and was perhaps ill-cast to begin with, suddenly stuck in the barrel about two feet from the powder charge. Apparently the crew did not realize that the shot had not been properly seated. When the gun was fired it instantly "burst into ten thousand pieces", repeating the October 13 tragedy on the North Redoubt. One man was killed and four wounded. At least one of the wounded later died. Most of the others must have lost limbs in the explosion. When McFeely was invited for tea that evening at the quarters of garrison surgeon Joseph West, he lost his appetite as soon as he saw "a pile of legs and arms lying in the corner on the floor." Doctor West was rather amused by the squeamishness of his commandant, who quickly excused himself. Four Americans were killed and seven wounded in the battle.[166] The capable Captain McKeon was not injured in the accident.

November 21 had been a terribly exhausting day for the garrison of Fort Niagara. McFeely's fears for his ammunition supply proved well-founded. The gunners fired off most of the powder and shot, and Major Walker K. Armistead spent the next day frantically requesting a fresh supply from Buffalo.[167] Fort Niagara's soldiers could be justly proud of their performance, having withstood a tremendous pounding from the enemy batteries. The British were impressed by the strength of Fort Niagara's masonry structures, particularly the Mess House and the stone towers. One observer noted of the American fort that "We made little impression on the stone buildings, which constitute its principal defence."[168] The tone of an American's letter to the *Buffalo Gazette* was more fulsome. The correspondent noted of the action of November 21 that:

> ... *Fort Niagara has received but little injury, the houses stand to cover, the stonework remains to protect men with courage, officers with intrepidity and skill, and guns to repel, avenge, and under Providence to frustrate the next attempt of the enemy to carry their* terrible *threat into effect.*[169]

Despite the much improved defense of the place, the basic flaws of the position had not been corrected. Mounting guns on the tops of the redoubts and the Mess House made the weapons more effective in returning the fire of Fort George but also badly exposed the gun crews. The British correspondent who noted that the buildings of Fort Niagara had been little damaged in the action of November 21 also reported that "we killed and wounded a good number of men stationed at the guns on top of them."[170] There was simply not enough protection on the gun decks of these buildings, even from the long distance fire directed on the post from Fort George. To have attempted to man guns on the tops of the redoubts during a siege from the land side would have resulted in monumental casualties. The same deficiency of cover for men and guns was noted for the Martello towers so popular in Britain at this period. A committee of engineers had noted in 1804, just as the massive seacoast Martello tower building program was about to begin in Britain, that:

> ... *It is admitted that upon first landing of an enemy a tower is not to be taken by assault; but a few shells thrown by small mortars brought on*

shore ... might in a short time destroy the carriages of the guns on the platform or top of the tower and thereby render its effect as a sea-battery useless ...[171]

The stone redoubt towers at Fort Niagara had been shown by wartime experience to have exactly the same advantages and the same deficiencies.

The actions of October 13 and November 21 had focused attention on the use of the redoubts as gun platforms. Their other functions had not been forgotten, however. It appears that the second floors of the buildings were used as quarters or additional guard rooms for the expanded garrison. These men soon settled into a winter routine following the dangerous excitement of late November. The infantry component of Fort Niagara's garrison consisted of two companies of McFeely's 22nd Regiment of Infantry and one of the 23rd. These were newly raised battalions which had only arrived from their Pennsylvania recruiting depots in November.[172] The men needed further drill and training, and they spent much time in these activities during the winter of 1812-13. At least two hours per day were spent at drill. The frequently inclement Lake Ontario weather could make this a hardship, however, and the "blockhouse" was specified as a sheltered location for drill in the event the day was wet or cold. Officers also learned the manual of arms so as to better instruct their men. In March, 1813, they were ordered to assemble with their muskets daily at 2:00 p.m. in the North Redoubt.[173]

The redoubts were also used for the purpose for which they were best suited: as strong points or "blockhouses" within the garrison. As early as February, 1813, the garrison order book included plans for last-ditch defense should it became necessary to abandon the gun positions on the main walls. The redoubts were considered important enough for each to be held by a full company of infantry plus whatever artillerymen were nearby when the signal to retire was given. Captain Daniel McFarland and his company of the 22nd Infantry were to withdraw to the North Redoubt while Captain David Millikin and his company, also of the 22nd, were to occupy the South Redoubt. They were to post their men at the loopholes to oppose a British assault. The lone company of the 23rd Infantry would hold the Mess House, and all officers commanding strong points were exhorted in the orders to "hold out to the last extremity."[174]

Such drastic measures would prove unnecessary during the winter and, in fact, for most of 1813. By spring, United States forces had taken the offensive on Lake Ontario. They were also meeting with success in their attempts to capture key points along the borders of Upper Canada. A combined naval and military force descended on the provincial capital of York (modern Toronto) on April 27 and captured the fort and town. One month later the same army and fleet, reinforced by additional troops from Sackets Harbor and the Niagara Frontier, took Fort George after a hard-fought action.[175] The artillery in Fort Niagara and in a number of new batteries along the east bank of the river played a crucial role in the prelanding bombardment. Fort George was effectively destroyed, its buildings burned and its guns dismounted before United States troops waded ashore on May 27. Guns on the redoubts took part in the general bombardment, and much of the success of the American attack on Fort George was attributed to the good services of the artillery.[176]

Col. Solomon Van Renssalaer ordered the French Castle unroofed and converted to an elevated battery in September, 1812. From Benson J. Lossing's *Pictorial Fieldbook of the War of 1812.*

These initial victories were soon followed by a series of disappointments on the Niagara front. British General John Vincent was able to extricate his shattered force from Newark and the ruins of Fort George, due largely to the lassitude of American commander Major General Henry Dearborn. Vincent's troops escaped to deal stinging defeats to units belatedly pursuing them at Stoney Creek on June 6 and Beaver Dams on June 23. The initiative had been lost by that time, and a substantial United States field army spent the summer and fall of 1813 bottled

Fort Niagara in 1814 by John Henry Slade. The South Redoubt (right) is shown without its roof and with only the stub of its chimney. In December, 1813, the British gained access to the fort through the gateway at center. *Courtesy, National Archives of Canada, C42570.*

up in Fort George while British and Canadian raiders annoyed their outposts. By autumn, most of the regular troops had been diverted for an offensive against Montreal, and the occupation of Fort George was largely in the hands of the New York Militia. Expiring enlistments and the weak strength of this force influenced its commander, New York Brigadier General George McClure, to order a withdrawal to the east bank of the Niagara River. On December 10 McClure had Fort George and the village of Newark destroyed. He then departed for Buffalo with his remaining militia leaving Fort Niagara in the hands of Captain Leonard and a garrison of United States regulars.[177]

Following the capture of Fort George, the role of Fort Niagara had become quite secondary. Throughout the summer and fall of 1813 the post guarded the mouth of the river and protected the rear of Fort George. Fort Niagara also served as a convenient depot for provisions and supplies needed by the army in Canada. No attempt was made by the British to attack this strong defensive complex. With the abandonment of Fort George, however, the old American fort was again on the front line. When McClure scurried off to Buffalo he left virtually every regular soldier still on the Niagara Frontier to defend Fort Niagara. This amounted, on December 15, to a garrison of one company of artillery and three of infantry for a total of 369 men. The addition of a number of sick from General William Henry Harrison's Northwestern Army pushed the total to 423.[178] The number of fit men was sufficient to defend Fort Niagara. McClure had left a number of instructions with Captain Leonard and warned him of the danger of a British attack in the wake of the destruction of Newark. The general departed for Buffalo with an expression of confidence in Leonard and a reminder of his responsibility. "Everything is expected of Captain Leonard from his long experience and knowledge of duty," he wrote as a General Order, "and the General feels confident he will be well supported by Lt. Loomis of the Artillery and ... the officers of infantry."[179] McClure's confidence would prove to be sadly misplaced.

Leonard and his officers certainly took measures to prepare for an attack. Standing orders specifying the positions of troops in the event of an emergency had continued to be a part of garrison life at Fort Niagara through the summer and fall of 1813.[180] These were carefully restated on December 13 by order of General McClure. As in earlier plans, the surviving men of the garrison were to retire to the defensible stone buildings if they could no longer hold their positions on the batteries and walls. The redoubts and the Mess House provided the main places of refuge. The signal for a withdrawal to the strong points was to be a drum beating the "retreat". Most of the troops were to occupy defensive positions in the Mess House, but twenty men under Captain Frank Hampton of the 24th Infantry were to take post in the South Redoubt. The guard detachment was to remain in front of the guard house (an indication that the South Redoubt no longer served this purpose in 1813) and join Captain Hampton if the situation warranted. Hampton's troops were to man the loopholes and "fire on any enemy who may come on to the parade or attempt to storm the works." Lieutenant Adam Peck, also of the 24th Infantry, was to take fifty men into the North Redoubt and defend it in the same manner. The artillerymen on the South (River) Bastion were to join Hampton while those manning guns on the "Marine Battery" on the lake side were to seek cover with Peck. The gunners were to disable their pieces and, upon reaching their new positions, "instantly man the guns placed in the block house."[181] McClure had further ordered that adequate quantities of hand grenades be placed in the blockhouses where these close range weapons could be thrown down on assaulting parties.[182] The troops practiced taking their positions on December 16, at which time Lieutenant Carey Trimble, by virtue of his seniority, was appointed to command the North Redoubt in place of Peck.[183] The plan was sound, and it probably seemed unlikely that the British would be able to bombard and storm a fortification of Niagara's strength so late in the season.

British troops had reoccupied the smoldering remains of Newark and Fort George before McClure's troops were out of sight. The officers and men were enraged by the senseless destruction of civilian property. Their commander, Lieutenant General Gordon Drummond, no doubt felt that the time was right to turn these sentiments on the most important American position along the Niagara. On December 17, his orders for an attack on Fort Niagara were passed to Colonel John Murray who had been appointed to lead the assault. The plan was a risky one. Drummond specified a night attack, and he was prepared to attempt an assault by a substantial force of valuable infantry unsupported by artillery. If the attack failed, it would do so in extremely bloody fashion, and there would be no possibility of a second chance or a siege. The troops were to carry axes and eighteen to twenty-foot scaling ladders. They were also to perform this perilous operation with unloaded muskets. The orders exhorted:

> *... The troops must preserve the profoundest silence and the strictest discipline. They must on no account be suffered to load without the orders of their officers. It should be impressed on the mind of every man that the bayonet is the weapon on which the success of the attack must depend.*[184]

Lt. Col. John R. Fenwick commanded Fort Niagara during September, 1812. Fenwick sat for this portrait by Gilbert Stuart about 1804 as a lieutenant in the Marine Corps. *Courtesy, The Gibbes Art Gallery / Carolina Art Association, Gift of Mrs. William Phillips.*

Drummond ordered the assault force to be composed of 350 men of the 100th Regiment of Foot, 100 grenadiers of the 1st or Royal Regiment, 100 men from the flank companies of the 41st Regiment, and 12 of the Royal Artillery. This number, totalling 562, was little more than the garrison of Fort Niagara. The troops were soon assembled, but a delay in obtaining boats made it impossible for them to cross the river before the evening of December 18.[185]

Murray's force successfully reached the New York shore at Five Mile Meadows and marched silently down the River Road. They overwhelmed an American picket in the hamlet of Youngstown and pressed on toward Fort Niagara. Various accounts speak of obtaining the garrison password from one or two sentries captured just outside the fort. The force divided into three columns with the largest continuing down the main road, through the glacis and "barrier gate" to the foot of the hill between the fort and river. Another group headed for the North Bastion and the North Redoubt while the third moved against the center of the land defenses. The advance party or "forlorn hope" of the main column, under the command of Lieutenant Irwin Dawson, moved up the hill to the main gate (roughly on the site of the modern Postern Gate). There they discovered the wicket of the gate open, apparently to admit an American soldier. Sergeant Andrew Spearman of the 100th Regiment stepped forward in the darkness. He was seen and challenged by the sentry. "Who comes there?" he called. Spearman, "imitating the nasal twang" of an American answered, "I guess, Mister, I come from

In December, 1813, Gen. George McClure ordered the redoubts to be well stocked with hand grenades in anticipation of a British assault. *Courtesy, Dan Glenney.*

British troops enter Fort Niagara in the predawn darkness of December 19, 1813. They came under "heavy and galling fire" from the South Redoubt in the background. Drawing by Frederic Ray. *Courtesy of the artist.*

Youngstown" and slipped the upper part of his body into the open wicket gate. The sentry's hesitation proved fatal for him and for Fort Niagara. Spearman bayoneted the man, the first of many to fall by that weapon on the night of December 19, 1813. The British were in the fort, and its American garrison was taken by surprise. It was one hour before dawn.[186]

The British were concerned about the strength of Fort Niagara, not only its defenses of regular construction but also its "three stone towers at the west, south-west and south angles of the fort."[187] These would have to be taken promptly if the post was to be secured. Colonel Murray had detached Captain John Martin with three companies of the 100th Regiment to "storm the eastern demi-bastion" (the North Bastion). Martin and his men entered the fort at about the same time as Spearman and the forlorn hope. They accomplished their task quickly and "in the most intrepid manner", and there seems to have been little or no resistance from the North Redoubt.[188] It seems unlikely that Lieutenant Trimble and his men were able to react. Captain Bailey and his 100 grenadiers of the 1st (Royal Scots) Regiment also entered Fort Niagara across the main wall without opposition.

The South Redoubt presented a greater challenge. As the main British column burst through the gate, they were faced with a formidable obstacle on each flank. To their left was the large stone Mess House with at least one gun mounted on its roof. To the right was the South Redoubt, also with artillery in a position to do much damage to the attackers. Spearman, Dawson and the rest of the forlorn hope were closely followed by the grenadiers of the 100th Regiment and the Royal Artillery detachment. Behind them came five more companies of the 100th and the grenadiers and light infantry of the 41st Regiment, all under the command of Lieutenant Colonel Christopher Hamilton of the 100th.[189] Once inside the gate, Hamilton's column turned to the left to assault the Mess House. On their way they encountered unexpected and fierce opposition from the sick in the "Red Barracks", located between the gate and the Mess House. The British troops turned on the heavily armed patients and went to work with their bayonets. Robert Lee, a civilian contractor who was in the fort that night, believed the building's defenders "were nearly all slaughtered."[190] The Mess House itself seems to have fallen without a fight.

As the column turned toward the Mess House, it suddenly received fire from the right. "A cannon, turned inwards, was fired from the roof of the south-western tower, followed by a slight pattering of musketry," recalled Lieutenant Henry Driscoll. Lieutenant Andrew Burke described it as a "heavy and galling fire from the southern stone tower ... from the six-pounder on the top and through two tiers of loopholes below."[191] It is not known whether Captain

Capt. David Davies and his men took shelter in front of the Provisions Storehouse (right) before rushing the door of the South Redoubt. *OFN 727/28C.*

Hampton had reached his post, but the men in the South Redoubt, who apparently included the guard, were following their instructions by firing "on any enemy who may come onto the parade." Two British soldiers were killed and one wounded in the "incessant tho' random fire" from the building. Captain David Davies of the 100th Regiment was "persuaded that had not the blockhouse been carried previous to the return of daylight, the enemy would have committed great destruction" in the assault column. Davies went to Lieutenant Colonel Hamilton and volunteered to lead his company in an attack on the tower.[192]

Hamilton ordered Davies to take the building, and the captain directed his thirty-three men of the 4th company, 100th Regiment of Foot against the South Redoubt. Davies led his troops along the north wall of the stone provisions storehouse. There they paused to catch their breaths. Davies then turned to an American prisoner who had been dragged along with the assault party. The captain spoke briefly with the man, "threatening him with instant death in default of guiding me up the inner stairs" of the tower.[193] Huddled in the shelter of the provisions storehouse were Lieutenant Burke, Lieutenant Francis Rawdon Fortune, Lieutenant Maurice Nowlan, and the men of the 4th company. Davies waited until the defenders had fired and he judged them to be reloading. Lieutenant Burke suddenly heard Davies shout "Follow me, my boys," and they dashed across the forty feet of open ground between the storehouse and the redoubt. The soldiers, many of whom had picked up sledges and "large billets of wood," began battering at the heavy double gate. Davies claimed that the door was partly open, but it still took "a few minutes" for them to get inside.[194]

As the British broke into the building, those defenders who had been firing through the ground floor loopholes retreated up the stairs. The attackers were right behind them, several carrying "large firebrands from which they blew immense sparks and flashes." This horrible lighting was supplemented by the flash of muskets and obscured by powder smoke. Lieutenant Nowlan and one British soldier were killed in the struggle to get up the stairs. Henry Driscoll reported that the lieutenant's body was found the next day to have been pierced by a deep bayonet wound with a musket ball and three buckshot at the bottom of it, testimony to the closeness of the fighting. In this fashion the British fought their way up the "narrow intricate staircase" to the second floor. It is not known if Davies dragged his unfortunate prisoner along.

With the prospect of another terrible melee on the second floor, Captain Davies cried out to his men to "bayonet the whole," which had the desired effect. The

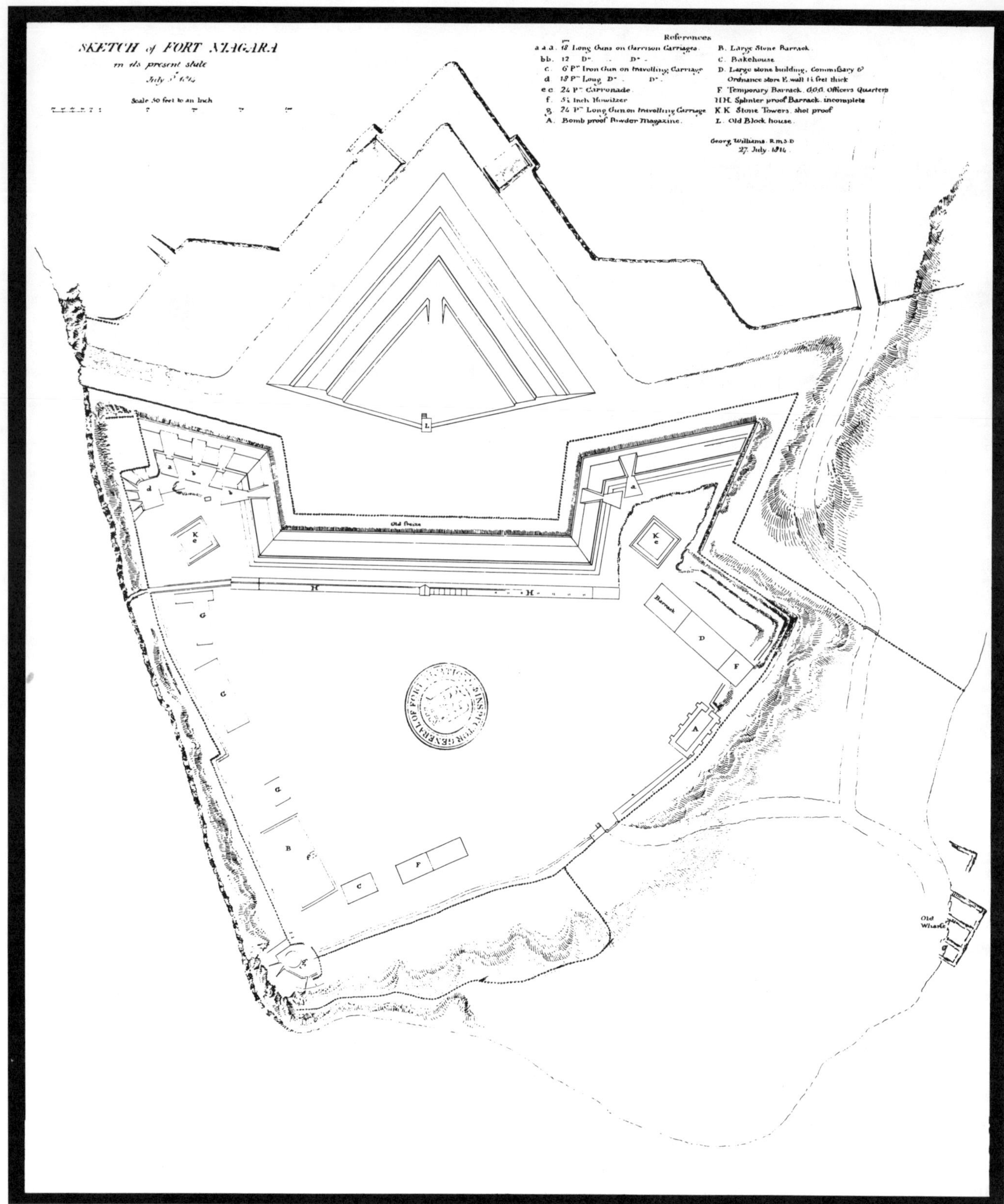

Fort Niagara in July, 1814. The redoubts were armed with twenty-four-pounder carronades. Seven months previously the British had assaulted the fort through the gate at right. *Courtesy, National Archives of Canada, H2/450/Niagara/1814, NMC23032.*

defenders, still shaken by the suddenness of the predawn attack, began to call for mercy. During the next few minutes a total of sixty-four United States soldiers surrendered to the men of the 100th. One American had been killed inside the South Redoubt. Lieutenants Burke and Fortune were put in charge of the prisoners, who numbered nearly double the attackers, and the building was secured by daybreak.[195]

Davies restrained his men, and in this he was more successful than many of his brother officers. Total American casualties that night were sixty-five killed and fourteen wounded, a disproportion that indicates the attackers used their bayonets freely. British casualties amounted to six killed and five wounded.[196]

Fort Niagara was firmly in British hands and would remain so for the balance of the War of 1812. During the next few weeks parties of British and Indians would lay waste to the New York side of the Niagara River as far south as Buffalo in retaliation for the destruction of Newark. With organized American resistance temporarily dispersed, the new garrison of Fort Niagara set to work to make the place tenable, this time against a land attack. Lieutenant Gaugreben of the Royal Engineers was ordered by General Drummond "to use every exertion in putting Fort Niagara in the best state of defence that circumstances and our means will permit." He had a formidable task ahead of him. Buildings and walls were in deplorable condition after eighteen months of war. Drummond disgustedly wrote to Governor Prevost that "Nothing can be in a more wretched state both as to the defences and the cover [quarters] than Fort Niagara at the time of its capture."[197]

The labor for repairing Fort Niagara's buildings and walls was provided by the soldiers of the garrison. Quartered in miserable barracks, isolated from the Canadian shore by drifting ice and hemmed in on the New York side by increasing local partisan activity, the troops worked through the winter. By March, morale among the men of the 8th (King's) Regiment had plummeted and desertion had soared. Major General Phineas Riall complained to Drummond that "The men are sick of the place, tired and disgusted with the labor to which they see no end." It became necessary to relieve the 8th Regiment with the 100th, and only the coming of spring and the high morale of the captors of Fort Niagara seems to have stabilized the situation.[198]

This incident with an otherwise fine regiment caused Riall to seriously question the utility of retaining Fort Niagara, at least in its current configuration. He suggested to Drummond that the works be compressed so as to hold the site with the smallest possible garrison.[199] Riall elaborated on his plan the same day and suggested:

> *... the idea of destroying that fort with the exception of the north eastern square tower or stone building and the rampart on the land side, which should be continued to the river and well picketed as a cover to the communications to the tower. The tower to be mounted with a gun of heavy calibre on top and three smaller within the work, to be surrounded by a strong picketing and a ditch ...*[200]

Riall envisioned a small outpost to the works on the Canadian side of the river. His recommendation of the use of the North Redoubt is reminiscent of the way in which Martello towers were then being employed on the coasts of England as isolated battery towers or defensive keeps for more conventional batteries.[201]

Riall almost immediately rethought his opinion of Fort Niagara. Two days after his initial contact with Drummond on the matter, he suggested abandoning and destroying the place altogether. Riall gave four reasons: first, the reduced fortress could probably not be held against a serious American attack because it lacked any shelter from mortar fire. Second, desertion was too easy for troops stationed on the American side, and this tendency had "manifested itself in more regiments than one in this army." Third, maintaining a garrison at Fort Niagara would require men badly needed in the field for the coming campaign. Fourth, Fort George and the new battery projected for Mississauga Point would adequately cover the entrance of the river and make a position on the American shore unnecessary.[202] Drummond did not wholly agree. Although he admitted that a substantial number of troops would be needed to hold Fort Niagara, he believed that they would tie down many more of the enemy by maintaining the position. He communicated this opinion to Riall and reminded him that, in the reduced state described in his first suggestion, the fortifications of Niagara could not hold out for even one day against a determined attack. Retention of Fort Niagara would not only tie down American troops, it would deny the Niagara River as a harbor to the enemy fleet.[203]

The question of what to do with Fort Niagara would occupy British officers for the rest of the month. Engineer Lieutenant Colonel R.H. Bruyeres recommended demolition and total withdrawal if additional troops were needed for the field. Colonel Edward Baynes informed Governor Prevost that he did not know what sort of defense the single square stone tower could make. He did know from experience in earlier campaigns that the North Redoubt was not covered by the guns of Fort George and that fire from the British post had earlier "produced little or no effect upon that building." Bruyeres believed that the position should be held as long as the British had naval superiority on Lake Ontario and abandoned if this advantage was lost.[204] The final word came from Governor Prevost on March 26. Niagara was to be retained in its existing form as long as it appeared that the Americans would not gain full control of Lake Ontario. Should this occur, the post was to be abandoned and destroyed.[205] The stone buildings would survive, and the war would come to an end before additional plans to alter Fort Niagara's fortifications had been developed.

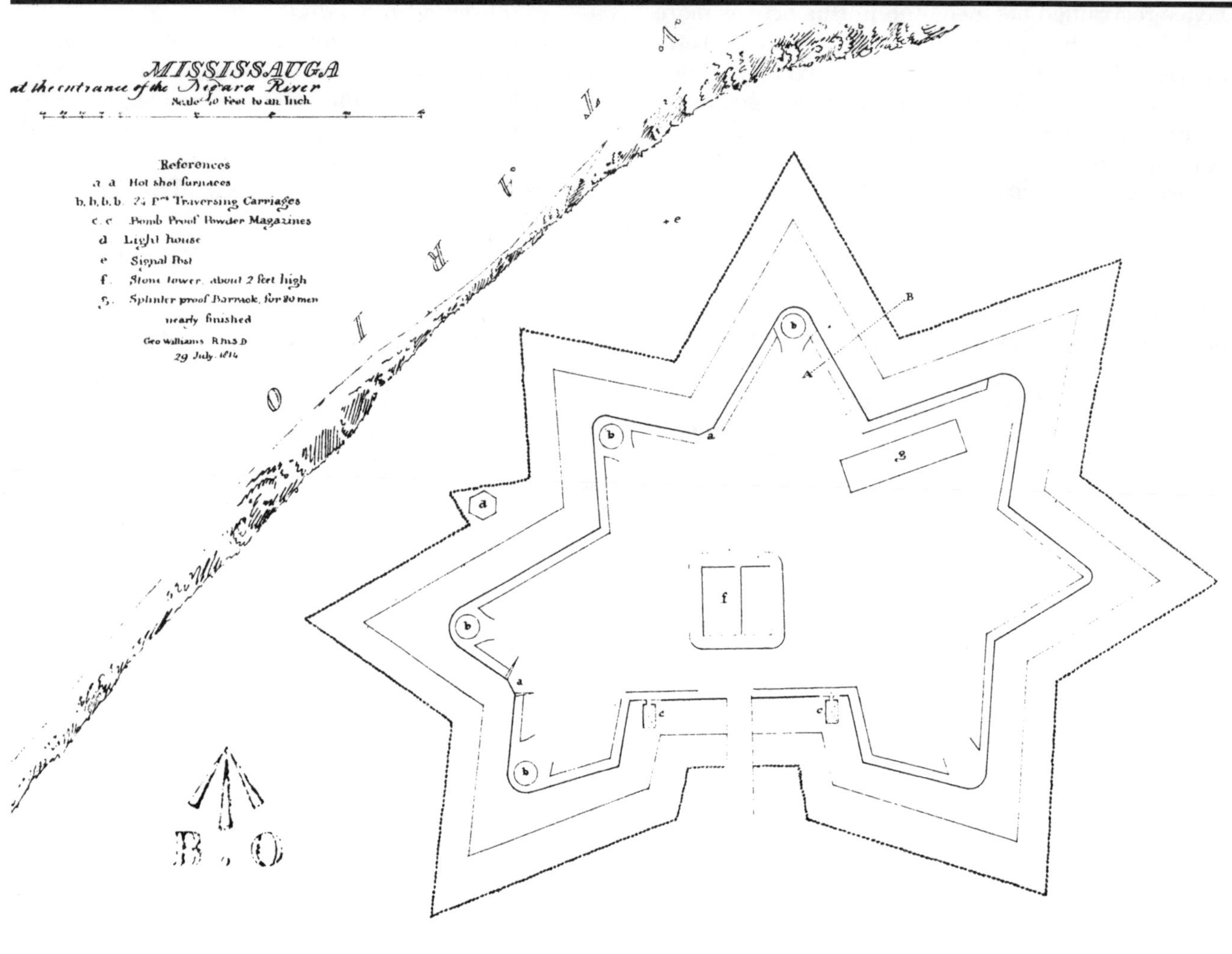

George Williams recorded the state of "the Fort erecting at Point Mississauga" on July 29, 1814. The "Stone tower" ("f") had been constructed to a height of two feet above the parade ground. This is the brick tower visible today in Fort Mississauga. *Courtesy, National Archives of Canada, H2 / 450 / Niagara / 1814, NMC42422.*

Repairs would continue throughout the summer of 1814. Some other alterations, notably a long, splinter-proof barracks built into the earthen curtain wall, were made to improve the post. American forces threatened Fort Niagara in July, but they were forced to withdraw before they could begin serious preparations for a siege. By mid-summer the redoubts were described as "Stone Towers, Shot proof", and each mounted a 24-pounder carronade on its gun deck.[206] The replacement of long guns by the much more powerful but shorter-range carronades reflects a reorientation of the defenses brought on by the British occupation. Rather than strike at the Canadian shore, the guns on the redoubts were once again intended for close-in work defending the ditch from infantry attack.

The greatest construction effort during the summer of 1814 took place on Mississauga Point, opposite Fort Niagara. The stone lighthouse of 1804 was demolished and replaced by an earthwork and a brick tower. Fort Mississauga was intended as a temporary work to cover the mouth of the river until a much more substantial fortress could replace it.[207] The projected larger fortification was to incorporate the tower in a bastion facing Fort Niagara.[208] The Fort Mississauga tower was an interesting structure, square with rounded corners and containing many of the features of a Martello tower. Its appearance and use are reminiscent of Riall's proposal for the contraction of Fort Niagara and employment of the North Redoubt as a citadel. The old stone buildings in Fort Niagara very likely had some influence on its design. The new post was nicely placed to fire into the exposed rear of Fort Niagara.

The campaign of 1814 was one of the hardest fought of the war, but the conflict was already beginning to wind down. The British held Fort Niagara as peace negotiations progressed at Ghent, Belgium,

Fort Mississauga's brick tower (right) served as an elevated gun platform and citadel. Fort Niagara is across the river in this 1840 watercolor view by Philip John Bainbrigge. Renovation of the North Redoubt (far left) has not yet begun. *Courtesy, National Archives of Canada, C11899.*

and the garrison continued to labor on the old earthen fortifications. Nature still defied their efforts. Heavy rains in September, 1814, caused great sections of the walls to slide into the ditch. The post was described as being "in a deplorable state as to defence against any attack by heavy cannon." [209] The stone redoubts, roofless and by now consistently described as "towers", remained in relatively good condition. The work of the eighteenth century New York masons had held up well to the battering of artillery and the ravages of Lake Ontario weather. In February, 1815, both buildings were in use as guard houses. They continued to mount short-range, anti-personnel artillery on their gun decks.[210]

British control of Fort Niagara was even then coming to an end. The treaty of peace had been signed in Ghent on Christmas Eve, 1814. It was ratified by Congress that winter, and plans were soon made to return captured territory. On May 20, 1815, United States troops in Buffalo were ordered to march down the river to take possession of Fort Niagara.[211] The war had finally come to an end for the long-suffering population of the Niagara Frontier.

"TWO HEAVY STONE BLOCKHOUSES... DAMP, BADLY VENTILATED AND UNWHOLESOME IN THE EXTREME"

1815 - 1922

United States troops peacefully took possession of Fort Niagara for a second time on May 22, 1815. The soldiers had departed Buffalo two days earlier under the command of Captain Henry Knox Craig and had an uneventful march down the River Road.[212] The men of the British garrison immediately crossed the river to Canada. They were no doubt delighted to see the last of the dilapidated fortress and its ruined buildings. Although the takeover involved no fighting, Fort Niagara was apparently not regained without a struggle. The *Niagara Journal*, reprinting an item from a New York paper, later reported:

> Little trick repeated, - *On surrendering the Fort of Niagara to the Americans the British cut away the haulyards and steps, and greased the flag staff, to prevent the immediate display of the American flag on it. The flag staff on the battery in this city was treated in the same manner on evacuation in 1783* - [213]

In 1815, Maj. Gen. Jacob Brown ordered Fort Niagara's stone buildings repaired.

If this incident actually occurred - and there is unfortunately no corroborating report from Captain Craig to prove that the story is not apocryphal - the little drama probably took place on the North Redoubt which, by 1815, supported the garrison flagstaff.[214]

It seems appropriate that the United States colors first flew from one of the redoubts. Not only had these buildings been the positions of honor during the long years of the War of 1812, but they were about the only structures of the fort still in reasonably good condition. The redoubts and the Mess House had, by this time, stood uncovered for nearly three years in the damp Niagara weather. The larger and older of the three buildings had suffered terribly, and it would experience a major structural collapse in 1817 before being entirely repaired.[215] American officers were soon surveying the condition of the repatriated post, but no repairs were made during the summer of 1815. In September, Captain Craig's immediate successor, Captain William Gates, carefully inspected all the quarters at Fort Niagara. He bluntly stated that repair of the Mess House would require so much expense that the building should be demolished. The sturdy "Block Houses" remained in good condition, however.[216] These great masonry piles had apparently been no more damaged by exposure than by British shot. Gates' assessment set the tone for most reports about the buildings for the next century. Complaints about the redoubts would focus not on their physical condition but rather on their unsuitability for use as storehouses and barracks, purposes for which the old buildings had never really been intended.

The process of repairing Fort Niagara in the aftermath of the War of 1812 would be a long and drawn-out procedure. Several problems existed for U.S. Army engineers and quartermasters. The buildings were in wretched condition and were both insufficient and unsuitable to accommodate a garrison. Chronic erosion on the Lake Ontario side of the post was threat-

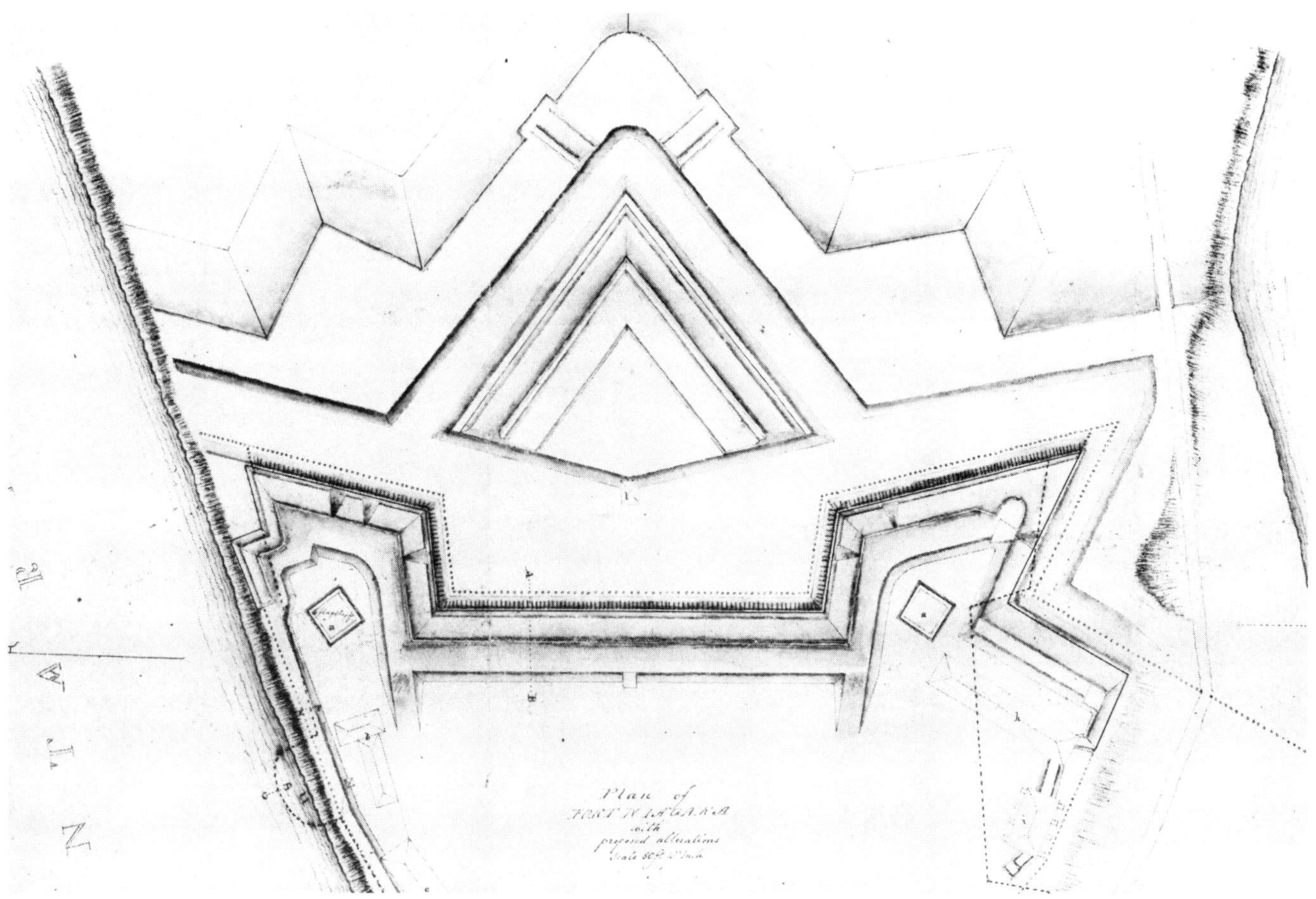

Lt. John L. Smith's "Plan of Fort Niagara with proposed alterations" was forwarded to his superiors on January 1, 1816. The redoubts are still roofless, and the northern building supports a flagstaff on its north corner. *Courtesy, National Archives and Records Administration, RG 77, Dr. 3, Sht. 6.*

ening several structures, particularly the Mess House, and even the very land on which the fort stood. Most alarming, the old problem of vulnerability to guns on the Canadian shore had only been emphasized by the experiences of the War of 1812. If the fortifications were to be held, they would have to be reoriented to face the main threat. For Captain Gates and his men, however, the immediate problem was the poor condition of their quarters and store houses. Two weeks after Gates' report, Major General Jacob Brown visited Fort Niagara. The general agreed that the sole United States fortification along the Niagara RIver was in "a ruinous condition" and wanted it put back into repair. The six stone buildings were very valuable, Brown believed. He noted the importance of keeping them "well covered" if they were to be preserved, and ordered Gates to work.[217]

Despite General Brown's attention, little was done. Captain Gates lacked the men, materials and funds to make a significant impact on the monumental problems facing the buildings of Fort Niagara. The Mess House and the redoubts remained totally uncovered, while all of the other structures were in various stages of disrepair. By April, 1816, Gates was still complaining that the "Public Buildings" were "going to ruin and we have not a nail to use in their repair." A month later the engineer at work on the seawall and fortifications at Fort Niagara advertised in the *Buffalo Gazette* for carpenters and laborers. One assumes that some of their duties included work on the buildings. Repairs probably began about that time.[218] Quarters were being renovated during the spring of 1817. When Major Joseph Delafield visited the post late that summer, he found Fort Niagara "undergoing repairs and in great confusion of course." Much of this was caused by work on the seawall, but the buildings were also receiving attention.[219] Reroofing of the redoubts must have been accomplished sometime during 1816-17, most likely in the latter year.

It is doubtful that much more was done to the two buildings because their very existence was, by this time, much in jeopardy. In October, 1815, Lt. John L. Smith of the Corps of Engineers had been ordered to proceed to Fort Niagara to report on the work required to place it once more in a defensible state. Smith reported promptly the next month, focusing on the erosion problem along the lake front and defense against guns on the Canadian shore.[220] On January 16, 1816, Lieutenant Smith forwarded a plan of Fort Niagara on which he had superimposed dotted lines

Fort Niagara viewed from Fort Mississauga in 1824. The North Redoubt is covered by a simple hipped roof. *Courtesy, National Archives of Canada, C4648.*

indicating "such alterations as have appeared to me best calculated to improve its defences and secure its site against further incursions of the Lake and river." Smith's plan included details for a stone seawall and proposed new bastions and curtain walls facing the Canadian shore. The Mess House, due to its location, would necessarily be destroyed if such lines were constructed. The powder magazine, built by the French in 1757, would also fall outside the new walls and therefore have to be abandoned. Smith proposed no alterations to the old land-side defenses, however, and the redoubts, which he termed "Stone Blockhouses", were shown intact on his plan. Both were clearly rendered as open towers, without roofs and were probably intended to mount guns in defense of the ditch. A flagstaff was shown in the extreme northern corner of the North Redoubt.[221] The old buildings did not fare so well in a later and more detailed set of plans, however. Drawings by engineer Lieutenant William Henry Chase refined Smith's suggestions and specified major changes to the land front as well as massive walls to oppose British guns across the river. Chase showed both demi-bastions much reduced and reshaped. Neither included a redoubt, so it must be assumed that it was intended to demolish the structures. Unfortunately, Chase's plans are not dated, but it is likely that they were prepared later in 1816 or early in 1817.[222]

This watercolor view of Fort Niagara was probably painted in the 1820's. It shows the flagstaff and the "peculiar construction" of the South Redoubt roof. *Courtesy, The Samuel E. Weir Collection and Library of Art.*

Smith's recommendations were soon followed, beginning with the essential construction of the seawall. In May, 1816, General Swift reported that plans for the alteration of Fort Niagara were to be executed, and money was available for the first phase of the project.[223] "Fortification" work continued through 1817, but nearly all the effort was expended on the seawall. Nothing was done to begin the massive works projected for the river side of the post, much less any alteration of the land defenses. Even this work was ordered to cease on May 6, 1818. Lieutenant Smith was instructed to halt construction as soon as the seawall was completed to the point that it could protect the fort from Lake Ontario.[224] The erosion problem had been temporarily checked, but the grand plans to make Fort Niagara tenable against an enemy on the Canadian shore had come to nothing. The river-side defenses were virtually nonexistent and would remain so for the next two decades.

Abandonment of the 1816 fortification plans saved the old British redoubts. The simple roofs covering their gun decks were apparently sufficient to protect the buildings since there is no mention of a need for repairs to either structure for the next fifteen years. It is apparent from drawings of the 1820's and 1830's that the North Redoubt was given a simple, low,

Fort Niagara from the Canadian shore, painted sometime in the 1830's. The garrison flag flies from the South Redoubt, and the crumbling buildings are covered with a gleaming coat of whitewash. The "Engineers' Barracks" is to the left of the South Redoubt. *Courtesy, The Samuel E. Weir Collection and Library of Art.*

hipped roof to cover its gun deck. The roof of the South Redoubt was more complex. Engineer Captain William D. Fraser noted, in 1841, that the "peculiar construction given to the roof of this building was to enable it to support a flagstaff."[225] Although no plans exist, views of the 1820's-30's depict a hipped roof topped by a square cupola. This was probably a platform with a wooden railing or a parapet from which the flag could be raised on a pole projecting from the center of the roof. After flying from a flagstaff on the North Redoubt for a number of years late in the War of 1812, the garrison colors would thereafter float above the South Redoubt until about 1841. Captain Fraser's report also provides one reason why the stone towers had survived their years without roofs so well. The gun deck floors were caulked to keep out the rain, and each building had "openings through the walls to drain off the water."[226]

The redoubts remained in such good condition for the next few years that it is difficult to find any but the most general reference to them or the way in which they were utilized. Late in 1826, with the garrison temporarily withdrawn, Fort Niagara's caretaker reported that "all the buildings are in a good state of preservation with the exception of the *Mess House*." Following the return of troops in 1828, the new commandant described the fort and quarters as "very much out of repair" and pledged to soon have the place back in good order. By November, the garrison buildings, presumably including the redoubts, had all been newly roofed (shingled), and other small repairs had been accomplished.[227]

With so little comment on the redoubts in the official records, it is difficult to judge exactly what purpose the buildings served between 1817 and 1841. It is most likely that they were not utilized for normal garrison activities, there being officers' quarters, barracks and storehouses in Fort Niagara sufficient for its small garrison. The nature of the redoubts did not make them attractive as quarters. It seems probable that the buildings simply awaited the next clash with Britain when they could again serve as shot-proof gun towers. One exception might have occurred in 1832, however, as United States soldiers were being moved rapidly westward to engage the Indians of Wisconsin in the Black Hawk War. Large numbers of dependents were left at Fort Niagara by the troops. There were so many families housed in the buildings that newly arrived Ordnance Sergeant Francis Powley was unable to find quarters there and was forced to seek lodgings in Youngstown.[228] The redoubts might have been pressed into service during that busy summer to shelter some of these temporary residents.

A few other references provide information on the state of the redoubts during the early 1830's. In 1832, a traveling British officer visited Niagara-on-the-Lake and recorded the first known reference to the use of whitewash on the exteriors of the buildings of Fort Niagara. He favorably compared "the neat white appearance of the American Fort Niagara" to that of the British fortifications across the river. A pair of watercolors from the early 1830's clearly show all the buildings brilliantly white.[229] Both redoubts and most other buildings retained a coat of whitewash well into the 1920's, and bits of it may still be found, particularly on the South Redoubt. Two years later, Lieutenant Amos B. Eaton was compelled to comment on the redoubts because they finally needed repair. Eaton made no mention of their use other than as blockhouses covering the land front:

> *The public buildings at this post consist of two two-story stone Blockhouses, within the half-bastion angles of a single bastion post; the walls strong & under little injury from past dilapidation, the wood work (including roofs, floors & timbers) in bad condition & needs to be renewed if it is intended to preserve the walls in a healthy condition*[230]

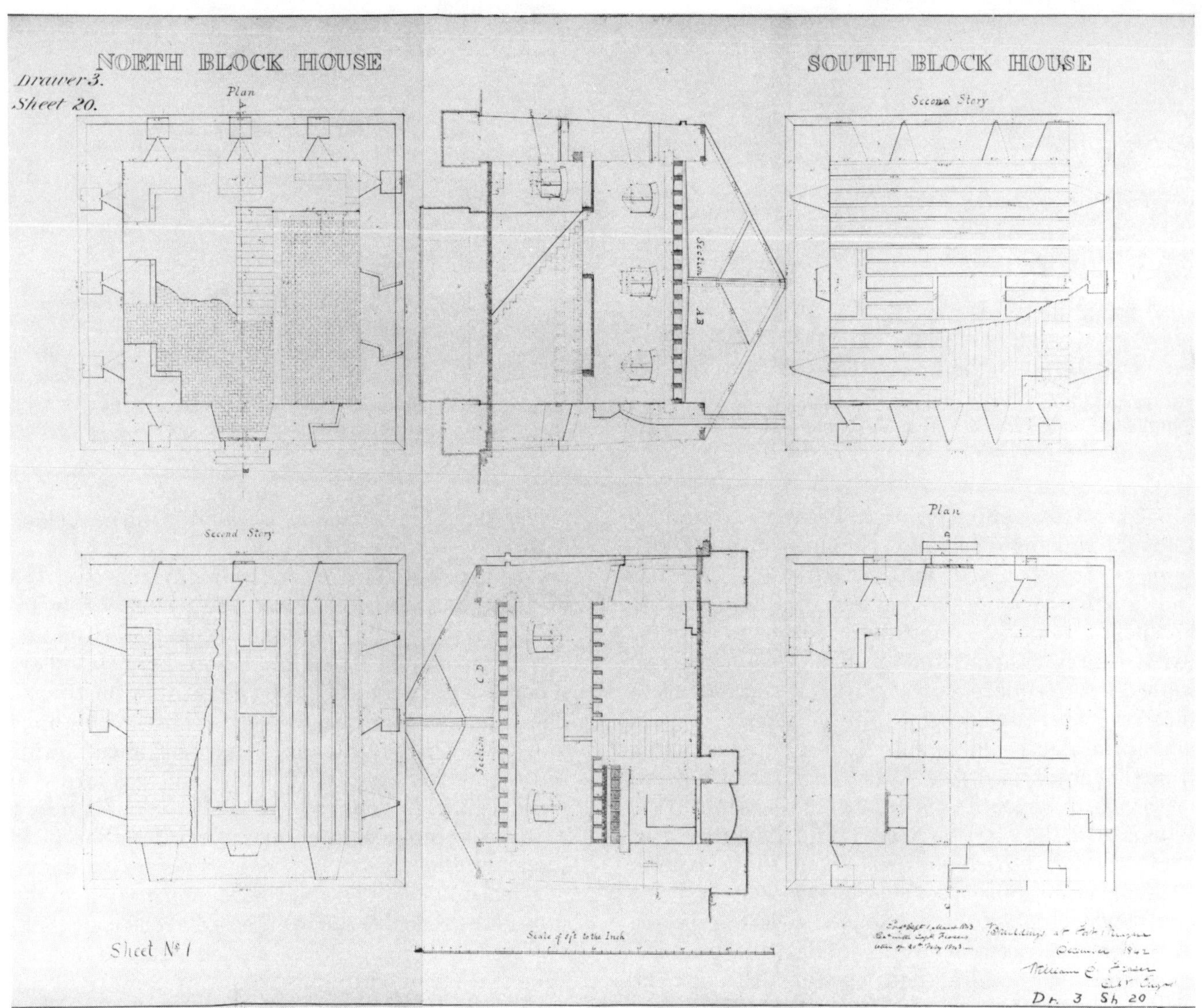

Sections and plans of the redoubts, prepared by Capt. William D. Fraser in December, 1842. The floor plans at left and the top section are of the North Redoubt. The bottom section and the plans at right show the South Redoubt. *Courtesy, National Archives and Records Administration, RG 77, Dr. 3, Shts. 21-1 and 21-2.*

No action was taken to authorize replacement of the post-War of 1812 roofs and the interior woodwork, much of which probably dated to the 1770's. Some patching and replacement of shingles was accomplished in 1837, but Fort Niagara's commandant again projected the need for new roofs (at $75.00 apiece) the following year. The work was accomplished in August, 1838, and the following month the two buildings were described as "recently re-roofed."[231]

The peaceful state of affairs along the United States-Canadian border in the years following the War of 1812 provided no incentive to renovate the defenses of Fort Niagara. What remained of the fortifications slid ever deeper into deterioration and ruin. The river front, more vulnerable than ever following construction of Fort Mississauga, was entirely defenseless.[232] This was tolerable so long as the boundary remained quiet. When Upper Canada exploded in rebellion during 1837, however, the inadequacy of the defenses of the northern frontier drew considerable attention. It came as no surprise that American citizens from Michigan and New York, raised in a tradition of defiance to British authority, sympathized with the rebels and involved themselves in Canada's civil strife.[233] Tensions escalated between the United States and Great Britain following the inevitable incidents, such as the British capture and destruction of the American steamer *Caroline* in the upper Niagara River. It appeared possible that Fort Niagara might again be on the front lines. Local concern grew, and with it came calls for renovation of Fort Niagara and the construction of new defensive works along the river.[234]

The entire scheme for defense of the Canadian border came under review at this time. Colonels Joseph G. Totten and Sylvanus Thayer examined the

Great Lakes-St. Lawrence boundary in the autumn of 1838 and made comprehensive recommendations for its defense. Their report served as the basis for Congressional action during the winter of 1838-39. Although there would be second thoughts about the cost of the new defense project within the next year, and delays would ensue, funds were finally available for renovating the fortifications of Niagara.[235] Plans for Fort Niagara would be prepared without delay, for the Chief of Engineers, Brigadier General Charles Gratiot, had dispatched Captain William D. Smith to Fort Niagara in the fall of 1838 to report on the condition of the fortifications and the measures necessary to once again put them in order.[236]

Captain Smith, who would legally change his name to "Fraser" in 1840, arrived at Fort Niagara in September, inspected the works and reported his findings. The post was again suffering from the effects of erosion which had only partly been corrected by the incomplete seawall of 1816-1818. Smith also found the place totally exposed to Fort Mississauga and the Canadian shore. The only good news was that the land-side defenses could be repaired along their original lines. Smith noted that, "Should the work as it now stands be merely repaired, it would be well defended on the Land-side." The redoubts formed part of these defenses. Smith found their masonry in need of some repairs, primarily repointing, "the mortar having in some places fallen out, leaving the stones loose." They had, of course, just been reroofed. In his report, however, Captain Smith sounded unsure as to whether the buildings would be retained as part of the defenses of Fort Niagara. He was convinced that, "were it considered necessary to preserve them, they could soon be put in as good a condition as they ever were."[237] Within the next three years not only would Captain Smith change his name, but also his opinion of the utility of the redoubts in the defense of Fort Niagara and his estimate of the amount of work needed to renovate the two structures.

Captain Smith was ordered back to Niagara in January, 1839, with orders to prepare an accurate survey of the post and detailed plans showing the work necessary to render Fort Niagara tenable against the natural and man-made threats of the 1830's. The seawall was to be completed, topped with a stockade and overhung by a one story wooden blockhouse to prevent enemy infantry from slipping along the beach. A tall stone wall along the river would cover the interior of the post from observation and fire from Fort Mississauga. Three batteries of guns placed along this wall would command the mouth of the river, the British fort and the village of Niagara-on-the-Lake. On the land side, the plank revetments of the old earthworks were to be replaced. Smith showed the redoubts intact on his plan, and he must have considered them integral parts of the defensive scheme.[238] It is likely that renovation of these existing towers of sturdy construction was viewed as a convenient and relatively inexpensive way to strengthen Fort Niagara's land-side bastions. The work proposed for the fort was much simpler than that projected after the War of 1812. It required no reconstruction of existing walls, almost certainly because Fort Niagara no longer possessed the strategic importance it had two decades before. Smith's design would correct, or at least conceal, the worst faults of the post.

George Ferguson photographed the derelict South Redoubt about 1929. The arch of the original gateway is visible. So too are the window alterations of 1842-43 and 1867. *OFN 674/28A.*

Work began under Smith/Fraser's supervision in the summer of 1839. The construction seasons of 1839, 1840 and 1841 were mostly spent completing the seawall and erecting the defensive wall along the river.[239] Considerable progress was made. The captain (now Fraser) reported in October, 1840, that "the whole work might easily be completed next year" if an appropriation for the repair of the post buildings could be obtained from Congress.[240] Funds did not be-

The southeast side of the South Redoubt, about 1929. The overgrown earthworks are in the foreground. The center loophole, added in 1842-43, has been cut into the arch of the old gateway. *OFN 4452/28A.*

A handsome study of the North Redoubt. The three slits in the first story are powder magazine ventilators. The purpose of the arch above the ventilator at left is unknown. The roof of this building was blown off in the storm of 1855 and subsequently replaced. This chimney was constructed sometime after 1879. *Courtesy, Buffalo and Erie County Historical Society.*

come available as quickly as Captain Fraser hoped, due to Congressional hesitancy over the expense of the new fortification plan for the northern border. It was September, 1841, before he could present his estimates and plans for repairs and alterations to the two redoubts. The work would significantly change the seventy year-old structures and mark them with many features visible today. Fraser's detailed description of his intentions was forwarded to Colonel Joseph G. Totten:

> *The changes contemplated in the block houses are only such as seem necessary to make them more servicable. These consist in, lowering the ground around them a little, in order that the height of the mouths of the loop holes and windows may at least be six feet above the surface of the ground; altering the slopes of the soles of all the openings to afford a better command over the exterior ground; increasing the number of loop-holes and windows, where it properly can be done; lowering the upper story about a foot and raising the walls another, so that, when it becomes necessary to dispense with the roofs, there may be height enough of wall to afford some protection to the men, changing the position of the stairs, that they may not in any way interfere with the use either of the loop-holes or embrasures; filling up the large door ways on both sides of the south block house, leaving only space enough for a door on the side facing the parade ground; and repairing the magazine in the north block house, and building one in the south.*
>
> *The reason why it is proposed to have a magazine in each block house is, that when they are required for the defence of the work, there may be in both, a place where the ammunition will not only be safe, but can be stored in such quantities, that each building will have to depend, for a considerable time, only upon itself.*
>
> *Besides the alterations suggested it is intended to repair the masonry wherever it is defective, to rough cast* [plaster or stucco] *the outside faces of the walls, to renew entirely the wood work, in many places now rotten, to add gutters to the roofs and to repair the openings through the walls to drain off the water that may collect, when the roofs are off, upon the upper decks.*

Fraser further noted that the new gun decks were to be constructed much as the old ones. Heavy, three-inch thick plank was laid on supporting timbers and joists to bear the weight of artillery. The deck was given a slight upward slant from each side of the building to the center, much like a hipped roof. This provided a slope which retarded the recoil of the guns and made it easier for the crews to return them to the "battery" position against the parapets. The decks were to be caulked. This, combined with the slant of the floor, would shed rainwater to small drains piercing the walls. Both buildings were to receive identical hipped roofs like that installed on the North Redoubt after the War of 1812. The "peculiar construction" of the South Redoubt roof was unnecessary since the building would no longer support a flagpole.[241]

These plans make it clear that Captain Fraser intended the redoubts to function much as they had during the War of 1812. They would provide strong points within the fort and mount guns to both cover the land side and fire against the Canadian shore. The former function would be enhanced by improving and increasing the number of loopholes while the latter would be made more efficient by ensuring that there was a magazine in each structure and that the parapets offered sufficient protection for the gunners. Closing the archways of the South Redoubt would remove an anachronism, unnecessary since the Gate of the Five Nations had been replaced, which made the building more difficult to defend from assaults such as that of 1813. Fraser concluded his description by emphasizing that *"As soon as these buildings are repaired, they should receive their proper armament, that they may be ready for use at a moments warning.*"[242] Unfortunately, he did not specify what type of guns were intended for them. The course of events never presented an opportunity to arm the buildings, and the new roofs were not taken down until reconstruction. Fraser's intention to install removable weather coverings on the towers is undoubtedly the origin of a frequently repeated story, incorrectly applied to the Chinese-style roofs, that they could be rapidly dismantled "on short notice in case of attack, thus obviating the danger of flying splinters from direct hits of artillery fire."[243]

Modification of the "two stone blockhouses" was to be funded from an appropriation of $20,000 passed by Congress earlier in 1841. This money would also allow completion of the fortifications proper and repairs to the French powder magazine of 1757.[244] Preparation of timber for the redoubt project began in October, 1841, and continued until work ceased for the winter. Renovations resumed in the spring of 1842. By April, the masons were closing up the great gateways of the South Redoubt and building the stone walls of a powder magazine on its ground floor. Cutting of new windows and loopholes began the following month. Masonry work continued for the balance of the season.[245] Just as work had initially concentrated on the South Redoubt in 1770, so it did in 1842. By mid-June, the magazine and ground floor loopholes of the South Redoubt were complete and the openings of the second floor nearly so. Difficulties in procuring proper timber had delayed the beginning of carpentry work, however, and nothing had as yet been done on the North Redoubt.[246]

By October, 1842, when Captain Fraser prepared his annual report, he could describe significant progress on both buildings. All of the masonry of the "South Blockhouse", except for detail work on two ground floor loopholes, paving of the ground floor and installation of a hearth for the second floor fireplace, had been completed. The roof had been erected and partly shingled, and some progress had been made on the interior woodwork and floors. The repairs and alterations to the stone elements of the North Redoubt had also been completed, a cellar had been excavated and some of the woodwork installed. In an interesting attempt to inhibit future deterioration of the wooden elements, all timber and plank for both buildings was treated with preservative.[247] The process, known as "Kyanizing" after its inventor, involved soaking the wood in a solution of "corrosive sublimate" (mercuric chloride). A huge vat had been constructed for this purpose two years earlier when the same method had been used to treat the plank and timber for the new revetments of Fort Niagara's earthworks.[248]

By the end of the 1842 season $2,842.37 had been spent on Niagara's stone redoubts. Work was not

Northeast facade of the North Redoubt. The loopholes all display evidence of the 1842-43 alterations. The two narrow slits probably mark the locations of small windows in the original British plan. *OFN 774/30A.*

completed, however, and Fraser estimated that an additional $500.00 would finish the job as well as the repairs to the large powder magazine.[249] Work resumed in the spring of 1843 with most of the laborers' time spent building hearths and laying brick to pave the ground floors of both buildings. On September 2, Captain Fraser reported completion of the seawall, magazine and "blockhouses".[250] This was followed by a much more detailed discussion in his annual report of October 10. In addition to finishing the alterations begun in 1842, Fraser's workmen had installed the wooden flooring of both buildings, erected a new chimney on the South Redoubt, plastered the inside and outside of both structures, built interior stairs, and placed a "conductor" or lightning rod on each building. Doors had been hung, and the ground around the buildings graded to smooth the surface and ensure that the loopholes were out of reach of anyone on the exterior. The North Redoubt had required somewhat more work than the southern building since it had lagged behind its sister in 1842. Work on the former had, in 1843, cost $746.87 while the South Redoubt had been completed for $297.27. Fraser could state, "Fort Niagara including the magazine and blockhouses has now received all the repairs contemplated by the [Engineer's] Department." Total cost of renovating the stone redoubts had been $3,886. 51.[251] Of the entire project, Fraser would proudly note that he had placed Fort Niagara "in a better state of defence than it had ever been before." The post was large enough to accommodate a garrison of four companies and would require thirty cannon for its proper defense. Captain Fraser tabulated the total cost of the 1839-43 work down to the penny - $90,592.92 - only $92.92 above the amount appropriated by Congress![252]

The improvements to the North and South Redoubts designed and supervised by Captain William D. Fraser are nearly all visible today. Fraser's reports

The land front of Old Fort Niagara, about 1920. Photo by George Ferguson. *OFN 3448/10A.*

and a set of plans prepared in December, 1842, document nearly all of the changes to the old British buildings.[253] Little remained by the end of the renovation project but the masonry shells constructed in 1770-71. Nearly all doors, windows and loopholes had been altered in some manner. The large, neatly cut sandstone blocks found around openings are a hallmark of the 1842-43 alterations. In some cases, loopholes were completely repositioned, such as those on the northwest facade of the North Redoubt. The original gunslits in both stories on that side were replaced by three new ones. The brick paving of the ground floor survives in the North Redoubt, as do the brick hearths and hearth arches in both structures. Original joists and floors remain in both structures, and the stairway openings and headers may be seen in the second and third floors of each. Some 1842-43 features, such as the powder magazine and brick floor in the South Redoubt, were later removed during restoration.

Ironically, all of this expensive work on Fort Niagara and its two redoubts was accomplished well after the border crisis of 1837-38 had passed. The redoubts would never again hear a shot fired in anger. In later years, the garrison would use the buildings for a variety of mundane purposes. They were still considered part of the defenses of Fort Niagara, however. As late as 1872, the post surgeon noted that the "two stone blockhouses or towers" were "fitted with loopholes for musketry and for cannon and have battlemented or parapet roofs, over which have been placed ordinary roofs, which can be thrown off."[254]

It was not long after completion of the 1842-43 renovations that the redoubts came into use as barracks, a purpose for which they had not been particularly well-suited in the 1770's and one for which they were woefully inadequate seventy years later. By October, 1845, the company at Fort Niagara was quartered in the "two stone blockhouses". It is not known why this was done, but it was probably because the wooden barracks, all of which had been constructed around the time of the War of 1812, had deteriorated to the point of ruin. Captain Fraser had only been the most recent in a long line of officers to advocate new barracks for Fort Niagara.[255] Nothing was done to alleviate the problem. Lieutenant Justus L. McKinstry complained of his men's quarters, in 1845, that the stone buildings had been "erected for defensive purposes" and that, as barracks, their interior arrangements were "inconvenient and confined."[256] The troops were withdrawn the following year to bolster United States forces fighting in Mexico. Some small repairs, chiefly the replacement of glass in the windows, were made in their absence, but this did nothing to significantly improve habitability. Just before the return of the garrison in October, 1848, Lieutenant Montgomery C. Meigs frankly informed the Chief of Engineers that the "Quarters and Barracks about to be occupied are not fit to be used by Man."[257]

The problem was finally addressed in 1849. Lieutenant Meigs designed and constructed a new frame barracks and a hospital near the lake front. The buildings would have provided comfortable quarters for Fort Niagara's garrison had they not been swept by fire on the morning of May 19, 1850. Most of the wooden structures between the Mess House (increasingly referred to as the "Old French Castle" by 1850) and the North Redoubt were totally consumed. These included a wooden barracks built about 1810, the small blockhouse constructed by Fraser in 1841, the nearly completed barracks and hospital, and most of the defensive stockade which topped the seawall.[258] This tragedy worsened the already abominable living conditions of Fort Niagara's enlisted personnel. When Engineer Lieutenant John Newton surveyed the fortifications for his annual report in the fall of 1850, he noted that the state of the defenses of Fort Niagara had worsened somewhat but that, "So far as regards the comfort of the troops it is very defective."[259]

There were distressingly few places where the soldiers and their families could be housed. The French

The North Redoubt peeks over the masonry scarp wall and casemates constructed in the 1860's. Photograph taken August 24, 1926.*Courtesy, Niagara Mohawk Power Corporation.*

Castle was in use as officers' quarters. Most of the other stone buildings were storehouses or service buildings generally unsuitable for habitation. Lacking other possibilities, minor repairs were made to the "Quartermaster Store House" and the enlisted men took shelter in the first story. The building had been constructed by the British as a provisions storehouse in 1762, and parts of it had served as barracks as early as the War of 1812. Some of the troops were also again billeted in the redoubts. Quarters for wives and children of the soldiers, the hospital, and the mess and cook rooms were moved into "an old frame building condemned long since." This was probably a two-story structure known as the "Engineers Barracks", built about 1816 and located in the southeast quadrant of the fort near the South Redoubt. The building was eminently unsuitable for the mess and cook rooms. Dust and dirt falling through the ceilings from the rooms above garnished every meal. This compelled the commanding officer to move the kitchens and mess rooms into one of the "Block-houses", probably the South Redoubt, and squeeze its tenants into the storehouse/barracks.[260]

United States soldiers of the Fort Niagara garrison would live under these appalling conditions for the next three years. Various commanding officers wrote repeatedly to the Quartermaster General to describe the state of the barracks and plead for new construction. The enlisted men were housed in the redoubts throughout this time. In 1854 the soldiers were being rotated seasonally. Summer was spent in "a portion of an old dilapidated one-story building erected in 1762." The former provisions storehouse was in such bad repair that the stone walls were "falling in" and the roof could not be patched to keep out the weather. During the winter the men moved into "two damp, ill-ventilated Stone blockhouses."[261] Most complaints about the redoubts thereafter centered on their unsuitability for quarters due to lack of ventilation and dampness. Lieutenant Edward M. Hudson's 1853 assessment was typical and probably perfectly accurate:

> *... The Troops at this post have no Quarters except two heavy stone Blockhouses, which, as such buildings must necessarily be, are damp, badly ventilated, and unwholesome in the extreme ...*[262]

There was no answer to the problem but the construction of new buildings. The army was temporarily spared this expense, however, when the garrison was again withdrawn from Fort Niagara in 1854.[263]

Upon departure of the troops, Fort Niagara was placed in the hands of Ordnance Sergeant Lewis Leffman. This veteran of several armies had watched over the physical plant of the post since 1839 and had served as caretaker in 1846-48 when the garrison was withdrawn for the Mexican War.[264] Leffman had no staff and, with the exception of visiting engineer officers and occasional workmen, would be the sole

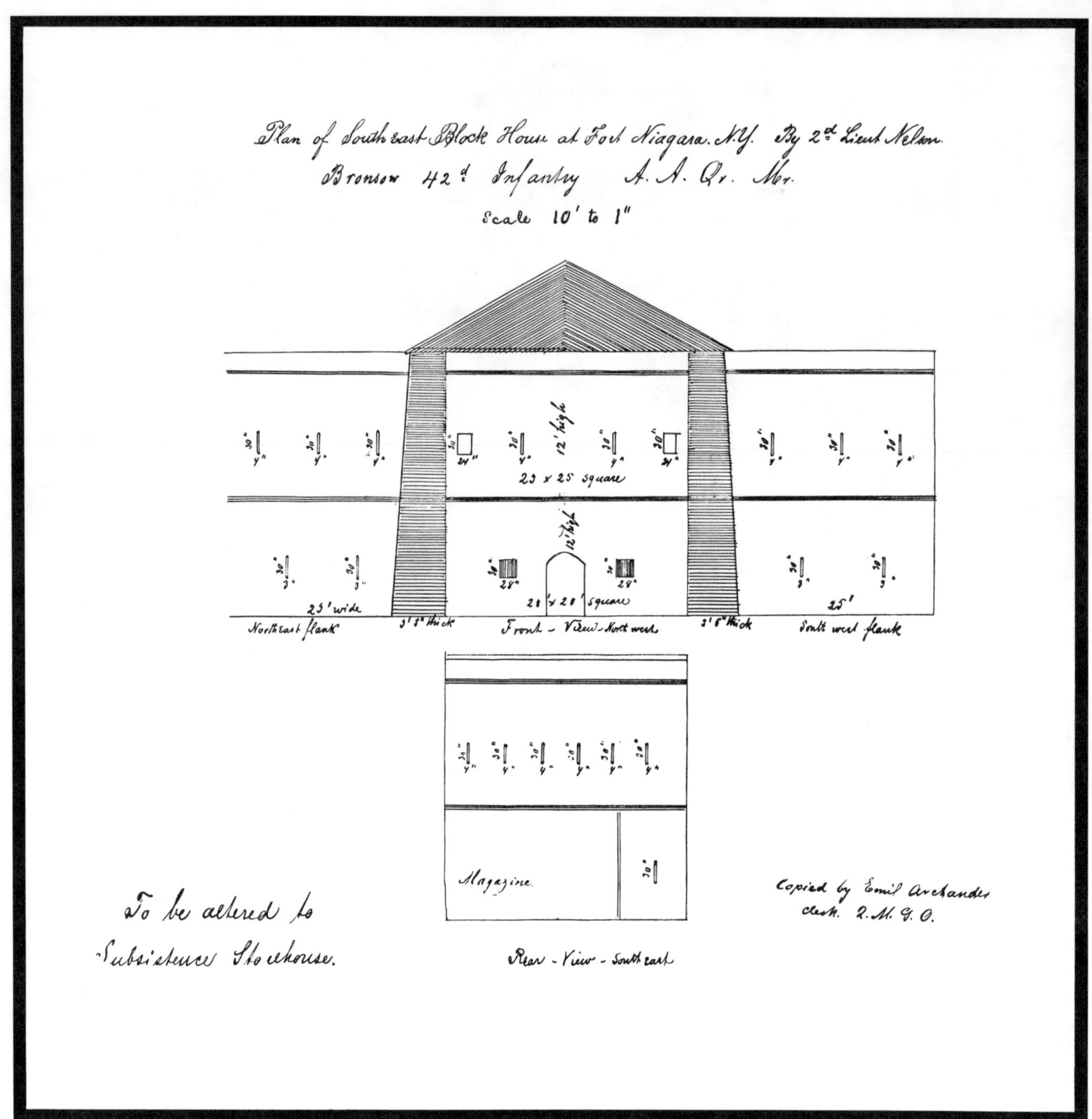

Lt. Nelson Bronson's 1867 plan projected conversion of the South Redoubt to a "Subsistence Storehouse". *Courtesy, National Archives and Records Administration, RG 77, Dr. 53, Sht. 3.*

individual responsible for Fort Niagara for the next seven years. Leffman's chief enemy was Nature, and it dealt the old walls and buildings some severe blows over the next few years. On April 18, 1855, a violent storm, described in the *Niagara Falls Gazette* as a tornado, struck Niagara County. Fort Niagara was in the path of the cyclone, and many of its buildings were damaged. The roof was blown off the North Redoubt, and that of the South Redoubt was "partially displaced" and its chimney knocked down. Engineer Lieutenant Charles E. Blunt was dispatched to the post upon Leffman's report of the storm. He estimated damage of $365.68 to the former building and $44.00 to the latter.[265] By October, the redoubts had been repaired along with most of the other structures with the exception of the old storehouse.[266] Most of the deterioration of the next few years was more insidious. Roofs, exterior and interior woodwork, plaster, and windows fell prey to neglect and vacancy despite Leffman's best efforts. By 1857 most of the buildings of Fort Niagara were described as being in "an almost ruinous state of repair." Only the "Blockhouses", "Old

The North Redoubt's chimney is down in the earliest photograph of the building, taken on October 1, 1879. Four Model 1857 twelve-pounder gun-howitzers ("Napoleons") and their limbers are ranged on the parade ground. *Courtesy, National Archives and Records Administration, RG 111, SC-88033.*

French Castle", powder magazine, and shot furnace were excepted. The post still lacked structures other than the French Castle which were adequate for use as quarters.[267]

Fort Niagara's housing problem remained a moot point so long as there was no garrison. The outbreak of the Civil War unexpectedly changed the post's inactive status, however, beginning with the arrival of one company of the 7th Regiment of Infantry in December, 1861. Although their reoccupation of the post was motivated partly by renewed friction with Great Britain over the "*Trent* Affair" of November, 1861, the soldiers were paroled men who were unable to serve against the rebels until properly exchanged. They were, however, free to guard the Niagara Frontier.[268] Additional British forces were soon sent to Canada. This action drew attention to the defense of the Great Lakes and to the fortifications of Niagara. These had deteriorated since Captain Fraser's improvements of 1839-43. The wooden revetments of the land side earthworks, although Kyanized for their preservation, had rotted, and the post was incapable of defense. Once again, U.S. Army engineers would alter the fortifications of Niagara.[269] While new plans were being prepared, the garrison officers were quartered in the French Castle and the enlisted men in the old storehouse which had been repaired for their accommodation by the Quartermaster Department. There is no evidence that the redoubts were used as barracks. The parolees of the 7th Infantry were exchanged in 1862. They departed Fort Niagara in October before any work had begun on the fortifications.[270]

Captain John A. Tardy, Jr. was ordered to Buffalo in June, 1863, to direct the work projected at the now empty Fort Niagara. His priority was to secure the land front by replacing the rotted timber revetments with concrete and brick and constructing casemated flanking galleries to better cover the ditch. Detailed instructions sent to Tardy by Brigadier General Totten do not describe what role the old redoubts were to play in the renovated land-side defenses. Since Totten referred to the buildings as "blockhouses" and carefully instructed Captain Tardy to construct the new concrete and masonry revetments *around* the old walls so as not to demolish them before the new ones were in place, it must be assumed that the redoubts were intended to remain, at least temporarily, as part of the fortifications.[271] In 1864 Captain Tardy described the redoubts as "masonry block-houses in the bastions of the land front", a further indication that they were still considered useful.[272] The buildings appear on several revised plans for new lake and river defenses through the 1860's. Even the final fortification plan for Fort Niagara, which would have removed the other eighteenth century structures, shows the redoubts in place.[273] In 1867, however, as the new walls neared completion, Captain Tardy informed Quartermaster Department Major Alexander Montgomery that "the [South] Block House will not be required for purposes of defense in the projected modification of the works."[274] Although Fort Niagara's surgeon reported, in 1872, that the roofs could quickly be removed and the buildings converted to

The South Redoubt, about the turn of the twentieth century. *OFN 673/28A.*

towers in the event of war, the useful defensive function of the old British redoubts seems to have ended as they neared the centennial of their construction.[275]

This is not to say that the army could find no service for the massive old structures. They would have been terribly difficult and expensive to remove in any case. During his inspection of the post buildings in 1864, Captain Tardy reported the "blockhouses" to be in good repair and "perfectly dry" while most of the other structures were in poor condition.[276] It was probably this assessment which resulted in the redoubts being converted to storehouses. Additional barracks and storage space became particularly important in the autumn of 1865 when Fort Niagara was again garrisoned. The redoubts had been in use as provisions storehouses for some time by the summer of 1867. They were not, however, well thought of by the officers who had to issue the rations stored in them. In their annual inspection report of the post buildings for 1867 the deficiencies of the redoubts as storehouses were outlined:

> *... the walls are thick and damp and there being no ventilation except small loop holes for Musketry, they are not considered safe places for the storage of perishable articles; some 3000 Pounds of bacon & ham which had been stored in one of the Blockhouses for six months (there being no other place to store it) had to be condemned and sold at auction, having become rotten & maggoty, owing to the dampness of the place, and want of proper ventilation. The construction of a storehouse for the storage and preservation of perishable articles is an absolute necessity.*[277]

This had apparently not been the first such complaint, but the post-Civil War army was concerned with avoiding undue expenses. Responsibility for provisions and the maintenance or construction of buildings to store them rested with the Quartermaster Department. Major Alexander Montgomery of the Northern District Office in Buffalo had received earlier requests for a new storehouse for Fort Niagara, but he did not believe this to be necessary. Montgomery thought that the deficiencies of the South Redoubt could be corrected. If, he suggested, the building was altered:

> *... By setting a door, of iron or wooden grating, inside the door of the Block House, and permitting the outer door to remain open, during the day, furring and plastering the walls and providing proper ventilation, all of which can be done at a trifling expense, No better Storehouse for all articles of Subsistence could be devised ...*

After determining from Captain Tardy, in June, 1867, that the South Redoubt was no longer necessary for defense so that "there can be no objection to piercing the walls, in places, to insure adequate ventilation," Montgomery submitted specifications and cost estimates to George Crosman, Chief Quartermaster of the Department of the East.[278] Three weeks later he forwarded more detailed estimates and a plan of the proposed changes. The latter was probably the set of elevations prepared by Lieutenant Nelson Bronson, Fort Niagara Post Quartermaster.[279]

Montgomery's estimate for the conversion was a trifling $146.75. General Crosman endorsed the request and forwarded it with his positive recommendation to Quartermaster General Montgomery Meigs. He also approved the plan and in turn recommended it to Secretary of War Edwin M. Stanton. The project was approved by highest authority on August 20.[280] The conversion appears to have been completed by June,1868, when the South Redoubt was reported to be in use as a storehouse. A further request that year for a new storehouse was turned down on the grounds that "the two blockhouses now in use" and the old stone barracks (provisions storehouse) provided ample room for the garrison's supplies.[281]

The plan prepared by Lieutenant Bronson gives some answers about the conversion of the South Redoubt to a "Subsistence Storehouse". It also presents a number of inconsistencies. Bronson's four elevations of the building neither accurately depict its appearance following the alterations of 1842-43 nor show the true arrangement of the facades in the later nineteenth century. The number and locations of Bronson's loopholes varies, in many cases, from those shown in the highly detailed plans drawn by Captain Fraser in December,1842. Most of the latter features may still be identified in the building. The ground floor powder magazine is also placed in the wrong location. It must therefore be surmised that Bronson's plan was merely a proposal, one which shows additional slits intended to serve as ventilators. It might also be that his plan incorporates a number of errors, particularly the misplaced powder magazine. The alterations actually made in 1867-68 were few in number. The arched loopholes flanking the doorway on the northwest side of the building and the single arched loophole on the southwest side of the ground floor were converted to windows. The pair of loopholes in the second story of the northwest facade were widened into simple square windows. All openings appear to have been barred for security.[282]

While the South Redoubt was being altered to better shelter provisions, the North Redoubt was put into use as a carpenter's shop.[283] It too might have undergone some changes. By 1870 the interior of the building was divided into two rooms and a loft.[284] It would thus seem that the original ground floor powder magazine, repaired in the 1840's, had been removed by this time. The North Redoubt would otherwise have been listed as containing three rooms and a loft. Perhaps the magazine was removed in 1867-68 to facilitate use as a carpenter's shop and lumber storeroom. In July, 1869, both redoubts were described as being in good order with storage capacities sufficient for the garrison. When Major General Irvin McDowell visited a few days later, he also noted their solid construction, good condition and utility as storehouses. McDowell wrote enthusiastically of all the old structures at Fort Niagara. He described the redoubts as having been built by the French between 1725 and 1727, no doubt confusing them with the Castle. He also felt that the buildings were misnamed. Perhaps because they lacked the machicolated second floor, McDowell insisted that they were actually "Two square towers, improperly called block houses!"[285]

Satisfaction with the usefulness of the redoubts as storehouses would not last for long. Positive comments seem, in fact, to have been most strongly expressed by officers who did not have to live on the post! By the end of 1869, the commandant, Captain Richard H. Jackson, was complaining that "the block houses in which the Subsistence will have to be stored are damp and unfitted for the purpose." He requested that a new storehouse be constructed at once.[286] Jackson's feelings were echoed by other officers whose concerns were also based on the dampness of structures which had been "built for defence" and not for the storage of food and lumber.[287] These complaints would soon be addressed. By June, 1872, the South Redoubt had finally been abandoned as a provisions storehouse. It was used instead as "Company Store rooms" and housed less perishable items such as equipment. The building was described as having four rooms and a loft. This arrangement had been

Many participants in the 1917 Fort Niagara Officer's Training Camp were accommodated in tents. A magazine ventilator slit is visible at left in the first story of the South Redoubt. *OFN 3976/28A.*

made by the construction of a wooden partition to divide the second floor into two rooms, a feature that lasted until restoration.[288] When a modern brick "Quartermaster & Commissary Storehouse" was constructed outside the walls, in 1888, the garrison's rations finally ended their odyssey and could at last be kept under proper conditions. In 1889 a new brick bakery was erected adjacent to the storehouse to replace the frame bakehouse built within the fort in 1870. The old bakery was then altered to serve as the carpenter's shop, thus removing the lumber from the moist atmosphere of the North Redoubt.[289] The stone buildings did not go out of use as storehouses, however. The army merely found more durable goods to keep in them. In 1905 the South Redoubt (alternately known as "Block House 1") was a storehouse for engineer, ordnance and signal equipment. The North Redoubt ("Block House 2") contained Quartermaster supplies.[290] The buildings appear to have remained secure and in use as storehouses at least through the First World War.

Although Fort Niagara's redoubts had been outstripped by technology and relegated to the mundane existence of storehouses, their original purpose as fortifications had not been forgotten. The army never ceased referring to the structures as blockhouses, and a 1908 atlas map also identifies the South Redoubt as "Old Guard Ho[use]."[291] Like the rest of the walled enclosure, however, now commonly known as "Old" Fort Niagara, the buildings had slipped into the realm of historical curiosities. They were maintained and preserved at very little expense because of their durability, and they still served secondary purposes for the early twentieth century garrison situated outside the obsolete fortifications.[292] Continued survival of the redoubts would soon depend upon their status as historic buildings and the growing consciousness within the local community of the perils which threatened the "Old Fort".

"TWO SQUARE TOWERS IMPROPERLY CALLED BLOCKHOUSES"

1922 - 1934

The dawn of the twentieth century found the windswept point at the mouth of the Niagara River occupied by a military post with two distinct elements. The tip of the peninsula was marked by the red brick and earthen walls of "Old" Fort Niagara with its six surviving eighteenth century buildings and a trio of later wooden structures. To the east, outside the fortifications, was the area of current military activity. By 1900, dozens of brick and frame barracks, officers' quarters and service buildings housed a substantial garrison in the unfortified "New" Fort Niagara. United States soldiers still walked post on the ramparts of the Old Fort, but the defenses no longer had any military significance. Although the last pieces of obsolete, muzzle-loading artillery were not removed until about 1903, their only purpose was to decorate the fort and perhaps fire an occasional salute.

Surprisingly, all of the old stone buildings were still in use. Aside from the powder magazine, however, their functions were far different than had been intended by their French and British designers. The Castle, the frame guardhouse of 1869 and the old Provisions Storehouse were quarters for married personnel or civilian employees, the latter reverting to a storage area by 1905. The Bakehouse of 1762 and the two redoubts served as storehouses.[293] The buildings of the Old Fort no longer had a very high priority in the army's plans for maintenance and repair, however. Photographs taken immediately preceding and during the First World War show that the historic structures were beginning to succumb to age and neglect.

The North Redoubt in the early 1920's. Percy Morgan feared that the historic buildings were being used for the storage of flammable materials. *Courtesy, National Archives and Records Administration, RG 111, SC-93528.*

In spite of the reduced status of what had once been the primary buildings of Fort Niagara, the old structures were recognized by tourists and local residents alike for their historical significance. Visitors to Niagara Falls had been stopping to inspect the walled fort and its colonial-period architecture since before the War of 1812. This interest had grown steadily throughout the nineteenth century.[294] The French Castle always received the most attention as a historical curiosity, but the massive redoubts ranked next in popularity. Samuel De Veaux included the "stone towers" in a romanticized catalog of the fort's buildings in his 1839 guidebook, and most publications after that time made reference to the redoubts.[295] When they were deleted from the defensive scheme of Fort Niagara in the years following the Civil War, mention of their age and historical context became more frequent in military inventories and correspondence. By 1872, Assistant Surgeon Bartholf was describing the century-old redoubts as "ancient structures". Three years earlier General McDowell had obviously been impressed by their antiquity and durability.[296]

For some reason, however, the later years of the nineteenth century witnessed growing confusion about the period of construction and the builders of the redoubts. The notion became popular that they dated to the French occupation. Earlier in the century, the redoubts were generally acknowledged to have been erected by the British, and Doctor Bartholf so described them as late as 1872. Three years earlier, however, General McDowell reported them to have been built by the French in 1725-26. By the end of the century, even such a local historical authority as Peter A. Porter was attributing the redoubts to the French and giving 1756 as the year of their construction. Porter's dating was accepted by other authors and by the U.S. Army when a detailed inventory of the post buildings was assembled in 1905.[297] Captions such as "Block House, Old French Fort Built in 1756" are found on postcards of the pre-World War I era. This misunderstanding would persist until the original plans were discovered in the British Museum. These were correctly dated as circa 1770. Despite this confusion, the redoubts were clearly perceived as interesting historical relics of an earlier age. The

The obvious deterioration of the South Redoubt, Provisions Storehouse and Powder Magazine, shown in a photograph taken August 24, 1926, illustrates the concern felt by local residents for the historic structures. Work began on the French Castle that year. *Courtesy, Niagara Mohawk Power Corporation.*

entire "Old Fort" was receiving wide public attention for this reason by the end of the nineteenth century. An 1899 editorial in the *Niagara Falls Gazette*, for example, lauded Fort Niagara for its value as a historic site. The writer extolled the completeness of its architecture when compared to other famous fortresses of colonial history which were, by then, nothing more than ruins.[298] This interest continued to grow throughout the first decades of the new century.[299]

Public recognition of the historic structures was sometimes expressed in rather peculiar ways. Two local buildings constructed in the twentieth century, for example, mimicked the form and details of Fort Niagara's redoubts. The first was based on the pre-restoration appearance of the North Redoubt and was located just outside Old Fort Niagara on the low ground occupied by the Coast Guard Station. Designed as a water filtration plant for the garrison of the "New" Fort and constructed of reinforced concrete, "Building 87" stood two stories tall and incorporated the low hipped roof and small classical doorway of the North Redoubt. Although it had large windows on the second floor and a wing to one side, the resemblance was unmistakable. This whimsical structure was completed in December, 1921 and demolished during the 1960's.[300] The second example employed exaggerated details of the restored buildings. In 1944, a highly romanticized "redoubt" was designed for the Niagara Frontier State Park and Recreation Commission as a public comfort station at Devil's Hole State Park. The building was completed six years later. It incorporated caricatures of the Chinese roofs, wall batter, loopholes, and doorways of the redoubts. The reason for the choice of this design is unknown. Perhaps the architect was aware that the site of one of Montresor's picketed redoubts of 1764, built to prevent a repetition of the Devil's Hole Ambush of 1763, was only a few dozen yards away from the park. Fort Niagara contained the only local examples of redoubts, and so they were copied. This comfort station still serves tourists and fishermen at Devil's Hole.[301]

If the respect of the local and visiting public for the value of Old Fort Niagara was increasing, that of the U.S. Army was not - at least not to the degree that scarce budget funds were likely to be devoted to its proper upkeep. The army expended slightly less than $200 on repairs to the South Redoubt between 1905 and 1929 and an even lesser sum on the northern building.[302] This was no doubt due, in part, to their relative imperviousness to the elements and the fact that the redoubts were in use only as secondary storehouses. The other historic buildings were in far worse condition, and they were receiving no more attention. The situation became desperate during the early 1920's when structural problems developed in the seawall and the French Castle making it appear likely that the fort's oldest building and the protective barrier for the entire north side of the Old Fort would collapse into Lake Ontario.[303]

Local residents soon became actively concerned about this problem as well as the possibility that vandals or arsonists might destroy the remaining buildings. An early and voluble proponent of Old Fort Niagara's preservation was Percy Morgan, a resident of Lewiston. In 1921 he began attempts to gain allies in a fight to save the site before it, "like Fort Erie, Fort Ticonderoga and other old frontier posts of the French and Indian and Revolutionary wars, will be nothing

The North Redoubt shortly before restoration. *OFN 6338/30A.*

William Wallace Kincaid, first President of the Old Fort Niagara Association. *OFN 5198/151.*

Col. Charles H. Morrow, 28th U.S. Infantry, commanded Fort Niagara from 1930 to 1935. He took a deep personal interest in the restoration of Old Fort Niagara and assisted in the search for artillery to arm the redoubts. *OFN 5190/151.*

but a pile of crumbling stone."[304] Morgan was particularly concerned that the old buildings were being used as storehouses with no protection from either fire or vandalism. Queries through local Federal representatives elicited the response that the structures were being inspected regularly by the garrison and that nothing dangerous was stored in them. Morgan was not mollified. He claimed that the buildings were open to "every Tom Dick and Harry who wanted to commit any desecration," and that at least one of the blockhouses was used for the storage of oil.[305] Colonel Frederic D. Evans, Fort Niagara's commandant, countered that he was keeping the fort patrolled, the buildings clean and the grass cut, and that no oil or lumber was kept in any of the historic structures. Evans even seems to have hoped for an appropriation to restore the fort, but this was not deemed to be a practical request at the time.[306]

The problem was one of money. It soon became apparent that the local advocates of Old Fort Niagara's preservation would have to take their case to Congress. Organized efforts began on March 6, 1922 at a meeting of the Youngstown Men's Club. A committee was formed which immediately opened contacts with Senator James W. Wadsworth, Jr., Congressmen S. Wallace Dempsey and other elected Federal officials from New York. Their first victory came in 1924 when nearly $25,000 was appropriated to repair the seawall. The work was completed in October. The Niagara Falls Chamber of Commerce reinforced the Youngstown men in 1925, and the 1926 Federal budget included $5,000 for preliminary restoration work on the French Castle. This was followed by appropriations of $15,000 each in 1927 and 1928. Again, the money was for work on the Castle. Removal of later additions from the building began in 1926 with restoration underway by the spring of 1927.[307]

Congress soon made it clear, however, that local resources would be needed if the Old Fort was to be completely restored. In order to achieve that goal, the various groups and committees which had begun advocacy efforts coalesced in June, 1927, to form the Old Fort Niagara Association, Incorporated. William Wallace Kincaid, a member of the original Youngstown Men's Club committee, was elected President. Kincaid had been tireless in his efforts to obtain the early appropriations, and he clearly wished to see the entire fort restored. Two other original committee members, Percy Morgan and George Ferguson, served on the new board. In a spirit of local and Federal cooperation, Congressman Dempsey and post commandant Colonel Ralph E. Ingram were named General Vice Presidents. The Association immediately began soliciting memberships and using the funds to supplement money provided through the War Department's budget.[308]

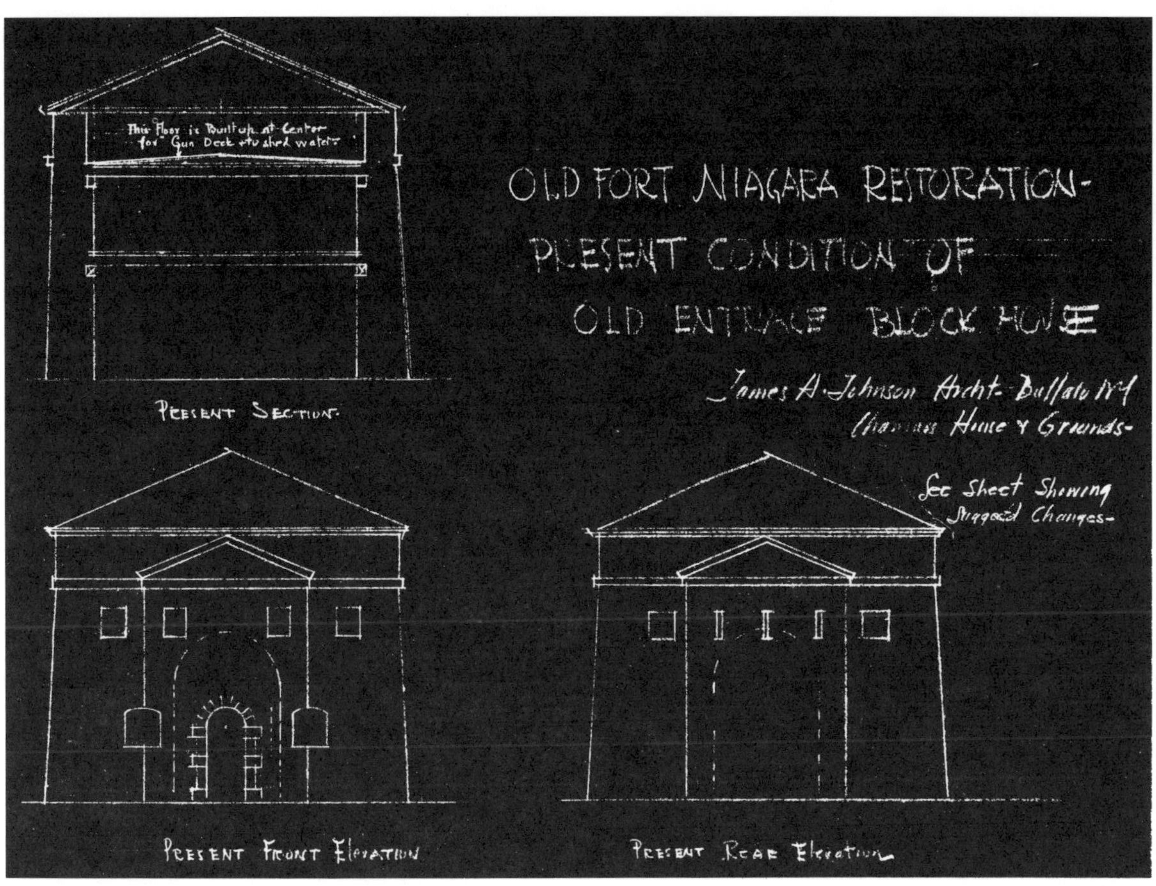

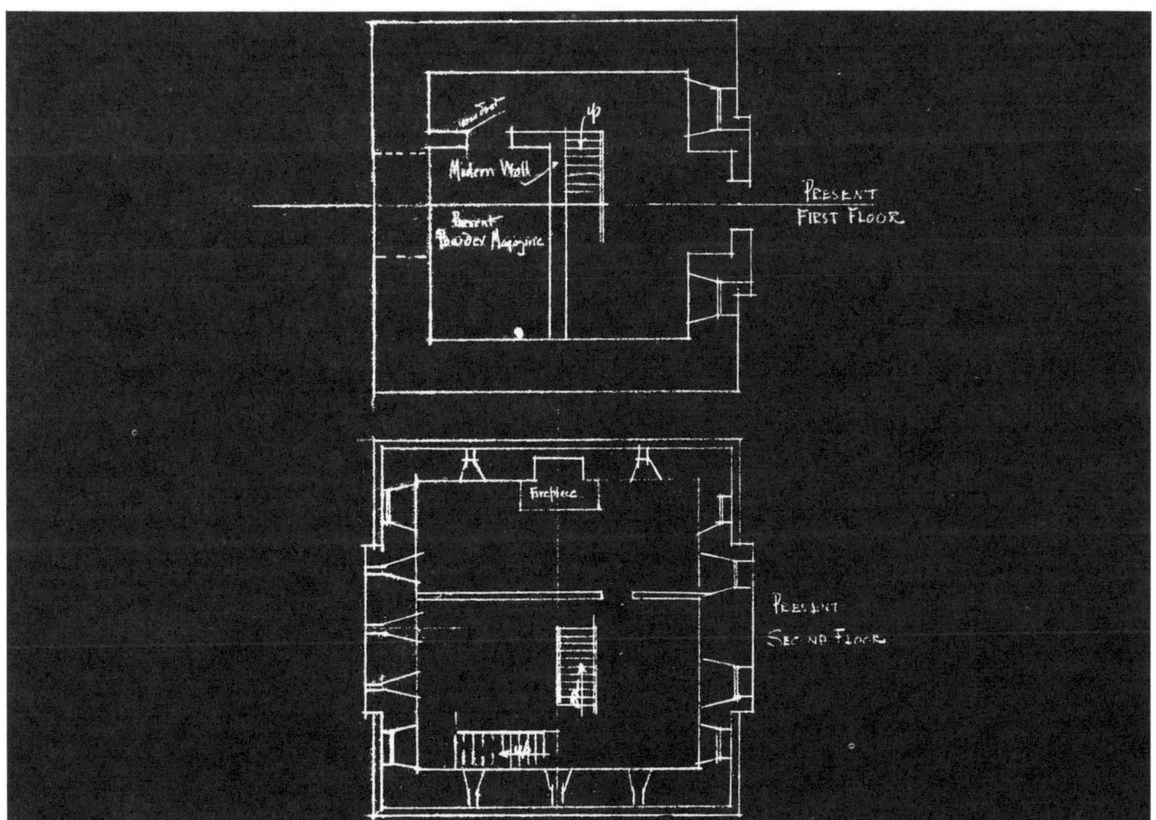

James H. Johnson drew plans, sections and elevations of the South Redoubt as it appeared prior to restoration. Some details, such as ventilator slits for the ground floor powder magazine, were omitted from these plans.

The South Redoubt on the eve of restoration. The ruined roof of the Provisions Storehouse has already been removed. *OFN 4429/28A.*

The French Castle was clearly the first priority of both the Association and the Army. The building was in terrible condition and threatened by major structural defects. Restoration efforts accordingly began there. The redoubts, once again by virtue of their rugged construction and their location away from the seawall, were not in such immediate danger nor in need of extensive repairs. When an initial survey was made, in the summer of 1922, the redoubts (this time correctly dated as having been constructed in 1770 and 1771) were each estimated to require only $250 in repairs. The Castle, by comparison, was listed for $7,650.[309] The redoubts therefore waited while the much more severe problems of the French Castle were addressed during the first two years of restoration.

While the Castle was the focal point of agitation for restoration of Old Fort Niagara, it is quite clear that Morgan, Kincaid and the many other advocates of the historic site wanted the whole place preserved and carefully restored. This was stated to the War Department in the summer of 1927 when Colonel Ingram reported the organization of the Old Fort Niagara Association. He wrote his superior, the Commanding General, Second Corps Area, that:

> *... Though not specifically declared, I am of the opinion, after discussion with the President and several members of the Old Fort Niagara Association, that said Association will desire to further the extension of the work of restoration to include all other buildings within the walls of the old masonry fort and the grounds therein.*

Furthermore, the Association wished to have the Old Fort declared a National Monument. Ingram believed that, so far as the military utility of the area was concerned, the Old Fort "may be so declared." He also recommended that future restoration projects follow the desires of the Association "under the general supervision and control of the Commanding Officer, Fort Niagara, New York, under such regulations as may be prescribed by the Secretary of War."[310]

While work progressed on the French Castle, the Association began to look toward restoration of the other buildings. War Department engineer Alfred G. Adams prepared new estimates late in 1927. The cost of rehabilitating the redoubts had increased to $4,890 each, probably because Adams and the Association were considering actual restoration rather than the simple repairs projected in 1922.[311] Much of 1928 was spent in discussions of priorities. By November, the decision had been made to first complete the Castle, then install public toilets somewhere within the fort and finally to proceed with restoration of the other buildings. Policies for the larger restoration project were hammered out at a Board of Directors meeting held on November 23. The Executive Committee was directed to proceed with preparation of plans in cooperation with the Buildings, Furnishings and Grounds Committee, the Commanding Officer of Fort Niagara and the engineer in charge of restoration. Several concerns were raised and resolved. James A. Johnson, Board member and an architect, asked whether the intention was to restore only the Castle and the French structures of Fort Niagara. President Kincaid answered that the idea was to have all buildings restored correctly to the period of their construction. The full Board concurred with this policy. Edward T. Williams, Association Historian, went on record as being "emphatically opposed" to the removal of any buildings. He firmly believed that the program should "involve no proposition outside of restoration and preservation." Johnson pointed out the need for proper plans for all restoration efforts. In this Kincaid and the others agreed. With these opinions on record, the Board reiterated the priorities set earlier in the month, and planning for the "restoration of the several old buildings within the triangle" began.[312] It is clear that the members were concerned about the accuracy and quality of the restoration.

Engineer Adams soon prepared additional estimates to accompany plans for restoration of the entire triangular enclosure. The cost of the North Redoubt remained the same as his earlier projection. That for the South Redoubt, however, had been combined with reconstruction of the old "Gate of the Five Nations". The expense of removing part of the concrete and brick revetment, altering the earthworks, constructing a drawbridge with its accompanying "headhouse" as well as the approaches to the South Redoubt significantly increased the estimate to $18,000. The total estimated restoration cost, with furnishings for all buildings, amounted to over $75,000.[313] Funds of this magnitude were simply not yet available, so the work proposed for 1929 had to be of more modest scope. In May, it was decided to proceed with a rest room addition to the Castle, restoration of the 1762 British Bakehouse and a new roof for the 1757 French Powder Magazine.[314]

These early priorities would soon be expanded, but there would first be considerable discussion. By June, the Buildings, Furnishings and Grounds Committee

Work progresses on the South Redoubt during the winter of 1929-30. The framework of the roof has been erected. *OFN 595/24B.*

was recommending a more ambitious plan of work for the year. For the first time this specifically included the two stone redoubts. As in 1770 and 1841, the North Redoubt would have a lower priority. The committee believed that, for the moment, it required only a few repairs to keep out the weather. The South Redoubt was given precedence on the list of 1929 projects. Copies of the original plans were then in the possession of the Association. These were, of course, the "Montresor" plans of circa 1770. It was known that, at a later date, "the large arched openings were closed up, windows were cut through the piers, and the building otherwise modified." Montresor's plans allowed these alterations to be identified. The committee also hoped to complete the drawbridge entrance since that would "add greatly to the public interest in the entire group of buildings, and increase very greatly the effect of age and mystery to the Fort."[315] These recommendations were accepted by the Executive Committee which again set priorities for the year. During 1929 its members hoped to complete the Castle with its rest rooms, restore the Bakehouse, rebuild the "French Barracks" (actually the 1762 British Provisions Storehouse), repair the Powder Magazine, and finally complete the "two block houses". This list was submitted to the commandant of Fort Niagara.[316]

There remained the problem of money. At the Board of Directors meeting of June 26, 1929, Claud H. Hultzén, the Association's Executive Vice President, announced that $15,000 would be available on July 1 from the latest War Department appropriation. This money had been approved in February for the Fiscal Year 1930 budget, but it would not be released until matched dollar for dollar by the Association. Success in obtaining the necessary private funds would thus provide $30,000 for the first restoration expenditure outside of the Castle.[317] This was still not enough for

The South Redoubt nears completion in the spring of 1930. Four windows on the northwest facade have been converted to 1770-period loopholes. Gratings from the 1867 storehouse conversion are still in place in the remaining windows. *OFN 691/28B.*

Northwest entrance of the South Redoubt near the end of restoration, spring, 1930. *OFN 692/28B.*

By the spring of 1930, little remained to be done to the exterior of the southeast facade of the South Redoubt other than to install windows and finish the archway. Jambs for the gate are in place. The reason for the peculiar shape of the chimney top is unknown. *OFN 690/28B.*

everything proposed, so several cuts had been made by the time President Kincaid submitted a final list to the Secretary of War. Because of the expense, and since the South Redoubt could be "restored as a unit and without affecting the restoration in the future of the French drawbridge," the latter project was deferred. Since the North Redoubt was still in fairly good repair, it was also proposed to wait for at least another year before commencing its restoration.[318] The project list was swiftly approved with minor revisions of plans, and work was underway by early fall. By the end of November, 1929, the Bakehouse and the roof of the Powder Magazine had been completed. The rest rooms were well advanced, and work had begun on the Provisions Storehouse. Last of all

Gates for the southeast entrance of the South Redoubt had been hung by December 8, 1929. *OFN 693/28B.*

these projects was the South Redoubt. Restoration was then in an early stage and only 5% complete.[319]

The South Redoubt would be primarily a winter project. This increased the cost slightly since the work had to be done in the cold season, and the wages of stone masons had recently increased.[320] By the first week of January, 1930, the job was 50% complete. The redoubt was at 90% completion by the end of April, and President Kincaid was able to report at the 1930 annual meeting that the building had been entirely restored according to the original plans.[321]

Details on exactly what was done to the South Redoubt are frustratingly vague. While reports and records about the restoration of the Castle are scanty, those for the stone towers are almost non-existent. It is known that copies of the original Montresor plans had been obtained from the Public Archives of Canada. These guided the restoration, and their influence on the project is apparent from the condition of both buildings today. Montresor's drawings were particularly valuable in providing construction details for the Chinese-style roofs. Plans of the building prepared by James A. Johnson about 1929 show the condition of the structure on the eve of restoration and give an idea of what was removed.[322] The low, hipped roof, the 1855 chimney, a wooden partition dividing the second floor, both sets of stairs, the stone powder magazine, and the brick paving of the ground floor were all torn out and discarded. The 1842-43 floors and masonry trim of most windows and gunslits were left in place, although four of the windows on the northwest facade (two from the 1840's work and two from 1867), which were shown as gunslits in the 1770 plans, were returned to their original form. Specifications and estimates prepared in December, 1929, show that a new roof was to have been constructed. This was done in conformance to the oriental style shown on the 1770 plan. Repairs were to be made to doors and windows. Eighteenth century-style windows were installed in the four remaining large openings in the northwest and southeast facades of the second story and the single one in the southwest facade of the first story. Two stair cases of hewn timber were specified. The stairway from the ground to the second floor was moved to correspond with the location against the northeast wall as shown on the Pfister plan of 1773. The old stair opening in the second floor was covered with a trap door and the headers left in place. A stone slab floor replaced the brick paving. Plans to repaint and replaster the interior and exterior walls do not seem to have ever been accomplished, although this was proposed as late as 1939.[323] Some of the material removed was salvaged for use in other parts of the restoration, notably white pine beams, probably from the framework of the roof, which were sawed into boards for panelling the Sir William Johnson Council Room in the French Castle.[324]

The brief specifications made no mention of several important parts of the work, particularly the largest job of all - reopening the two gateways. The old arches could be clearly distinguished in the masonry facades. After both large doors had been reopened, massive iron-bound wooden gates were hung to close up the building. This work provided a gateway to nowhere, since the drawbridge reconstruction had been deferred. The chimney was also reconstructed but with a peculiar narrowing at the top which was totally unlike that shown on Montresor's plans. This might have been intended to enhance the draft for an oil space heater later placed in the ticket booth on the ground floor. The chimney top was rebuilt in 1987 to conform to its eighteenth century appearance. A small wooden booth, used today for the sale of tickets, was probably added at this time since it had earlier been proposed that a gatekeeper's station be located in the South Redoubt.[325]

The 1929 appropriation had allowed a great deal of progress. As the year neared its end, it was time for the Association to approach the Federal government for another year's restoration funding. Kincaid and Hultzén could at least appear before the House Sub-Committee on Military Appropriations with some powerful ammunition. The 1929 appropriation of $15,000 had been fully matched by the Old Fort Niagara Association. To date, the local community had contributed $32,344.27 directly to the restoration effort and nearly $30,000 to related projects. The Association asked for a 1930 appropriation (for FY 1931) of $49,539.79 to continue the work begun in 1929. This would complete most of the restoration. Kincaid also hoped that Congress would not "call upon the citizens of the Niagara Frontier to further contribute to the restoration."[326]

Kincaid and Hultzén traveled to Washington to meet with New York Senator Royal S. Copeland and Congressman Dempsey. A bill was prepared, and Dempsey and the Association representatives presented it to the House Sub-Committee. Kincaid also took the opportunity to seek legislation legalizing the relationship of the Association with the War Department. This would eventually result in the not-for-profit organization's first license to operate and maintain the Old Fort. The two men also met with representatives of the War Department where, according to Hultzén, they "found unqualified sympathy and support on the part of all War Department officials in their attitude toward the restoration of Old Fort Niagara."[327] Draft legislation for the 1931 fiscal year appropriation included "repair, restoration and rehabilitation" of the "east [north] blockhouse, French gateway, drawbridge, [and] headhouse."[328]

While Kincaid and Hulzén reported a generally favorable reception in Washington, there was evidence that the cost of restoring Old Fort Niagara was

An interior view of the northwest gateway of the South Redoubt, December 8, 1929. "Original bolts" for holding the door frame to the walls were found in place. The timber lintel was salvaged from "a local settler's cabin built about 1804." *OFN 685/28B.*

creating some discontent. During his presentation to the House Sub-Committee on Military Appropriations, Kincaid was questioned at some length by its Chairman, Congressman Barbour of California. The tone of the interview was impatient and rather strained. The Association's President patiently answered Barbour's queries and corrected some errors in the Chairman's information. He also maintained that the sum requested, $49,539.79, would complete everything that remained to be done. Just as Barbour had been satisfied on this point, Hultzén chimed in, "Everything except the restoration of the French breastworks." The final exchange was sharp:

> **Mr. BARBOUR. How much is this on the outside going to be? That will come later, I suppose?*
>
> **Mr. HULTZEN. Perhaps, if you see fit to do it.*
>
> **Mr. KINCAID. Now, you can go just as far as you please, gentlemen. This is not my job. This is the Nation's job.* [329]

Kincaid was expressing the depth of his commitment to preserving Old Fort Niagara, but it was clear that he had no great ally in Congressman Barbour.

The wheels of government then began to turn. Plans and estimates submitted for the continuation of restoration work were examined by officers of the Quartermaster Corps and judged reasonable. They pointed out, however, that the $49,539.79 requested would not be adequate to complete the restoration. The War Department then approved only one of the many projects listed - that for restoration of the North Redoubt. Due to the expense of the remainder and the fact that "any funds appropriated for their accomplishment would be a charge against the War Depart-

Reconstructed stairway to the second floor of the North Redoubt. The narrowing of the second floor joists at top right was done in 1842-43 to accommodate the roof of the ground floor powder magazine. *OFN 812/30C.*

ment appropriations which are required for many more urgent purposes," the balance of the program was not favorably considered. Major General H.E. Ely, commanding Second Corps Area, informed the commandant of Fort Niagara that needs for maintenance at his other posts meant that there were no extra resources for the Fort Niagara restoration project.[330] Funds for continuing the work had not, in fact, even been included in the 1931 Army Bill, although Senator Copeland was preparing an amendment to correct the omission. The expenses of restoration had been constant, and they were increasing. The army was obviously tiring of the costs, despite the goodwill and interest shown Kincaid and Hultzén by War Department officials in December. In January, 1930, the Quartermaster General suggested that the time might have come to consider naming Old Fort Niagara a National Monument in order to place the site "in the same relative position as other historical memorials."[331] The matter of completing the restoration of Old Fort Niagara hung in the balance. Kincaid confided to Frank Steele, a counsel to the Senate, that "restoration work at Old Fort Niagara is at a standstill until Congress decides how much they are going to contribute for the coming year."[332]

Second floor guard room of the North Redoubt as restored. The furnishings were constructed during the winter of 1933-34. *OFN 811/30C.*

It was Senator Copeland who came to the rescue. On January 6, 1930, he introduced an amendment to bill H.R. 7955 "making appropriations for the military and nonmilitary activities of the War Department for the fiscal year ending June 30, 1931." It included the projects requested by Kincaid and Hultzén with no provisions for matching by the Association.[333] By the time the War Department Appropriation Bill for 1931 had been completed in April, however, it contained only $25,000 for continued repairs and preservation at Old Fort Niagara. This was lumped in with Quartermaster Corps funds for a number of Civil War battlefield memorials and a monument to the Wright brothers to be placed on Kill Devil Hill at Kitty Hawk, North Carolina. The appropriation was approved when the bill was voted on May 26. The Old Fort Niagara Association would still be raising funds, however. This appropriation also contained qualification that none of the money could be released until an equal amount had been deposited with Headquarters, Second Corps Area at Governor's Island, New York.[334]

Kincaid and the Association immediately began looking for the money. The Executive Committee met on June 18 to consider how to carry out the wishes of the Board which had voted to accept the appropriation.[335] The result was a major fund-raising effort intended to obtain $100,000 for completion of the restoration. The goal proved to be an impossible one. At one point in the summer of 1930, Kincaid plaintively requested that Major General C.F. Summerall, Chief of Staff of the U.S. Army, come to Buffalo to address a luncheon group in an effort to raise funds. Kincaid bemoaned the fact that:

> *... we are gradually wearing out our welcome among those who have the means to contribute to the work, Vision is none too high and patriotism is dormant in far too many, and we cannot carry the entire burden ourselves, nor should we for the good of the cause.*[336]

Despite the difficulties of fund raising, sufficient money was obtained to match the 1930 (1931 fiscal year) appropriation. By October, 1930, the Old Fort Niagara Association had turned over to the War Department a grand total of $59,763.38, including the $25,000 necessary to continue work on the North Redoubt and the Gate of the Five Nations complex.[337]

James A. Johnson made a number of concept drawings for the Gate of the Five Nations in 1930.

It is fortunate that the Old Fort Niagara restoration was nearing its end, for Congress was definitely tiring of the expense. When Senator Copeland sought funds in 1931 to finish the Provisions Storehouse and restore the earthworks and brick casemates during the 1932 fiscal year, he had "quite a battle" in the Military Appropriations Committee. Copeland was able to obtain $35,000, which again had to be matched by the Association, but he also had to "promise not to ask for more another year." The Senator agreed, with the stipulation that if the seawall required further repairs this request would be excepted from his pledge. Senator Copeland warned Kincaid, "Be sure to have Congressmen Dempsey watch the House Conferees. We must keep what we have." The $35,000 appropriation remained in the budget.[338] In the search for funds to match this Federal money, the Old Fort Niagara Association eventually went to New York State with a request for support. Early in 1931, Senator William W. Campbell of Lockport introduced a bill that would grant $20,000 to the Association. This was passed by both houses of the legislature but vetoed by Governor Franklin D. Roosevelt. The Governor's decision was influenced by two factors: the poor economic situation during the winter of 1931 and the questionable legality of using State funds on a Federal project. Although asked to reconsider his veto, Roosevelt refused.[339] The balance of non-Federal support for the project would come from Association membership fees and donations and labor from the Niagara County Work Relief Bureau.[340]

Restoration of the North Redoubt and reconstruction of the old French entrance gateway to the South Redoubt at last commenced in the fall of 1930 with the $25,000 appropriated that spring and the Association's matching funds. Information on both projects is, again, distressingly scarce. Work on the two structures had begun by November, again under the direction of Alfred G. Adams.[341] Presumably, the North Redoubt was completed by spring, although none of the Association's records acknowledge a specific date. The drawbridge was finished in September, 1931, thanks to financial support from the Paul Schoellkopf family of Niagara Falls.[342]

Details of the restoration of the North Redoubt must be pieced together from the few references to the project and the physical evidence remaining in the building itself. Estimates prepared in January, 1930, indicated that the North Redoubt was to be treated in much the same fashion as the southern building. Work was to include general repairs to masonry, new roofs and stairs, stone flags on the ground floor, and replacement of windows and doors.[343] By the time restoration was ready to begin in November, the scope of work seems to have been reduced to include a roof, pointing and patching of walls, a new door, and stairs.[344] The end result was much as in the South Redoubt. The eighteenth century roof was duplicated using the Montresor plan as a guide. The stairs were replaced, but the openings constructed by Captain Fraser in the 1840's were reused. New windows were constructed for the second floor openings. The loophole and the ventilator slit flanking the entrance door were enlarged, converted to windows and fitted with iron bars like those in the first story of the French Castle. The pair of powder magazine ventilators on the southeast facade were closed up. Fraser's brick floor remained in place, however, and the walls were not plastered or painted. The North Redoubt, as anticipated, proved to be the simplest single element of the Old Fort Niagara restoration.

Reconstruction of the "French Gateway" was, by contrast, far more complicated and expensive. A drawbridge gate had pierced the river face of the South Bastion since 1756. Dubbed the "Gate of the Five Nations" by the French, this provided the primary access to Fort Niagara until the first decade of the nineteenth century. The South Redoubt greatly strengthened this entrance. Sometime before 1810, however, the old bridge was removed and replaced by a gate on the river side of the fort. Later renovation projects in 1839-43 and 1863-72 had incorporated the former drawbridge area as part of the walls. During the latter project, a thick concrete and brick revetment with a sheltered position for a gun commander had been added in front of the earthworks. All this

The angle of the River Bastion as it was on September 25, 1929. Notations indicate proposed demolitions to allow reconstruction of the Dauphin Battery and Gate of the Five Nations. *OFN 925/36A.*

construction, plus 3,675 cubic yards of earth, would have to be removed in order to reconstruct Captain Pouchot's gate. The plan included a wooden drawbridge with a "headhouse" to cover the lifting mechanism, a stationary wooden bridge spanning most of the ditch plus sodded earthworks and palisades around the gate and along the "Dauphin Battery" to its right. Total cost was estimated in January, 1930, at $22,687.50.[345]

No copies of the final plans for the Gate of the Five Nations are known to have survived. It is obvious, however, that the design went through a number of changes before construction began late in 1930. The original concept apparently called for a wooden headhouse. A pair of renderings prepared by James A. Johnson depict this and a ramp-like stationary bridge.[346] As constructed, the headhouse is stone with a thick, arched roof. Final planning for the Gate of the Five Nations reveals some of the perils of attempting to reconstruct buildings of another era by interpreting existing and incomplete documentation. It is possible only to speculate on the process of deciding to rebuild the headhouse in stone rather than timber. The design for the bridge and gate complex was probably based on a 1759 plan which depicted Fort Niagara shortly after its capture by the British.[347] On it, the "headhouse" structure is simply represented by an "x" within a square. Since standard engineering notation of the eighteenth century often employed a *dotted* "x" to indicate a bombproof arch (the Powder Magazine is so rendered on this and other plans), it is most likely that the gate was assumed to have been bombproof and therefore built of stone like the magazine. This is a misinterpretation. By 1768, the entrance had deteriorated to the point that the double gates "could not be Shutt from the Sides that Support the Earth being Rotten, and press'd in," a clear indication that any structure was of wood and not masonry.[348] Francis Pfister's detailed 1773 plan of Fort Niagara shows that the gateway, as repaired in 1768, was nothing more than an opening in the earthworks,

The North Redoubt restored, probably after completion of repairs following the 1933 fire. *OFN 3499/60.*

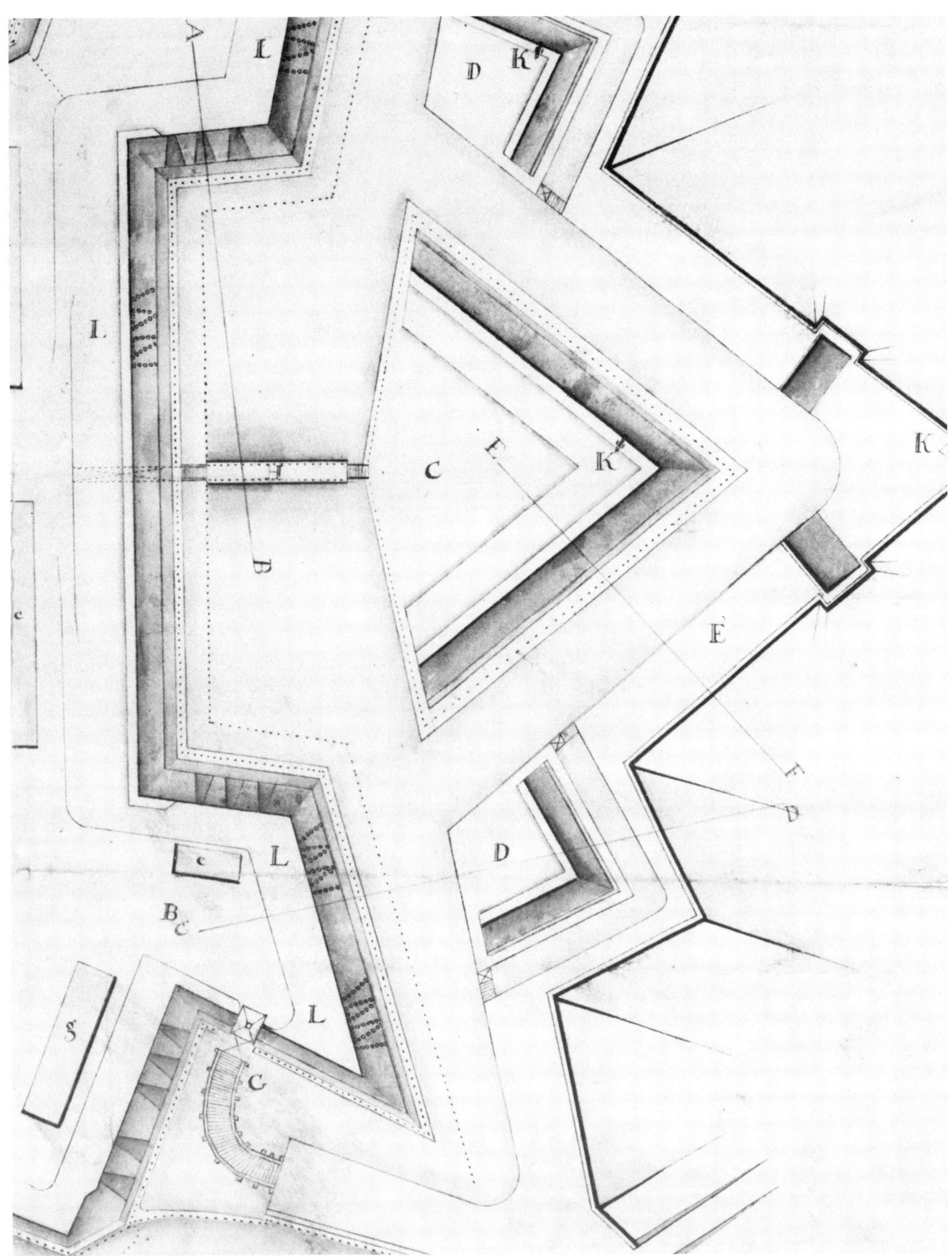

This plan, probably by Lt. Thomas Sowers, shows Fort Niagara after the siege of 1759. A misinterpretation of the way in which the drawbridge "headhouse" was rendered on this and other contemporary plans resulted in construction of the massive stone entry building in 1930-31.
Courtesy, Public Record Office, MPG 342.

The impressive Gate of the Five Nations entrance as completed in September, 1931. The pool below the bridge holds water- temporarily. *OFN 1178/38C.*

closed by two sets of wooden gates.[349] The lifting mechanism was probably an open bascule with counterweights. It is likely just this sort of gear which Sowers depicted by the *solid* "x" within a square on his 1759 plan.

Demolition of the 1860's concrete and brick scarp revetment, probably in the late autumn of 1930. The headhouse for the Gate of the Five Nations was reconstructed in the angle at right. *OFN 942/36B.*

Thomas Sowers' 1769 plan of a drawbridge for Fort Niagara was also known in 1930. Efforts were made to obtain a clear copy during the winter of 1931, so it must have figured in the planning process for the stationary wooden bridge.[350] The structure designed by Sowers had a gracefully curving deck, however, and the angular design completed by Alfred Adams for the Old Fort Niagara Association corresponds with the French bridge shown on the 1759 Sowers plan.

A massive amount of work was required to complete the Gate of the Five Nations. The concrete and brick revetment was torn out by workmen wielding pickaxes. The earth was then reshaped to open the gateway and build the ramparts of the Dauphin Battery. Wicker "gabions" or baskets filled with earth were emplaced to duplicate those used to protect the batteries of Fort Niagara in 1759.[351] The moat below the drawbridge was deepened and lined to hold water. Since the ditch was a "fosse" or dry ditch, and even had drains installed during the 1860's to keep it so, it understandably proved impossible to keep water in the area beneath the bridge. The practice was soon given up.

Final construction details would have to await a future year's work. The $35,000 provided by Congress in 1931 was used, in part, during the spring of 1932 to construct stone retaining walls flanking the walk between the Gate of the Five Nations and the South Redoubt and to pave the path with flagstones. A 110 volt electrical cable was installed to connect the South Redoubt and headhouse to the transformer room in the Provisions Storehouse.[352] Detail work also continued on the gateway. On May 19, 1932, the drawbridge was raised for the first time to test the mechanism with its stone counterweights.[353]

There remained only a need for furniture and equipment. The Furnishings Committee had been very active in planning rooms for the French Castle and were committed to progressing slowly and carefully. "We do not want errors," proclaimed President Kincaid in 1933, "We do want authentic work. We are taking every precaution to make sure that we have the proper thing in the right place."[354] Furnishings for the redoubts, including tables, benches, bunks, and firing steps were constructed during the winter of 1933-34.[355] A number of contemporary pencil sketches in the Old Fort Niagara Collection show an interior arrangement identical to that seen today. Unlike the highly fanciful creations designed for the French Castle, however, the furnishings installed in the redoubts were simple, practical pieces reflecting the buildings' 1771 use as guard rooms for twenty men. Lacking more detailed information on the original furniture, the reproductions seem valid.

In order to complete the redoubts to their appearance during the British occupation, artillery was needed for their gun decks. Finding authentic pieces proved to be difficult. Considerable research had been done on the artillery appropriate for Old Fort Niagara. Alfred G. Adams prepared a memo on the guns necessary, including "4 Brass field pieces, six-pounders" of English manufacture, circa 1770. The identification of appropriate ordnance was based on Thomas Sower's plan of late 1768 which showed the small stone blockhouses originally proposed in 1766. Sowers noted that these were each to mount a pair of six-pounders.[356] A September, 1930, query to Francis Bannerman & Son, well-known supplier of antique military equipment, about the availability of such weapons, "complete with carriage," drew a negative response.[357] In March, 1931, President Kincaid sought appropriate ordnance in Canada. He even suggested that "Perhaps the Canadian Government may have some cannon of the period of 1770 which they would like to contribute to the restoration work to be mounted on the top of the Block Houses."[358] They did not. Frustrated in attempts to locate eighteenth century British guns, Kincaid found a compromise with the assistance of Fort Niagara commandant Colonel Charles H. Morrow and the U.S. Army. A visit to the Chief of Ordnance in Washington resulted in advice to seek obsolete ordnance from Federal arsenals. Morrow and Kincaid visited several places and selected a number of brass muzzle-loading guns. Most were from the Mexican War and Civil War, but many were equipped with "dolphins" or handles and so superficially resembled weapons of the eighteenth century. The cannon were delivered to Old Fort Niagara in 1931.[359] Eighteenth century-style field carriages were later constructed for the pieces selected for the gun decks. The North Redoubt received a pair of brass six-pounders from the period of the Mexican War, while

The caption of this pre-1916 postcard attributed construction of the South Redoubt to the French in 1756. *OFN 5624/30A.*

Vehicles crowd the parade ground as weekend visitors inspect restoration of the French Castle in 1927. The North Redoubt awaits its turn. *OFN 6/10B.*

Mass for the garrison at the Millet Cross monument, Easter, 1941. The North Redoubt overlooks the scene. *OFN 1701/60.*

South Redoubt restoration complete, about 1934. The plaster and whitewash were never renewed. ***OFN 725/28C.***

the South Redoubt was equipped with a pair of brass Model 1857 twelve-pounder Napoleon gun-howitzers with handles.

Restoration of the redoubts, and indeed of Old Fort Niagara, was nearly complete. It was fortunate, however, that the newly obtained cannon had not yet been placed in the redoubts by the summer of 1933. Early on the morning of August 18, Niagara County was ravaged by driving rain and severe electrical storms. A bolt of lightning struck the chimney of the North Redoubt and, within minutes, the reconstructed roof was ablaze. The fire was reported as a spectacular one with flames shooting out all four sides of the gun deck. According to official reports, the military fire company from Fort Niagara responded promptly, aided by many men of the 28th Infantry and the young summer trainees of the Citizen's Military Training Corps (CMTC). Walter Barrs arrived soon after with the Youngstown Volunteer Fire Department to support the effort to save the historic building.[360]

"New" Fort Niagara's 1921 water filtration plant, visible beyond the River Wall, September 11, 1936. Although constructed of reinforced concrete, the building employed many stylistic elements of the North Redoubt. *OFN 28 / 10C.*

This picture of cool efficiency varies somewhat from the memories of Merle S. Clark, then a soldier in the 28th Infantry. Clark's colorful account agrees with other reports but adds a few details:

> *Early one morning (a Sunday I believe) a hard thunderstorm came in off the Lake with a heavy downpour. During the storm lightning struck the old blockhouse in the northeast corner of the Old Fort setting the interior woodwork afire. The flames burned the ropes letting the trapdoors drop shut under the eaves of the roof which left only the lower entrance door open. The Post Fire Department was summoned, along with the usual ceremonies which included firing a signal gun. Many fellows thought it was ... reveille and ignored it. The fire truck driver was soon on his way to the entrance on the river side of the Old Fort. He got a bit over-zealous and attempted to drive the fire truck across the grassed area inside the Old Fort, promptly burying the truck to the axles in the wet ground. The would-be firemen strung hose from a hydrant to the fire truck pump and then to the blockhouse and attempted to fight the fire from the small entrance door. Someone shut off the hose nozzle which resulted in too much back pressure on the line, promptly blowing out gaskets in the engine. Some official sent a call to the Youngstown fire department who immediately responded and, with long ladders, their crew got the trap doors open so that water could be put on the interior fire ... the Post fire truck was constructed from the chassis of a WW I Liberty Truck with hard rubber tires. The engine had to be hand-cranked and had a magneto ignition system. It didn't need any warning devices as one could hear it coming a long way off.* [361]

Damage to the roof and the gun deck was severe.[362] Fortunately, the fire had not migrated to the second floor nor completely destroyed the third floor deck itself which dated to 1842-43. The worst damage was confined to reconstructed features of the building.[363]

To the great relief of the Old Fort Niagara Association, the North Redoubt was insured. A lease to operate and maintain the site had been finalized between the War Department and the Association on March 6, 1931. Section 12 of this document required fire insurance "in such amount as the said Commanding Officer shall require, the policy or policies to name the United States as beneficiary." Insurance policies amounting to $30,000 had been forwarded to the commandant of Fort Niagara on March 31. The North Redoubt was valued at $1,000.[364] An adjustment was made promptly. Payment was received on November 6, 1933, from local agent Richard Cary. One third each of the total insured amount came from Aetna Insurance Company, Great American Insurance Company and Underwriters Insurance Company.[365] Estimates for repairs were submitted during September. The total cost of replacing the burned structure was set at $546.66, provided that staff labor of the Association was used to do the work. All damage had been repaired by the time the Executive Committee of the Association met on November 28.[366]

The North Redoubt still bears scars of the 1933 fire. Charring may be found on most of the heavy timbers of the roof framework, especially on the northwest and northeast sides of the building. Most of these members were salvaged and the blackened surfaces planed down to fresh wood. The shingles, roof sheathing and rafters were destroyed and had to be replaced. The existing gun deck floor appears to be original to the 1840's, and it too was reworked to remove evidence of the fire after the planks were discovered to be otherwise sound. All flooring supports for the gun deck survived the conflagration.

Little more remained to be done to either redoubt. Gun carriages were reproduced and the cannon mounted during the winter of 1933-34.[367] By spring, the redoubts, along with the rest of Old Fort Niagara, had been completely restored. The Association was ready to dedicate the results of more than a decade of effort by local residents and the Federal Government. A grand "Four Nations Celebration" was planned with activities and ceremonies at the Old Fort and a huge pageant at Hyde Park Stadium in Niagara Falls. In the midst of all this hoopla, the South Redoubt was briefly used for one final service. During dedication activities early in September, 1934, it provided working space for the press contingent covering the event. The second floor guard room was a lively place according to a somewhat hyperbolic item in the *Buffalo Evening News*. The correspondent reported that:

> *... Walls three feet thick echo the clicks of typewriters just as they did the cracks of musketry and the war whoops of Indians more than 100 years ago.*
>
> *In the room where British and later American Colonial Soldiers slept on their arms ready to rush to the defense of the outer gate, modern reporters are chronicling their heroic achievements. Two gun racks clamped to the stone walls are utilized to hold copy paper, and the tables where the soldiery used to pound pewter tankards and carve venison steaks now are used to hold typewriters, paste pots and editorial shears.*[368]

A redoubtable comfort station constructed in 1950 at Devil's Hole State Park, Niagara Falls, New York.

One wonders what John Montresor and Francis Pfister would have thought of this activity, so foreign to their understanding of the purposes of a redoubt.

The conclusion of the Four Nations Celebration found Old Fort Niagara firmly established as a popular outdoor historic site and Niagara Frontier tourist attraction. Concern would shift from restoration of the historic structures to their preservation and interpretation for the public. The Old Fort Niagara Association, now responsible for the site by the terms of its license with the War Department, was perhaps not entirely certain of how to proceed. In his Annual Report for 1934 President William Wallace Kincaid noted:

> *There has been some discussion of what we are going to do with Old Fort Niagara after we had it restored and it seems to me that we can make something more out of it than is being made out of most buildings that have been restored, most of which have settled down to be a museum ... It has occurred to some of us that it might be a better use made of this restoration here than a museum in which to place the relics of historical furnishings of the past ...*
>
> *We cannot stop here. I do not think*

When the stairway to the second floor of the South Redoubt was moved in 1929, the 1842-43 stairway opening was simply covered with a trap door.

Charring from the 1933 fire still marks many roof timbers of the North Redoubt.

The second floor hearths in both redoubts are supported by plastered brick arches installed during the 1842-43 renovations.

Distinctive cut stone trim readily identifies window and gunslit alterations of the 1840's.

South Redoubt fireplace showing brick lining installed in the nineteenth century. The stovepipe thimble was for a twentieth century space heater. This might account for the peculiar shape of the reconstructed chimney.

A forlorn North Redoubt, photographed on August 24, 1926. *Courtesy, Niagara Mohawk Power Corporation.*

> *I am in favor of allowing this Institution to become static. I think this restoration can be made a very interesting and helpful source of teaching local history ...*[369]

President Kincaid's hopes would not be realized in the next few years, and a World War would intervene to interrupt further development. Much of Kincaid's enthusiasm was lost in the aftermath of the conflict. In 1948 the Fort Niagara Military Reservation was given up by the War Department. Future licenses would be between the Old Fort Niagara Association and the State of New York. The Association today maintains the historic site and structures under license from the New York State Office of Parks, Recreation and Historic Preservation. Substantial rehabilitation of the exteriors of the North and South Redoubts has occurred during the 1980's as a cooperative venture of the two organizations reminiscent of the relationship between the Association and the War Department during restoration. The redoubts have been preserved, and, like the rest of Fort Niagara, their many scars bear witness to the long history of the site. They contain elements of eighteenth and nineteenth century alterations for military purposes as well as evidence of the enthusiastic restoration work of the early twentieth century preservationists who ensured that the buildings would not be lost.

APPENDIX A

CHANGING FACADES, 1770 - 1934

While graphic evidence is incomplete for many phases of the history of Old Fort Niagara's redoubts, existing documentation permits an accurate reconstruction of their general appearance at different periods. The accompanying drawings concentrate on the chief features, primarily the shape of roofs and placement of windows and loopholes. The drawings have been simplified for clarity.

SOUTH REDOUBT

1770 - 1812 (1)

The South Redoubt as completed, based on the "Montresor" plans of 1770 and the Pfister plan and elevation of 1773. The two sources disagree on the existence of the two loopholes above the gateway. This sketch follows the Montresor plan.

1812 - 1817 (2)

The roof has been removed and the chimney shortened in November, 1812, converting the redoubt to an open tower. Sod has been stacked on the stone parapet to provide cover for the gunners. No alterations have been made to the facades.

1817 - 1842 (3)

The South Redoubt retains its original arrangement of windows, loopholes and doors. The new roof of "peculiar construction" includes a flagpole and a cupola or platform to facilitate raising and lowering of the garrison colors.

1842 - 1929 (4)

Massive changes to the facades in 1842-43 have resulted in the closing up of the gateways and the enlargement or reconstruction of several loopholes and windows. Additional loopholes and powder magazine vents (northeast and southeast sides of the first story) mark the exterior. The roof has been simplified. The pair of second floor loopholes above the door on the northwest facade were opened into square windows in 1867.

1929 - PRESENT (5)

Restoration has included reconstruction of the Chinese roof and reopening of the gateways. The arrangement of loopholes is still much as altered in 1842-43 except for restoration of the eighteenth century-style loopholes on the northwest side.

NORTH REDOUBT

1771 - 1812 (1)

The North Redoubt as built. Details of the second floor window and loophole arrangements are conjectural and based largely on what is known of the South Redoubt. There is no evidence that loopholes were located above the entrance between the second floor windows. Slits on the first story of the southwest and southeast facades are powder magazine vents.

1812 - 1817 (2)

The roof has been removed, the chimney shortened and sod stacked atop the parapet. At least one additional loophole appears to have been added to the first story of the northwest facade before 1798. A flagpole was added to the north corner of the third floor between 1812 and 1816.

1817 - 1842 (3)

A simple hipped roof covers the gun deck. There has been no alteration of windows or loopholes.

1842 - 1930 (4)

Substantial changes have been made to the arrangement of loopholes on the northwest, northeast and southeast sides during the 1842-43 work. The powder magazine vents remain in place on the first story facade. The simple hipped roof dates to the 1842-43 renovations and later replacement in 1855.

1930 - PRESENT (5)

Little has been done to the North Redoubt aside from reconstruction of the Chinese roof and closing up of powder magazine vents on the southeast facade. The first story loophole and ventilator on the southwest facade have been converted to barred windows.

Drawings by Dennis P. Farmer.

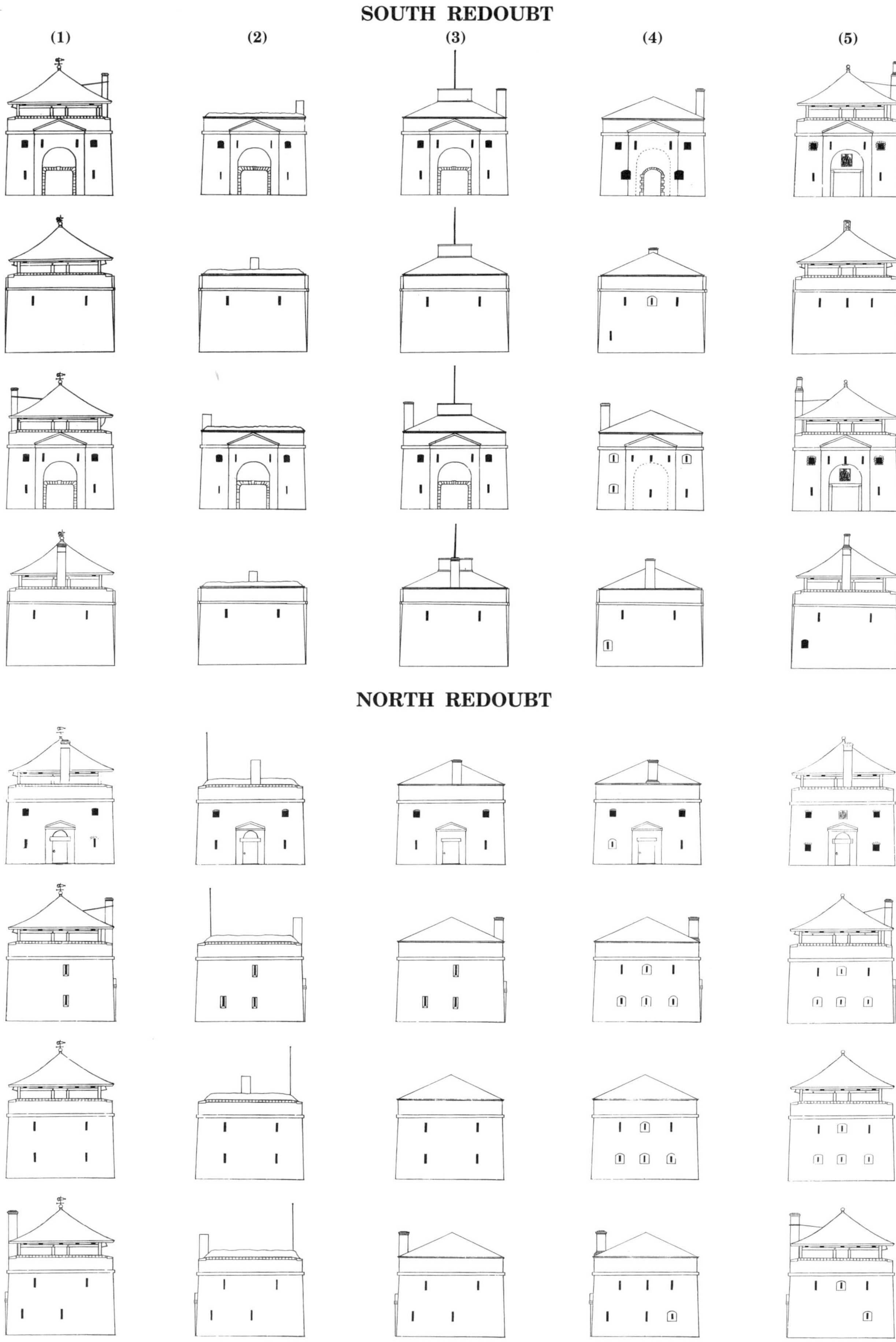
SOUTH REDOUBT
(1)
(2)
(3)
(4)
(5)
NORTH REDOUBT

APPENDIX B

ARMAMENT OF THE REDOUBTS

Artillery defined the chief role of Fort Niagara's redoubts from their construction in 1770-71 until the middle of the next century. The buildings originally mounted light field guns to cover the ruined land-side defenses. During the first year of the War of 1812, their top floors bore the weight of heavier cannon emplaced to fire against enemy positions across the Niagara River. Short-range guns on the redoubts again covered the land front following the British capture of the post, this time guarding against an American counterattack. From 1815 to 1867, during their final years as part of the fortifications, the redoubts were again maintained as elevated gun positions, useful in the event of another war with Britain. Throughout these phases, artillery of one kind or another was mounted on the gun decks. The following summary details the weapons with which the North and South Redoubts are known to have been armed.

Breech of a British light brass six-pounder. Guns of this type were the original armament of the redoubts. Such weapons might later have been mounted in the buildings by the U.S. troops for, in December, 1813, the British recaptured a brass six-pounder lost to the Americans in 1777. *OFN 1603/50F.*

The earliest proposals for stone blockhouses on the salients of the bastions make no mention of the type of guns intended for them. The plans only indicate that fire from the towers was to "plunge into the Ditches and Flank the Land Front".[370] The implication is that the plunging would be done by artillery. When Captain Thomas Sowers prepared his "Plan of the Fortifications of Niagara", late in 1768 or early in 1769, he was the first to note that "two six Pounders were to be mounted on their Roofs."[371] Captain John Montresor's "Section and Elevation of a Stone Redout", drawn in 1769 or 1770, shows a single piece of light artillery on a field carriage placed to fire over the parapet.[372] The redoubts were presumably armed upon completion for, in July, 1773, Jabez Fisher noted that the upper parts of the "2 large Redoubts" had "several brass cannon" which could cover the ground outside the old walls. The first exact statement of the artillery mounted in the redoubts comes from a garrison ordnance return dated September, 1774. Each "Block House" was armed with "2 6 prs on traveling Carriages."[373]

This type of weapon would provide the armament of the redoubts for the remainder of the British occupation. The field carriages with their relatively light brass guns could be easily moved to face a threat. The brass six-pounders were obviously the guns preferred for the redoubts. When Lieutenant Colonel Mason Bolton was asked to send brass sixes to other posts in 1779, he pointed out that "we have only those left belonging to the Block Houses, one of which burst lately".[374] Light brass six-pounders appear on ordnance returns for Niagara for the rest of the British period.[375]

These guns were removed when British troops evacuated Fort Niagara in 1796. The new United States garrison brought only "four small field pieces" which were "planted at the four corners of the fort."[376] These were probably brass six-pounders, and six such weapons remained in Fort Niagara between 1810 and the outbreak of the War of 1812.[377] There is no evidence that any of the American guns were placed on the gun decks of the redoubts prior to the War of 1812. As early as 1798, however, Major John J.U. Rivardi reported that there was "a platform covered with a roof fit for light artillery & provided with Port & Loop

Iron twenty-four-pounder carronades, similar to these weapons, were mounted on the redoubts in 1814 to pour destructive, short-range fire into the ditches of the land front. *OFN 1546/50E.*

holes" at the top of each of the redoubts.[378] The new threat to Fort Niagara was across the river, not along the land front. The small amount of artillery available to the garrison was probably placed on the walls rather than in the redoubts during this period.

The first months of the War of 1812 found the garrison of Fort Niagara frantically mounting artillery and reinforcing defenses. The roof was removed from the French Castle in September, and brass cannon were mounted on its third floor. By the first part of that month, each of the redoubts was armed with "six-pounders."[379] These were probably of brass since guns of this metal were the most common type of six-pounder in Fort Niagara during the War of 1812.[380] The need to strike at Fort George prompted a change in armament that occurred by the next month. On October 13, Fort Niagara returned fire against the British batteries with a single six-pounder on the South Redoubt and a twelve-pounder on the North Redoubt. During the course of the action the latter gun, probably of iron construction, burst and killed two of its crew.[381]

The tragedy of October 13 led to a redistribution of Fort Niagara's artillery. By November 20, the South Redoubt had been rearmed with a twelve-pounder and the North Redoubt with a six. The latter was probably of brass and the former iron. The prolonged exchange of fire with Fort George the next day resulted in another disaster with an iron twelve-pounder when the newly mounted gun on the South Redoubt shattered during the heat of the action.[382]

It is uncertain what ordnance was mounted in the redoubts for the remainder of the American occupation. The guns were probably the dependable brass six-pounders. Although of light caliber, they were capable of striking the Canadian shore, even from the North Redoubt. Artillery was mounted atop the roofless towers in the fall of 1813, but the only indication of its type comes from British accounts of the capture of Fort Niagara. These mention fire from a six-pounder on the South Redoubt.[383] Among the twenty-seven pieces of cannon taken by the British on December 19,

A brass 5 1/2-inch howitzer of British manufacture. The howitzer mounted on one of the redoubts in the winter of 1815 was probably similar to this 1756 piece. *Courtesy, New York State Office of Parks, Recreation and Historic Preservation, New Windsor Cantonment State Historic Site.*

American iron six-pounder and field carriage of the style used during the War of 1812. It is not known whether the six-pounders mounted on the redoubts were of iron or brass. Iron twelve-pounders burst with disastrous effect during two exchanges of fire with Fort George.

A British light brass six-pounder mounted on a field carriage. *Courtesy, Museum Restoration Service.*

1813, was a brass six-pounder of British manufacture captured by the Continental Army at Trenton, New Jersey (or perhaps Princeton judging from the date) on January 3, 1777.[384] It is not known where this weapon had been mounted.

When British engineers made recommendations for the decrepit fortifications of Niagara in March, 1814, one suggestion was that all buildings other than the North Redoubt be demolished. That stone tower would be retained as an advance post on the American shore with a single gun "of heavy calibre" on its gundeck.[385] The plan was not carried out, and by the summer of 1814 each building mounted one twenty-four-pounder carronade.[386] This represented a significant shift in the armament plan for the redoubts and reflected the threat perceived by Fort Niagara's British garrison. An American counterattack would come from the land side. Long-range guns intended to fire across the river were no longer necessary. Carronades provided a heavy calibre for relatively little weight and were extremely destructive in short-range situations. These guns were probably intended to fire anti-personnel canister shot into the ditch and along the glacis of the land defenses, much the same function intended for six-pounders in the 1770's. The final months of British occupation found a carronade mounted atop one redoubt and a howitzer on the other.[387] The latter was probably of 5 1/2-inch caliber, another useful weapon for short range work. It could fire either canister or explosive shell against assaulting infantry.[388]

The British evacuated their artillery for a second time on May 22, 1815. It is unlikely that the redoubts were ever rearmed. The buildings were covered with simple weather roofs later in the decade, and there is no indication that these were removed until the renovations of 1842-43. Captain Fraser's improvements were clearly intended to make the redoubts more useful as gun platforms in time of war. He designed the new roofs to be removable and the stone parapet strong enough to afford some protection to gun crews. The new third floor decks were slanted to facilitate the use of guns, presumably still intended to be mounted on field carriages since no provision was made for permanent mountings. Perhaps it was felt that the buildings would not be able to support anything heavier than a field gun. In September, 1841, Fraser emphasized that the redoubts should receive their proper armament as soon as repairs were completed.[389] There is no evidence that this was ever done, and the 1842-43 roofs, repaired in 1855, remained in place until restoration. A quantity of unmounted iron ordnance stored at Fort Niagara in 1864 probably included the guns intended for arming the redoubts in the event of war. Counted among these were two twelve-pounder and two six-pounder field guns and three twenty-four-pounder howitzers.[390] Any of these would have been appropriate.

Completion of the new concrete and brick walls spelled the end for the redoubts as defensive structures. By the summer of 1867, the old stone buildings were reported to no longer be required for the defense of the post.[391] No more guns would be mounted in anger at Old Fort Niagara. Only with the restoration of the buildings would antique brass ordnance be emplaced in the redoubts to represent their armament of the 1770's.

NOTES

[1] M. Le Blond, *The Military Engineer or, A Treatise on the Attack and Defence of All Kinds of Fortified Places* (London: J. Nourse, 1759), p. 105.

[2] John Muller, *A Treatise Containing the Elementary Part of Fortification, Regular and Irregular* (London: J. Nourse, 1774), p. 237. See also the edition of 1782.

[3] Captain George Smith, *An Universal Military Dictionary* (London: J. Millan, 1779), p. 92.

[4] Smith, p. 100.

[5] D.H. Mahan, *A Complete Treatise on Field Fortification with the General Outlines of the Principles Regulating the Arrangement, the Attack, and the Defence of Permanent Works* (New York: Greenwood Press, reprint of 1836 edition), p. 20.

[6] Richard J. Young, "Blockhouses in Canada, 1749-1841: A Comparative Report and Catalogue", *Canadian Historic SItes: Occasional Papers in Archaeology and History, No. 23* (Ottawa: National Historic Sites Branch, Parks Canada, 1980), pp. 7-8.

[7] Brian Leigh Dunnigan, "The Post of Mackinac, 1779-1812", Unpublished Master's Thesis for the Cooperstown Graduate Programs, State University of New York at Oneonta, 1979, pp. 101-06.

[8] Young, pp. 90-104.

[9] Mahan, pp. 101-02.

[10] Ivan J. Saunders, "A History of Martello Towers in the Defence of British North America, 1796-1871", *Canadian Historic Sites: Occasional Papers in Archaeology and History* (Ottawa: National Historic Sites Branch, Parks Canada, 1976), pp. 9-17.

[11] *Ibid.*, pp. 9-11.

[12] For a discussion of Fort Mississauga see David McConnell, "A Study of the British Military Buildings at Niagara-on-the-Lake, 1814-1837", Manuscript Report No. 191 (Ottawa: Parks Canada, 1977), pp. 18-31 and David Flemming, *Fort Mississauga, Ontario, 1814-1972* (Ottawa: Parks Canada, 1982). Neither author attributes any influence of the Fort Niagara redoubts on the design of the Fort Mississauga tower.

[13] Lewis Lochée, *Elements of Field Fortification* (London: By the Author, 1780), pp. 36-37.

[14] Account of René-Robert Cavelier, Sieur de La Salle, Aug. 22, 1682, in Frank H. Severance, *An Old Frontier of France* (2 vols.; New York: Dodd, Mead and Company, 1917), I, p. 42.

[15] Brian Leigh Dunnigan, *History and Development of Old Fort Niagara*. (Youngstown, New York: Old Fort Niagara Association, 1985), pp. 13-14.

[16] Le Blond, p. 105.

[17] Gaspard-Joseph Chaussegros de Léry, *"Traité de Fortifications divisé en huit livres..."* 1714, National Archives of Canada (hereafter NAC), MG18, K2.

[18] Brian Leigh Dunnigan, *Glorious Old Relic: The French Castle and Old Fort Niagara* (Youngstown, NY: Old Fort Niagara Association, 1987), pp. 19-22.

[19] Maj. W.H. Betsch, "The Defenses of Oswego", *Proceedings of the New York State Historical Association*, XIII, 1934, 108-10.

[20] Lt. Col. William Browning to Lt. Gen. Jeffery Amherst, Sept. 16, 1763 and enclosed List of Casualties, Sept. 14, 1763, Public Record Office (hereafter PRO), Amherst Papers, W.O. 34/22.

[21] Browning to Amherst, Sept. 16, 1763, PRO, W.O. 34/22.

[22] Col. John Bradstreet to Maj. Gen. Thomas Gage, March 26, 1764, William L. Clements Library (hereafter WLCL), Thomas Gage Papers (hereafter GP), Vol. 16.

[23] Journal of John Montresor, June 4, 1764, in G.D. Scull (ed.), "The Montresor Journals", *Collections of the New-York Historical Society for the Year 1881* (New York: The New-York Historical Society, 1882), p. 261.

[24] "Plan of the Road and River Between Niagara and Fort Schlosser with the different Posts Erected on the Communication, by order of Colonel Bradstreet in June 1764", by Lt. Bernard Ratzer, WLCL.

[25] Gregory Furness and Timothy Titus, "Master Plan for Crown Point State Historic Site", Unpublished Report for the New York State Bureau of Historic Sites, December, 1985, pp. 13, 16 and 30-32.

[26] Charles Morse Stotz, "Defense in the Wilderness", *The Western Pennsylvania Historical Magazine*, XLI, Nos. 3-4 (Autumn, 1958), 175-76.

[27] *Ibid.*, 175-76 and facing 188-89.

[28] Smith, p. 103.

[29] For a concise account of the earliest forts on the site see Dunnigan, *History and Development*, pp. 13-20.

[30] Gov. Francois Pierre de Rigaud de Vaudreuil to M. de Machault, July 24, 1755, E.B. O' Callaghan (ed.), *Documents Relative to the Colonial History of the State of New York* (hereafter *DRCHSNY*) (15 vols.; Albany: Weed, Parsons & Co., 1856-77), X, p. 307.

[31] Severance, II, pp. 94-141.

[32] Vaudreuil to Machault, Sept. 25, 1755, *DRCHSNY*, X, pp. 325-26.

[33] Franklin B. Hough (ed.), *Memoir Upon the Late War in North America* (2 vols.; Roxbury, MA: W. Elliott Woodward, 1866), I, p. 94.

[34] Dunnigan, *History and Development*, pp. 19-24.

[35] See Brian Leigh Dunnigan, *Siege - 1759: The Campaign Against Niagara* (Youngstown, NY: Old Fort Niagara Association, 1986) for a full account of the siege of Fort Niagara.

[36] Lt. Col. William Farquhar to Brig. Gen. Thomas Gage, Aug. 27, 1759, WLCL/GP, 3.

[37] Farquhar to Gage, Sept. 20, 1759, WLCL/GP, 3.

[38] Lt. Col. John Vaughan to Gage, Jan. 3, 1765, WLCL/GP, 29.

[39] Lt. Col. William Eyre to Amherst, July 10, 1762, PRO, W.O. 34/69.

[40] Lt. Col. John Wilkins to Amherst, June 15, 1763 and Wilkins to Amherst, June 25, 1763, PRO, W.O. 34/22.

[41] Vaughan to Gage, Oct. 21, 1764, WLCL/GP, 8.

[42] Gage to the Earl of Shelburne, April 3, 1767, Clarence Edwin Carter (ed.), *The Correspondence of General Thomas Gage with the Secretaries of State, and with the War Office and the Treasury, 1763-1775* (2 vols.; New Haven: Yale University Press, 1933), I, pp. 124-28.

[43] Gage to Sec. of State H. Seymour Conway, May 6, 1766, Carter, I, pp. 89-91.

[44] *Ibid.*

[45] Gage to Sec. at War Lord Barrington, May 7, 1766, *Ibid.*, II, pp. 349-52.

[46] Wilkins to Amherst, June 15, 1763, PRO, W.O. 34/22.

[47] Vaughan to Gage, Jan. 3, 1765, WLCL/GP, 29; Vaughan to Gage, March 1, 1765, WLCL/GP, 31; Gage to Vaughan, March 18, 1765, WLCL/GP, 32; Gage to Vaughan, April 18, 1765, WLCL/GP, 34.

[48] Capt. Harry Gordon to Gage, Aug. 27, 1765, WLCL/GP, 41.

[49] Capt. John Brown to Gage, Sept. 1, 1766, WLCL/GP, 56; Gage to Brown, Oct. 5, 1766, WLCL/GP, 58.

[50] Brown to Gage, September 28, 1766, WLCL/GP, 57. The plan is preserved as "Plan of Niagara", 1766, in the British Library (hereafter BL), Crown Maps, cxxi, 74.

[51] "Estimate of the Expenses of the Works at the Forts in the District of New York for 1766", May 9, 1766, WLCL/GP, 51.

[52] *Ibid.*

[53] Brown to Gage, Sept. 28, 1766, WLCL/GP, 57.

[54] "Estimate of Expences ... for the year 1767 at Niagara", Nov. 10, 1766, WLCL/GP, 59.

[55] Gage to Shelburne, Dec. 23, 1766, Carter, I, p. 117.

[56] Brown to Gage, April 25, 1767, WLCL/GP, 64; Gage to Sowers, May 28, 1767, WLCL/GP, 65.

[57] Sowers to Gage, July 16, 1767, WLCL/GP, 67; Brown to Gage, Oct. 25, 1767, WLCL/GP, 71.

[58] Gage to Brown, Feb, 22, 1768, WLCL/GP, 74; Gage to Brown, April 2, 1768, WLCL/GP, 75; Gage to Sowers, April 2, 1768, WLCL/GP, 75.

[59] Earl of Hillsborough to Gage, April 15, 1768, Carter, II, pp. 61-66.

[60] Gage to Hillsborough, June 16, 1768, Carter, I, pp. 175-79.

[61] Gage to Sowers, June 21, 1768 and Gage to Brown, June 21, 1768, WLCL/GP, 78.

[62] "Plan of Fort Niagara with a design for Contracting the same", June, 1768, by Capt. John Montresor, BL, Crown Maps, cxxi, 75.

[63] Brown to Gage, Aug. 2, 1768, WLCL/GP, 79; Gage to Brown, Sept. 4, 1768, WLCL/GP, 80.

[64] Brown to Gage, Nov. 6, 1768, WLCL/GP, 82.

[65] Gage to Brown, Dec. 19, 1768, WLCL/GP, 83; "Plan of the Fortifications of Niagara showing the new Stockade as Ordered to be begun in 1767. Likewise the new Stockade Fort for forty men agreeable to an order receiv'd 30th July 1768", by Capt. Thomas Sowers, plan known to have been in the British War Office, Caxton House, London in 1929 but now believed lost. Copy in the Old Fort Niagara Library.

[66] Gage to Sec. at War Lord Barrington, March 4, 1769, Carter, II, pp. 501-02.

[67] Hillsborough to Gage, Jan. 18, 1770, Carter, II, pp. 95-97.

[68] Brown to Gage, Feb. 4, 1770, WLCL/GP, 89; Brown to Gage, Feb. 25, 1770, WLCL/GP, 90.

[69] Gage to Brown, April 7, 1770, WLCL/GP, 91; Abstract of Cash Disbursed, April 24, 1770, WLCL, Gage Warrants, 24:114.

[70] *British Army List* (London: War Office, 1759), p. 111; *British Army List* (London: War Office, 1763), p. 98; Sowers to Gage, April 15, 1760, WLCL/GP, 6; Amherst to Lt. Col. William Browning, Oct. 6, 1763, PRO, W.O. 34/23.

[71] Gage to Lt. Bernard Ratzer, Aug. 16, 1764, WLCL/GP, 23; Capt. Joshua Loring to Gage, Sept. 9, 1764, WLCL/GP, 24; *British Army List* (London: War Office, 1768), p. 115; Ralph Izard, *An Account of a Journey to Niagara, Montreal and Quebec in 1765* (New York: William Osborn, 1846), pp. 9-10; Gage to Barrington, Oct. 9, 1767, Carter, II, p. 437.

[72] Brown to Gage, Sept. 28, 1766, WLCL/GP, 57; Brown to Gage, Oct. 20, 1768, WLCL/GP, 82; Brown to Gage, Feb. 4, 1770, WLCL/GP, 89.

[73] "Section and Elevation of a Stone Redout", [1770], BL, Crown Maps, cxxi, 78.1.

[74] "Plan, Section and Elevation of a Stone Redout, for 40 men Projected for Beacon Hill, in the Town of Boston, Augt. 1774", WLCL.

[75] See G.D. Scull (ed.), "The Montresor Journals", *Collections of the New-York Historical Society for the Year 1881* (New York: New-York Historical Society, 1882).

[76] *Ibid.*, pp. 3-8; R. Arthur Bowler, "John Montresor", *Dictionary of Canadian Biography* (12 vols; Toronto: University of Toronto Press, 1966-), IV, pp. 552-53.

[77] Saunders, pp. 10-11.

[78] "Plan of Niagara with an Explanation of its present State", Sept. 28, 1773, by Lt. Francis Pfister, BL, Crown Maps, cxxi, 76; "Plan of the Northern Blockhouse", June 10, 1798, by Maj. John J.U. Rivardi, National Archives and Records Administration (hereafter NARA), RG 77, Dr. 3, Sht. 13.

[79] "Plan of the Northern Blockhouse", June 10, 1798, by Maj. John J.U. Rivardi, NARA, RG 77, Dr. 3, Sht. 13.

[80] *Ibid.*

[81] Brown to Gage, July 20, 1770, WLCL/GP, 93.

[82] Brown to Gage, Feb. 4, 1770, WLCL/GP, 89.

[83] Brown to Lt. Francis Pfister, Aug. 20, 1770, WLCL/GP, 95.

[84] Pfister to Brown, Aug. 20, 1770; Brown to Garrison Officers, Aug. 27, 1770; Garrison Officers to Brown, Aug. 27, 1770; Brown to Gage, Aug. 27, 1770; Brown to Pfister, Aug. 27, 1770, all WLCL/GP, 95.

[85] Brown to Gage, Sept. 21, 1770; Copies of Certificates, Sept. 21, 1770, both WLCL/GP, 96.

[86] Brown to Pfister, Sept. 26, 1770; Pfister to Brown, Sept. 26, 1770; Brown to Pfister, Sept. 26, 1770, all WLCL/GP, 96.

[87] Brown to Gage, Sept. 27, 1770, WLCL/GP, 96.

[88] Gage to Brown, Sept. 28, 1770, WLCL/GP, 96.

[89] Gage to Brown, Oct. 24, 1770, WLCL/GP, 97.

[90] Brown to Gage, Oct. 16, 1770, WLCL/GP, 96; Brown to Gage, Nov. 4, 1770, WLCL/GP, 97.

[91] Brown to Gage, Oct. 18, 1770, WLCL/GP, 96; Minutes of an Indian Council, Oct. 30 - Nov. 2, 1770, WLCL/GP, 97; Brown to Gage, Nov. 4, 1770, WLCL/GP, 97; Gage to Sir William Johnson, Nov. 19, 1770, WLCL/GP, 98; Johnson to Gage, Dec. 31, 1770, James Sullivan and Milton W. Hamilton (eds.), *The Papers of Sir William Johnson* (hereafter *SWJP*) (14 vols; Albany: University of the State of New York, 1921-65), VII, pp. 1053-54.

[92] Isabella M. Graham to Janet H. Marshall, Feb. 3, 1771, Joanna Bethune, *The Unpublished Letters and Correspondence of Mrs. Isabella Graham for the Years 1767 to 1814* (New York: John S. Taylor, 1838), pp. 48-52.

[93] Brown to Gage, Nov. 12, 1770, WLCL/GP, 98.

[94] Brown to Gage, Feb. 7, 1771, WLCL/GP, 99; Gage to Bradstreet, April 8, 1771 and Gage to Brown, April 8, 1771, both WLCL/GP, 101; Abstract of Cash Disbursed, May 8, 1771, WLCL, Gage Warrants, 28:59; Gage to Brown, June 16, 1771, WLCL/GP, 104.

[95] Gage to Hillsborough, April 2, 1771, Carter, I, p. 292.

[96] Brown to Gage, Aug. 11, 1771 and Brown to Gage, Aug. 26, 1771, both WLCL/GP, 105.

[97] Computed from a compilation of Abstracts of Cash Disbursed, all WLCL, Gage Warrants, April 24, 1770 (24:114), July 22, 1770 (26:3), Sept. 22, 1770 (26:22), Oct. 29, 1770 (26:50), Jan. 31, 1771 (27:40), March 25, 1771 (30:53), May 8, 1771 (28:59), July 4, 1771 (29:3), and Dec. 25, 1771 (30:30).

[98] Ordnance Return, Sept. 2, 1774, WLCL/GP, 123.

[99] Journal of Jabez Fisher, July 21, 1773, Oneida Historical Society MSS.

[100] Lt. Col. John Caldwell to Gage, Sept. 11, 1774, WLCL/GP, 123.

[101] See "Plan of Niagara", 1771, by Lt. Francis Pfister, WLCL; also "Plan of Niagara with an Explanation of its present State," Sept. 28, 1773, by Lt. Francis Pfister, BL, Crown Maps, cxxi, 75. For a comprehensive account of events at Fort Niagara just before and during the first two years of the American Revolution see Paul L. Stevens, *A King's Colonel at Niagara, 1774-1776: Lt. Col. John Caldwell and the Beginnings of the American Revolution on the New York Frontier* (Youngstown, NY: Old Fort Niagara Association, 1987).

[102] Lt. Col. Mason Bolton to Gov. Frederick Haldimand, Sept. 18, 1778, BL, Frederick Haldimand Papers, Add MSS 21756.

[103] Barbara Graymont, *The Iroquois in the American Revolution* (Syracuse: Syracuse University Press, 1972), pp. 192-222.

[104] Capt. Diedrich Brehm to Haldimand, Aug. 2, 1779, BL, Add MSS 21759.

[105] Bolton to Haldimand, Sept. 16, 1779, BL, Add MSS 21760.

[106] See, for example, "Return of Work done in the Engineer's Department at Niagara & its Dependencies, between 25th Decr. 1780 & 24th June 1781 inclusive", June 24, 1781, BL, Add MSS 21761.

[107] Capt. Robert Mathews to Bolton, March 25, 1779, BL, Add MSS 21760; "A Plan of Niagara", n.d. [believed 1780], PRO, MPH 275; Plan, "Fort Niagara", n.d. [1781-1782], by John Luke, American Antiquarian Society, John Bradstreet Papers.

[108] Journal of John Enys, July 21, 1787, Elizabeth Cometti (ed.), *The American Journals of Lt. John Enys* (Syracuse: Syracuse University Press, 1976), pp. 144-46.

[109] "Return of Work done", June 24, 1781, BL, Add MSS 21761; "Return of Work done", June 24, 1782, BL, Add MSS 21762; "Return of Work done", June 24, 1783, BL, Add MSS 21763.

[110] "Plan of Niagara", n.d. [probably 1795], by Ens. James M. Hamilton, PRO, MPI 211; Plan of Fort Niagara, n.t., June 10, 1798, by Maj. John J.U. Rivardi, NARA, RG 77, Dr. 3, Sht. 2; "Plan of the Northern Blockhouse", June 10, 1798, by Maj. John J.U. Rivardi, NARA, RG 77, Dr. 3, Sht. 13.

[111] Observations on Niagara by Lt. Gov. John Graves Simcoe, March 24, 1794, E.A. Cruikshank (ed.), *The Correspondence of Lieut. Governor John Graves Simcoe* (5 vols.; Toronto: Ontario Historical Society, 1923-31), II, pp. 192-93.

[112] Maj. Robert Mathews to Evan Nepean, July 9, 1790, E.A. Cruikshank (ed.), *Records of Niagara: A Collection of Contemporary Letters and Documents, 1790-92* (Welland, Ontario: Niagara Historical Society, No. 41, 1930), p. 54.

[113] Journal of Thomas Hughes, Aug. 6, 1786, Thomas Hughes, *A Journal by Thomas Hughes* (Port Washington, NY: Kennikat Press, 1947), p. 151.

[114] Journal of John Enys, July 21, 1787, Cometti, pp. 144-46.

[115] La Rochefoucault, duc de Liancourt, *Travels through the United States of North America, the country of the Iroquois, and Upper Canada, in the years 1795, 1796 and 1797* (London: Phillips, 1799) quoted in Peter A. Porter, *A Brief History of Old Fort Niagara* (Niagara Falls: By the Author, 1896), p. 61.

[116] Capt. James Bruff to the Secretary of War, Aug. 20, 1796, *Philadelphia Gazette and Universal Daily Advertiser*, Philadelphia, Sept. 10, 1796.

[117] Isaac Weld, Jr., *Travels Through the States of North America and the Provinces of Upper & Lower Canada During the Years 1795, 1796 & 1797* (New York: Augustus M. Kelley, 1970), pp. 95-97.

[118] Maj. John J.U. Rivardi to Maj. Gen. Alexander Hamilton, April 3, 1799, Library of Congress, Alexander Hamilton Papers (hereafter LOC/AHP).

[119] Weld, p. 97.

[120] Dunnigan, *Glorious Old Relic*, pp. 47-48.

[121] La Rochefoucault, quoted in Porter, p. 61.

[122] Rivardi to Hamilton, April 3, 1799, LOC/AHP.

[123] Plan of Niagara, n.t., June 10, 1798, by Maj. John J.U. Rivardi, NARA, RG 77, Dr. 3, Sht. 2.

[124] "Plan of the Northern Blockhouse", June 10, 1798, by Maj. John J.U. Rivardi, NARA, RG 77, Dr. 3, Sht. 13.

[125] Rivardi to Hamilton, April 3, 1799, LOC/AHP; Plan of Fort Niagara, n.t., June 10, 1798, by Maj. John J.U. Rivardi, NARA, RG 77, Dr. 3, Sht. 13.

[126] Rivardi to Hamilton, April 3, 1799, LOC/AHP.

[127] Sec. of War James McHenry to Hamilton, July 8, 1799 and Hamilton to Rivardi, Oct. 2, 1799, both LOC/AHP.

[128] Senator Uriah Tracy to Sec. of War Samuel Dexter, Dec. 20, 1800, NARA, RG 77, Entry 221, Engineer's Book.

[129] "Statement of the Works & buildings at Fort Niagara when Majr Rivardi gave up the Command to Maj[r] Porter", n.d. [Oct. 23, 1800], Essex Institute, Moses Porter Papers; Maj. Moses Porter to Sec. of War Henry Dearborn, Aug. 10, 1803, Danvers Archival Center, Moses Porter Papers.

[130] Journal of DeWitt Clinton, Aug. 1, 1810, William W. Campbell, *The Life and Writings of DeWitt Clinton* (New York: Baker and Scribner, 1849), pp. 124-25.

[131] "Plan of Fort Niagara", n.d. [c. 1805], NARA, RG 77, Dr. 3, Sht. 1; "View of the American Garrison at Old Niagara from Lake Ontario, U.C.", July 21, 1806, by Sempronius Stretton, NAC, C18775 clearly shows the Chinese-style roof of the North Redoubt.

[132] "Plan of the Northern Blockhouse", June 10, 1798, by Maj. John J.U. Rivardi, NARA, RG 77, Dr. 3, Sht. 13.

[133] Samuel De Veaux, *The Falls of Niagara* (Buffalo: William B. Hayden, 1839), pp. 122-24.

[134] James J. Fuld and Mary Wallace Davidson, *18th-Century American Secular Music Manuscripts: An Inventory* (Philadelphia: Music Library Association, Inc.), pp. 38-47.

[135] "Plan of Niagara", n.d. [c. 1805], NARA, RG 77, Dr. 3, Sht. 1; "Plan of Niagara", Nov. 20, 1810, by A. Gray, NAC, H2/440/Niagara/1810, NMC19551.

[136] "Observations on Niagara by John G. Simcoe", March 24, 1794, Cruikshank, *The Correspondence of Lieut. Governor John Graves Simcoe*, II, pp. 192-93.

[137] Garrison Orders, Jan. 19, 1813, Archives of Ontario, Fort Niagara Order Book, 1812-13, (Hereafter FNOB), typescript, p. 29.

[138] Journal of DeWitt Clinton, Aug. 1, 1810, Campbell, pp. 124-25.

[139] Garrison Return, April [30], 1812, Buffalo and Erie County Historical Society, MSS B00-11.

[140] Dunnigan, *History and Development*, pp. 29-30.

[141] Lt. Col. Philetus Swift and Benjamin Barton to Gov. Daniel D. Tompkins, June 24, 1812, E.A. Cruikshank (ed.), *The Documentary History of the Campaign Upon the Niagara Frontier* (hereafter *DHCNF*) (9 vols.; Welland, Ontario, 1902-1908), III, pp. 71-73.

[142] Brig. Gen. William Wadsworth to Tompkins, July 6, 1812, *DHCNF*, III, p. 102; Gen. Peter B. Porter to Tompkins, July 9, 1812, *DHCNF*, III, p. 117.

[143] Ordnance Return, Dec. 31, 1811, Buffalo and Erie County Historical Society, Fort Niagara Garrison Papers, MSS A00-439; Wadsworth to Tompkins, July 6, 1812, *DHCNF*, III, pp. 101-04.

[144] Article from the *Buffalo Gazette*, *DHCNF*, III, pp. 231-32.

[145] John Melish, *Travels in the United States of America in the Years 1806 & 1807 and 1809, 1810 & 1811* (2 vols.; Philadelphia: T. & G. Palmer, 1812), II, pp. 328-30.

[146] Inspector Gen. Nicholas Gray to Tompkins, July 22, 1812, *DHCNF*, III, pp. 139-40.

[147] Col. Solomon Van Renssalaer to Abraham Van Vechten, Sept. 5, 1812, *DHCNF*, III, pp. 237-38; Lt. Col. John Fenwick to Maj. Gen. Stephen Van Renssalaer, Sept. 10, 1812, *DHCNF*, III, pp. 251-52.

[148] Stephen Van Renssalaer to Dearborn, Sept. 5, 1812, *DHCNF*, III, pp. 238-39.

[149] Solomon Van Renssalaer to Maj. Gen. Morgan Lewis, Sept. 11, 1812, *DHCNF*, III, pp. 253-55.

[150] *Ibid.*

[151] Journal of George McFeely, Nov. 14, 1812, Cumberland County Historical Society (Hereafter CCHS). This document may be found more readily in John C. Fredriksen (ed.), "Chronicle of Valor: The Journal of a Pennsylvania Office in the War of 1812", *The Western Pennsylvania Historical Magazine*, LXVII, No. 3 (July, 1984), 243-84.

[152] Solomon Van Renssalaer to Lewis, Sept. 11, 1812, *DHCNF*, III, pp. 253-55.

[153] Lt. G. Ridout to his brother, Oct. 21, 1812, *DHCNF*, IV, p. 147.

[154] For a description of the Battle of Queenston Heights see Louis L. Babcock, *The War of 1812 on the Niagara Frontier* (Buffalo: Buffalo Historical Society, 1927), pp. 35-58.

[155] For American and British accounts of this action see, respectively, Letter to the Philadelphia *Aurora*, Nov. 4, 1812 , *DHCNF*, IV, pp. 127-28 and Letter from Maj. Thomas Evans, Oct. 15, 1812, *DHCNF*, IV, pp. 108-14.

[156] Letter to the Philadelphia *Aurora*, Oct. 16, 1812, *DHCNF*, IV, pp. 127-28.

[157] *Ibid.*; "Accident at Fort Niagara", *Buffalo Gazette*, Oct. 27, 1812, *DHCNF*, IV, p. 167.

[158] Capt. Ninian Pinckney to Col. William Winder, Oct. 22, 1812, Maryland Historical Society, William Winder Papers; Winder to Brig. Gen. Alexander Smyth, Nov. 3, 1812, *DHCNF*, IV, p. 177.

[159] Journal of George McFeely, November 14, 1812, CCHS.

[160] Garrison Orders, Nov. 20, 1812, FNOB, pp. 4-5.

[161] Journal of George McFeely, Nov. 20, 1812, CCHS.

[162] Journal of George McFeely, Nov. 21, 1812, CCHS; Lt. Col. George McFeely to Smyth, n.d. [Nov. 22, 1812], *DHCNF*, IV, pp. 233-35.

[163] Lt. Col. Christopher Myers to Maj. Gen. Roger Hale Sheaffe, Nov. 22, 1812, *DHCNF*, IV, pp. 227-29.

[164] McFeely to Smyth, n.d. [Nov. 22, 1812], *DHCNF*, IV, pp. 233-35.

[165] Myers to Sheaffe, Nov. 22, 1812, *DHCNF*, IV, pp. 227-29; McFeely to Smyth, n.d. [Nov. 22, 1812], *DHCNF*, IV, pp. 233-35; Maj. Walker K. Armistead to Smyth, Nov. 22, 1812, *DHCNF*, IV, p. 227.

[166] Journal of George McFeely, Nov. 21, 1812, CCHS; McFeely to Smyth, n.d. [Nov. 22, 1812], *DHCNF*, IV, pp. 233-35.

[167] Armistead to Smyth, Nov. 22, 1812, *DHCNF*, IV, p. 227.

[168] Letter to the *Quebec Mercury*, Dec. 5, 1812, *DHCNF*, IV, pp. 277-79.

[169] Letter to the *Buffalo Gazette*, Nov. 25, 1812, *DHCNF*, IV, pp. 292-93.

[170] Letter to the *Quebec Mercury*, Dec. 5, 1812, *DHCNF*, IV, pp. 277-79.

[171] Report of April 26, 1804, quoted in Saunders, p.13.

[172] See Journal of George McFeely, CCHS, for an interesting account of the formation of the 22nd Regiment and its march to the Niagara Frontier.

[173] Garrison Orders, Dec. 10, 1812, FNOB, p. 9; Garrison Orders, March 22, 1813, FNOB, pp. 54-55.

[174] Garrison Orders, Feb. 20, 1813, FNOB, pp. 41-42.

[175] See E.A. Cruikshank, *The Battle of Fort George* (Welland, Ontario: The Niagara Historical Society, 1912).

[176] Letter to the New York *National Advocate*, June 3, 1813, *DHCNF*, V, p. 268.

[177] Babcock, pp. 77-138.

[178] Morning Report, Dec. 15, 1813, *DHCNF*, VIII, p. 279; Return of American Losses, Dec. 19, 1813, *DHCNF*, IX, p. 13.

[179] General Orders, Dec. 13, 1813, FNOB, p. 106.

[180] Garrison Orders, Oct. 22, 1813, FNOB, p. 97.

[181] Garrison Orders, Dec. 13, 1813, FNOB, pp. 106-09.

[182] General Orders, Dec. 13, 1813, FNOB, p. 106.

[183] Garrison Orders, Dec. 16, 1813, FNOB, p. 111.

[184] Lt. Col. John Harvey to Col. John Murray, Dec. 17, 1813, *DHCNF*, IX, pp. 3-4.

[185] Lt. Gen. Gordon Drummond to Sir George Prevost, Dec. 18, 1813, *DHCNF*, IX, pp. 6-8.

[186] There are quite a number of accounts of how the British gained entrance to Fort Niagara. Most agree on the main points. E.A. Cruikshank, *Drummond's Winter Campaign* (Lundy's Lane, Ontario: Lundy's Lane Historical Society, n.d.) provides a comprehensive account of the capture of Fort Niagara and subsequent events. Some of the main contemporary accounts are: Murray to Drummond, Dec. 19, 1813, *DHCNF*, IX, pp. 11-13; "The Capture of Fort Niagara", by Lt. Henry Driscoll, n.d., *DHCNF*, IX, pp. 18-20; General Orders, Dec. 19, 1813, *DHCNF*, IX, pp. 14-15.

[187] "The Capture of Fort Niagara", by Lt. Henry Driscoll, n.d., *DHCNF*, IX, pp. 18-20.

[188] Murray to Drummond, Dec. 19, 1813, *DHCNF*, IX, pp. 11-13; Diary of Charles Askin, Dec. 18-19, 1813, *DHCNF*, IX, pp. 26-29.

[189] Murray to Drummond, Dec. 19, 1813, *DHCNF*, IX, pp. 11-13.

[190] Deposition of Robert Lee, Jan. 18, 1814, *DHCNF*, IX, pp. 16-18.

[191] "The Capture of Fort Niagara", by Lt. Henry Driscoll, *DHCNF*, IX, pp. 18-20; Lt. Andrew C. Burke to Bvt. Maj. David Davies, Dec. 15, 1814, *DHCNF*, IX, pp. 297-98.

[192] Murray to Col. Edward Baynes, April 17, 1814, *DHCNF*, IX, pp. 298-300; Burke to Davies, Dec. 15, 1814, *DHCNF*, IX, pp. 297-98.

[193] Murray to Baynes, April 17, 1814, *DHCNF*, IX, pp. 298-300.

[194] *Ibid.*; Burke to Davies, Dec. 15, 1814, *DHCNF*, IX, pp. 297-98.

[195] Murray to Baynes, April 17, 1814, *DHCNF*, IX, pp. 298-300; Burke to Davies, Dec. 15, 1814, *DHCNF*, IX, pp. 297-98; "The Capture of Fort Niagara", by Lt. Henry Driscoll, n.d., *DHCNF*, IX, pp. 18-20.

[196] Returns of Killed and Wounded, Dec. 19, 1813, *DHCNF*, IX, p. 13.

[197] Drummond to Prevost, Dec. 22, 1813, *DHCNF*, IX, pp. 35-38.

[198] Maj. Gen. Phineas Riall to Drummond, March 15, 1814, *DHCNF*, IX, p. 238; Riall to Drummond, March 17, 1814, *DHCNF*, IX, pp. 240-41.

[199] Riall to Drummond, March 15, 1814, *DHCNF*, IX, p. 238.

[200] Drummond to Prevost, March 15, 1814, *DHCNF*, IX, pp. 238-39.

[201] See Saunders, pp. 8-16.

[202] Riall to Drummond, March 17, 1814, *DHCNF*, IX, pp. 240-41.

[203] Drummond to Prevost, March 22, 1814, *DHCNF*, IX, pp. 247-48; Harvey to Riall, March 23, 1814, *DHCNF*, I, pp. 3-6.

[204] Lt. Col. R.H. Bruyeres to Prevost, March 25, 1814, *DHCNF*, IX, pp. 257-58; Baynes to Prevost, n.d. [March 25, 1814], *DHCNF*, IX, p. 258.

[205] Prevost to Drummond, March 26, 1814, *DHCNF*, IX, pp. 261-62.

[206] Extract of Capt. Morton's Report on the Defences in Upper Canada, July 3, 1814, NAC, RG 8, C Series, Vol, 388, p. 139; "Sketch of Fort Niagara in its present state", July 27, 1814, by George Williams, NAC, H2/450/Niagara/1814, NMC23032.

[207] See Flemming, *Fort Mississauga, Ontario, 1814-1972*.

[208] Plan of the Mouth of the Niagara River, n.t., April 8, 1816, by G. Nicolls, PRO, MR 127.

[209] Drummond to Prevost, Sept. 21, 1814, *DHCNF*, I, p. 226; Drummond to Prevost, Sept. 28, 1814, *DHCNF*, II, p. 235.

[210] Plan of the Mouth of the Niagara River, n.t., April 8, 1816 showing Fort Niagara as it was on February 7, 1815, by G. Nicolls, PRO, MR 127.

[211] Lt. Col. Josiah Snelling to Brig. Gen. Daniel Parker, May 20, 1815, *Niles Weekly Register*, June 3, 1815, Vol. 8, No. 14, p. 237.

[212] "Fort Niagara given up", *Buffalo Gazette*, No. 188, May 23, 1815.

[213] "Little trick repeated", *Niagara Journal*, No. 22, Nov. 28, 1815.

[214] "Plan of Fort Niagara with proposed alterations", Jan. 16, 1816, by Lt. John L. Smith, NARA, RG 77, Dr. 3, Sht. 6.

[215] Dunnigan, *Glorious Old Relic*, pp. 59-64.

[216] Capt. William Gates to Brig. Gen. Daniel Parker, Sept. 5, 1815, NARA, RG 107, Letters Received by the Secretary of War, Micro 221.

[217] Maj. Gen. Jacob Brown to Sec. of War A.J. Dallas, Sept. 22, 1815, NARA, RG 107, Micro 221.

[218] Gates to Parker, April 10, 1816, NARA, RG 107, Micro 221; *Buffalo Gazette*, No. 239, May 14, 1816.

[219] Gates to Acting Sec. of War Graham, April 7, 1817, NARA, RG 107, Micro 221, Reel 73, p. 634; Journal of Joseph Delafield, Aug. 26 and Sept. 3, 1817, Robert McElroy and Thomas Riggs (eds.), *The Unfortified Boundary: A Diary of the First Survey of the Canadian Boundary Line from St. Regis to the Lake of the Woods by Major Joseph Delafield* (New York: Privately Printed, 1943), pp. 164-67.

[220] Brig. Gen. Joseph G. Swift to Lt. John L. Smith, Oct. 27, 1815, NARA, RG 77, Buell Collection of Historical Documents Relating to the Corps of Engineers; Swift to Sec. of War William H. Crawford, Nov. 30, 1815, NARA, RG 77, Entry 221, Engineer's Book, pp. 80-81.

[221] Smith to Swift, Jan. 16, 1816, NARA, RG 77, Entry 221, Engineer's Book, pp. 107-08; "Plan of Fort Niagara with proposed alterations", Jan. 16, 1816, by Lt. John L. Smith, NARA, RG77, Dr. 3, Sht. 6.

[222] Plan, "Niagara River and Fort Niagara", n.d. [c. 1816-17], by Lt. William H. Chase, NARA, RG 77, Dr. 3, Sht. 5.

[223] Swift to Crawford, May 8, 1816, NARA, RG 77, Entry 221, Engineer's Book, pp. 123-25.

[224] Swift to Sec. of War John C. Calhoun, Dec. 8, 1817, NARA, RG 77, Entry 221, Engineer's Book, p. 175; Swift to Smith, May 6, 1818, NARA, RG 77, Buell Collection.

[225] Capt. William D. Fraser to Col. Joseph G. Totten, Sept. 3, 1841, NARA, RG 77, Records of the Chief of Engineers, (Hereafter RCE), F164.

[226] *Ibid.*

[227] Ezekiel Jewett to Brig. Gen. Thomas S. Jesup, Dec. 2, 1826; Lt. Col. Alexander Cummings to Col. Roger Jones, Sept. 26, 1828; Capt. Henry Smith to Jesup, Nov. 5, 1828, all NARA, RG 92, Consolidated Correspondence File on Fort Niagara, New York (Hereafter CCF).

[228] Sgt. Francis Powley to Col. George Bamford, July 3, 1832; Jewett to Jesup, July 28, 1832, both NARA, RG 92, CCF.

[229] "A Subaltern's Furlough", *Waldie's Select Circulating Library*, Philadelphia, 1832; Undated watercolor of Fort Niagara, artist unknown, Samuel E. Weir Collection and Library of Art, Queenston, Ontario; Watercolor of St. Mark's Church and Fort Niagara, 1834, artist unknown, Niagara Historical Society, Niagara-on-the-Lake, Ontario.

[230] Lt. Amos B. Eaton to Jesup, May 29, 1834, NARA, RG 92, CCF.

[231] "Report of Expenses incurred by repairs &c during the year ending 30th of June 1837", June 30, 1837 and Capt. Samuel L. Russell to Brig. Gen. Roger Jones, July 11, 1838, both NARA, RG 92, CCF; Capt. William D. Smith to Brig. Gen. Charles Gratiot, Sept. 21, 1838, NARA, RG 77, RCE, S307.

[232] Dunnigan, *History and Development*, pp. 33-34.

[233] For a brief account of Western New Yorkers in the Rebellion of 1837 see Stuart D. Scott, "The Patriot Game: New Yorkers and the Canadian Rebellion of 1837-1838", *New York History*, LXVIII, No. 3 (July, 1987), 281-95.

[234] Charles F. Mitchell to Sec. of War Joel R. Poinsett, June 15, 1838, NARA, RG 77, RCE, M95.

[235] Nuala Drescher, *Engineers for the Public Good: A History of the Buffalo District, U.S. Army Corps of Engineers.* Buffalo: Buffalo District, U.S. Army Corps of Engineers, n.d., pp. 122-30.

[236] Smith to Gratiot, Sept. 21, 1838, NARA, RG 77, RCE, S307.

[237] *Ibid.*

[238] Col. Joseph G. Totten to Smith, Jan. 9, 1839, Old Fort Niagara Collection (Hereafter OFNC), Engineer's Journal, 1839-48; "Plan of Fort Niagara Showing the contemplated Repairs, July 1839", by Capt. William D. Smith, NARA, RG 77, Dr. 3, Sht. 14.

[239] Smith/Fraser's work at Fort Niagara is copiously documented in the "S" and "F" files of NARA, RG 77, RCE and in the OFNC, Engineer's Journal, 1839-48.

[240] Fraser to Totten, Oct. 1, 1840, NARA, RG 77, RCE, F102.

[241] Fraser to Totten, Sept. 3, 1841, NARA, RG 77, RCE, F164.

[242] *Ibid.*

[243] Claud H. Hultzén, *Old Fort Niagara: The Story of an Ancient Gateway to the West* (Youngstown, NY: Old Fort Niagara Association, 1939), p. 48.

[244] Fraser to Totten, Oct. 23, 1841, NARA, RG 77, RCE, F184.

[245] Entries for Oct., 1841 and April-Sept., 1842, OFNC, Engineer's Journal.

[246] Fraser to Totten, June 15, 1842, NARA, RG 77, RCE, F245.

[247] Fraser to Totten, Oct. 5, 1842, NARA, RG 77, RCE, F281.

[248] *The Builder's Practical Directory or Buildings for All Classes* (London: J. Hagger, 1860), p. 154; John Thomas Hurst, *A Hand-Book of Formulae, Tables, and Memoranda for Architectural Surveyors and Others Engaged in Building* (London: E. & F.N. Spon, 1882), p. 332.

[249] Fraser to Totten, Oct. 5, 1842, NARA, RG 77, RCE, F281.

[250] Entries for April-June, 1843, OFNC, Engineer's Journal.

[251] Fraser to Totten, Oct. 10, 1843, NARA, RG 77, RCE, F410.

[252] Fraser to Totten, Oct. 16, 1844, NARA, RG 77, RCE, F575.

[253] Plans and sections, "Buildings at Fort Niagara: North Block House; South Block House", Dec., 1842, by Capt. William D. Fraser, NARA, RG 77, Dr. 3, Sht. 20.

[254] Report of Asst. Surgeon John H. Bartholf, July 24, 1872, printed in *Niagara Falls Gazette*, Oct. 8, 1937, p. 35:1.

[255] Fraser to Totten, Oct. 10, 1843, NARA, RG 77, RCE, F410.

[256] Lt. Justus L. McKinstry to Jesup, Oct. 5, 1843, NARA, RG 92, CCF.

[257] Lt. Montgomery C. Meigs to Totten, Oct. 2, 1848, NARA, RG 77, RCE, M1816.

[258] Lt. John Newton to Totten, May 25, 1850 enclosing Board of Survey report of May 21, 1850, NARA, RG 77, RCE, N116.

[259] Newton to Totten, Oct. 5, 1850, NARA, RG 77, RCE, N133.

[260] Newton to Totten, July 10, 1851, NARA, RG 77, RCE, N183.

[261] Lt. Edward M. Hudson's Report on Public Buildings, May 23, 1853 and "Annual Report of Public Buildings", June 30, 1854, both NARA, RG 92, CCF.

[262] Hudson to Jesup, April 15, 1853, NARA, RG 92, CCF.

[263] See Compilation of United States Commanding Officers, OFNC.

[264] See Donald E. Loker, *Lewis Leffman, Ordnance Sergeant, U.S. Army* (Lockport, NY: Niagara County Historical Society, 1974) for an account of Leffman's long association with Fort Niagara.

[265] "A Tornado", *Niagara Falls Gazette*, April 25, 1855, p. 2:3; Estimate for repair of storm damage enclosed in Lt. Charles E. Blunt to Totten, May 15, 1855, NARA, RG 77, RCE, B6536.

[266] Blunt to Totten, Oct. 9, 1855, NARA, RG 77, RCE, B6647.

[267] Blunt to Totten, Oct. 9, 1857, NARA, RG 77, RCE; Blunt to Totten, Aug. 16, 1858, NARA, RG 77, RCE, B7843.

[268] *Niagara Falls Gazette*, Dec. 18, 1861.

[269] Drescher, pp. 139-42.

[270] Capt. John A. Tardy to Brig. Gen. RIchard Delafield, Oct. 7, 1864, NARA, RG 77, RCE, T3035; *Niagara Falls Gazette*, Oct. 15, 1862.

[271] Totten to Capt. John A. Tardy, Jr., June 17, 1863, NARA, RG 77, Letters to Engineers. Vol. 35, p. 322; Totten to Tardy, July 6, 1863, NARA, RG 77, Letters to Engineers, Vol. 35, pp. 401-14.

[272] Tardy to Delafield, Oct. 7, 1864, NARA, RG 77, RCE, T3035.

[273] "Sketch of Fort Niagara ... Showing location of proposed Light House", May 4, 1871, NARA, RG 77, Dr. 3, Sht. 45.

[274] Maj. Alexander W. Montgomery to Bvt. Maj. Gen. George H. Crosman, June 22, 1867, NARA, RG 92, CCF.

[275] Report of Asst. Surgeon John H. Bartholf, July 24, 1872, "New Light Thrown on Old Fort's History ...", *Niagara Falls Gazette*, Oct. 8, 1937, p. 35:1.

[276] Tardy to Delafield, Oct. 7, 1864, NARA, RG 77, RCE, T3035.

[277] "Annual Inspection Report of the public buildings ...", June 30, 1867, NARA, RG 92, CCF.

[278] Montgomery to Crosman, June 22, 1867, NARA, RG 92, CCF.

[279] Montgomery to Crosman, July 13, 1867, NARA, RG 92, CCF; "Plan of Southeast Block House at Fort Niagara, N.Y.", 1867, by Lt. Nelson Bronson, NARA, RG 77, Dr. 53, Sht. 3.

[280] Brig. Gen. Montgomery C. Meigs to Sec. of War Edwin M. Stanton, Aug. 7, 1867, endorsed Aug. 20, 1867, NARA, RG 92, CCF.

[281] "Annual Inspection Report of the public buildings ...", June 30, 1868 and Bvt. Maj. William T. Howell to Bvt. Maj. Gen. Rufus Ingalls, Oct. 26, 1868, both NARA, RG 92, CCF.

[282] See plan "Buildings at Fort Niagara: North Block House; South Block House", Dec., 1842, by Capt. William D. Fraser, NARA, RG 77, Dr. 3, Sht. 20; "Plan of Southeast Block House at Fort Niagara, N.Y.", 1867, by Lt. Nelson Bronson, NARA, RG 77, Dr. 53, Sht. 3; Plan, "Old Fort Niagara Restoration. Present Condition of Old Entrance Blockhouse", n.d. [c.1929], by James A. Johnson, OFNC.

[283] "Annual Inspection Report of the public buildings ...", June 30, 1868, NARA, RG 92, CCF.

[284] Annual Report of Public Buildings, June 30, 1870, NARA, RG 92, CCF.

[285] Lt. James E. Bell to Meigs, July 24, 1869 and Maj. Gen. Irvin McDowell to Meigs, July 26, 1869, both NARA, RG 92, CCF.

[286] Capt. Richard H. Jackson to Maj. Alexander Montgomery, Nov. 26, 1869, NARA, RG 92, CCF.

[287] Bvt. Maj. Stewart Van Vliet, *Outline Description of Posts & Stations of Troops in the Military Division of the Atlantic* (Philadelphia: Headquarters, Military Division of the Atlantic, Oct., 1870), p. 185. Similar opinions were expressed in the publications of 1871 and 1872.

[288] "Annual Report of Public Buildings ...", June 30, 1872, NARA, RG 92, CCF; Plan, "Old Fort Niagara Restoration. Present Condition of Old Entrance Blockhouse", n.d. [c.1929], by James A. Johnson, OFNC.

[289] "Building No. 14, Q.M. & Com. Storehouse" and "Building No. 16, Post Bakery", Post Engineer's Record Book, 1905-31, OFNC.

[290] "Building No. 32, Block House [South]" and "Building No. 33, Block House #2 [North]", Post Engineer's Record Book, 1905-31, OFNC.

[291] *Outline Description of Military Posts and Reservations in the United States and Alaska and of National Cemeteries* (Washington: Government Printing Office, 1904), p. 349; Plan, "Fort Niagara Military Reservation", *New Century Atlas* (Philadelphia, 1908).

[292] See repair records for Buildings 32 and 33, Post Engineer's Record Book, 1905-31, OFNC.

[293] See Post Engineer's Record Book, 1905-31, OFNC.

[294] Dunnigan, *Glorious Old Relic*, pp. 81-82.

[295] De Veaux, p. 120.

[296] Report of Asst. Surgeon Bartholf, July 24, 1872, *Niagara Gazette*, Oct. 8, 1937, p. 35:1; McDowell to Meigs, July 26, 1869, NARA, RG 92, CCF.

[297] Porter, pp. 51 and 82; Archer Butler Hulbert, *The Niagara River* (New York: G.P. Putnam's Sons, 1908), reprinted as *History of the Niagara River* (Harrison, NY: Harbor Hill Books, 1978), pp. 216-17; "Building No. 32 Block House" and "Building No. 33 Block House #2", Post Engineer's Record Book, 1905-31, OFNC.

[298] "As It Seems to a Man Up a Tree", *Niagara Falls Gazette*, Sept. 1, 1899, p. 2.

[299] See Dunnigan, *Glorious Old Relic*, pp. 81-82 for a brief summary of growing local interest in the history of Fort Niagara during this period.

[300] "Building No. 87 Water Filter Plant", Post Engineer's Record Book, 1905-31, OFNC.

[301] Plans, "Proposed Comfort Station, Devil's Hole State Park", Feb. 1, 1944 and "Proposed Comfort Station, Devil's Hole State Park", Nov. 15, 1950, both in the engineering office, Niagara Region, New York State Office of Parks, Recreation and Historic Preservation, Prospect Park, Niagara Falls, New York.

[302] "Building No. 32 Block House" and "Building No. 33 Block House #2", Post Engineer's Record Book, 1905-31, OFNC.

[303] Dunnigan, *Glorious Old Relic*, pp. 82-86.

[304] Percy Morgan to Henry W. Hill, Oct. 3, 1921, Percy Morgan Papers, OFNC.

[305] Hill to Morgan, Oct. 6, 1921 and Morgan to Peter A. Porter, Feb. 25, 1922, both Percy Morgan Papers, OFNC.

[306] Sen. James W. Wadsworth, Jr. to Percy Morgan, April 13, 1922, Percy Morgan Papers, OFNC.

[307] Edward T. Williams, *An Interpretation of Old Fort Niagara* (Youngstown, NY: Old Fort Niagara Association, 1929), pp. 66-69.

[308] *Ibid.*, pp. 69-72; See also Dunnigan, *Glorious Old Relic*, pp. 88-99 for an overview of the formation of the Old Fort Niagara Association and the search for funding to restore the French Castle.

[309] Estimate of Repairs to Seawall and Buildings, July 29, 1922, Old Fort Niagara Association Correspondence (hereafter OFNAC).

[310] Colonel Ralph E. Ingram to Commanding General, 2nd Corps Area, Aug. 5, 1927, OFNAC.

[311] Board Meeting Minutes, Jan. 9, 1928, Old Fort Niagara Association Minutes (hereafter Minutes), I, p. 22.

[312] Board Meeting Minutes, Nov. 23, 1928, Minutes, I, p. 46; Semi-annual Report of Officers and Executive Committee, Nov. 23, 1928, Minutes, I, p. 55.

[313] Executive Committee Minutes, Dec. 4, 1928, Minutes, I, p. 56.

[314] Board Meeting Minutes, May 7, 1929, MInutes, I, pp. 67-68.

[315] "Suggested Program of Work to be Done at Old Fort Niagara", June 6, 1929, OFNAC.

[316] Executive Committee Minutes, June 11, 1929, Minutes, I, p. 74; Claud H. Hultzén to Col. George E. Stewart, July 5, 1929, OFNAC.

[317] Board Meeting Minutes, June 26, 1929, Minutes, I, p. 78.

[318] William W. Kincaid to Secretary of War, Sept. 7, 1929, OFNAC.

[319] Stewart to Commanding General, 2nd Corps Area, Nov. 30, 1929, OFNAC.

[320] Alfred G. Adams to Kincaid, Dec. 10, 1929, OFNAC.

[321] Board Meeting Minutes, Jan. 7, 1930, Minutes, I, p. 84; "Report of Restoration of Old Fort Niagara", April 30, 1930, OFNAC; Annual Meeting Minutes, June 21, 1930, Minutes, I, p. 98.

[322] Plan, "Old Fort Niagara Restoration. Present Condition of Old Entrance Block House", n.d. [c.1929], by James A. Johnson, OFNC.

[323] Project Estimates, Dec. 7, 1929, OFNAC; Special Board Meeting Minutes, May 31, 1939, Minutes, II, pp. 314-15.

[324] "To Discuss Plans for Completion of Fort Restoration", *Niagara Falls Gazette*, March 28, 1930, p. 24:1.

[325] "Suggested Program of Work to be Done at Old Fort Niagara", June 6, 1929, OFNAC.

[326] Kincaid to the House Sub-Committee on Military Appropriations, Dec. 13, 1929, OFNAC.

[327] Kincaid to Sen. Royal S. Copeland, Dec. 18, 1929; Kincaid to Congressman S. Wallace Dempsey, Dec. 18, 1929; Hultzén to Kincaid, Dec. 19, 1929, all OFNAC.

[328] Draft Bill, n.d. [Dec., 1929?], OFNAC.

[329] Transcript of Discussion of War Department Appropriation Bill, 1931, n.d. [Dec., 1929], OFNAC.

[330] Col. P.W. Guiney to Adjutant General John H. Shuman, Jan. 7, 1930; Shuman to Commanding General, 2nd Corps Area, Jan. 24, 1930; Maj. Gen. H.E. Ely to Commanding Officer, Fort Niagara, N.Y., Jan. 28, 1930, all OFNAC.

[331] Brig. Gen. H.F. Rethers to Shuman, Jan. 18, 1930, OFNAC.

[332] Kincaid to Frank Steele, Jan. 28, 1930, OFNAC.

[333] Amendment to H.R. 7955, Jan. 6, 1930, OFNAC.

[334] War Department Appropriation Bill for 1931, April 21, 1930; Congressman John Taber to Kincaid, May 26, 1930; Brig. Gen. L.H. Bash to Quartermaster, 2nd Corps Area, June 3, 1930, all OFNAC.

[335] Executive Committee Minutes, June 18, 1930, Minutes, I, p. 95; Annual Meeting Minutes, June 21, 1930, Minutes, I, p. 98.

[336] Kincaid to Maj. Gen. C.F. Summerall, July 11, 1930, OFNAC.

[337] "Statement re Funds Appropriated by Congress and raised by the Association", Oct. 18, 1930, OFNAC.

[338] Copeland to Kincaid, Jan. 29, 1931 with enclosed Military Appropriation Bill, 1932, OFNAC.

[339] "Delegation to Urge That Governor Give Consent to Measure", *Niagara Falls Gazette*, April 23, 1931, p. 1:1.

[340] "Report on Construction", May 20, 1932, OFNAC.

[341] Executive Committee Minutes, Nov. 12, 1930, Minutes, I, p. 103; Lt. E.R. Stevens to Hultzén, Nov. 14, 1930, OFNAC.

[342] Report of the President at Annual Meeting, June 20, 1931, Minutes, I, p. 133; Executive Committee Minutes, Aug. 12, 1931, Minutes, I, p. 137; Hultzén to Paul J. Speyser, Sept. 22, 1931, OFNAC.

[343] "Estimate of Work Contemplated ... During the Fiscal Year 1931", Jan. 8, 1930, OFNAC.

[344] Stevens to Hultzén, Nov. 14, 1930, OFNAC.

[345] "Estimate of Work Contemplated ... During the Fiscal Year 1931", Jan. 8, 1930, OFNAC.

[346] Untitled rendering of Gate of the Five Nations, 1930, by James A. Johnson, OFNC.

[347] Untitled plan of Fort Niagara, n.d. [1759], probably by Lt. Thomas Sowers, PRO, MPG 342.

[348] Capt. John Brown to Maj. Gen. Thomas Gage, March 28, 1768, WLCL/GP, 75.

[349] "Plan of Niagara with an Explanation of its present State", Sept. 28, 1773, by Lt. Francis Pfister, BL, Crown Maps, cxxi, 76.

[350] See "Elevation, Plan and Section of the New Draw-Bridge built at Niagara, 1769", by Capt. Thomas Sowers, BL, Crown Maps, cxxi, 77; Mabel B. Goshorn to Kincaid, Jan. 18, 1931, OFNAC.

[351] Stevens to Hultzén, Nov. 14, 1930, OFNAC.

[352] "Tabulation of Projects to be Carried on in the Restoration of Old Fort Niagara", Jan. 14, 1932, Minutes, I, pp. 148-49.

[353] "Report on Construction", May 20, 1932, Minutes, I, pp. 152-55.

[354] Report of the President at the Annual Meeting, July 15, 1933, Minutes, I, pp. 181-82.

[355] Report of Claud H. Hultzén, Sept. 10, 1934, Minutes, I, following p. 200; "List of Materials Required for Various Proposed Projects at Old Fort Niagara", n.d. [1933-34], OFNAC.

[356] "Schedule of Guns for Old Fort Niagara, N.Y.", March 7, 1931; Kincaid to Adjutant General, His Majesty's Forces in Canada, March 5, 1931, both OFNAC.

[357] Kincaid to Francis Bannerman & Son, Sept. 13, 1930, OFNAC.

[358] Kincaid to Adjutant General, His Majesty's Forces in Canada, March 5, 1931, OFNAC.

[359] "Report of Activities", March 17, 1931, Minutes, I, pp. 118-19; "Report of Operations", Aug. 20, 1931, Minutes, I, pp. 140-41.

[360] "Blockhouse, Barns Burned", *Niagara Falls Gazette*, Aug. 18, 1933; Hultzén to Commanding Officer, Fort Niagara, Aug. 19, 1933 and Hultzén to Chief Howard Pierson, Aug. 19, 1933, both OFNAC.

[361] Merle S. Clark to Brian Leigh Dunnigan, October, 1983, Merle S. Clark file, Old Fort Niagara Oral History Collection.

[362] "Blockhouse, Barns Burned", *NIagara Falls Gazette*, Aug. 18, 1933.

[363] Hultzén to Pierson, Aug. 19, 1933, OFNAC.

[364] Lease Between the Secretary of War and the Old Fort Niagara Association, March 6, 1931, Minutes, I, pp. 120-22; Hultzén to Commanding Officer, Fort Niagara, March 31, 1931, OFNAC.

[365] A.E. Peterson to Hultzén, Aug. 31, 1933 and Loss Endorsements and Receipts, Nov. 6, 1933, all OFNAC.

[366] Hultzén to Capt. McKeever, Sept. 12, 1933, OFNAC; Executive Committee Minutes, Nov. 28, 1933, Minutes, I, p. 191.

[367] "List of Materials Required for Various Proposed Projects at Old Fort Niagara", n.d. [1933-34], OFNAC.

[368] "Ancient Blockhouse Used as Press Room", *Buffalo Evening News*, Sept. 5, 1934.

[369] Report of the President at the Annual Meeting, Sept. 10, 1934, Minutes, I, following p. 200.

[370] "Estimate of the Expenses of the Works at the Forts in the District of New York for 1766", May 9, 1766, WLCL/GP, 51.

[371] "Plan of the Fortifications of Niagara ...", n.d. [1768], by Capt. Thomas Sowers, plan in the British War Office, Caxton House, London in 1929 and now believed lost.

[372] "Section and Elevation of a Stone Redout", n.d. [1770], attributed to Capt. John Montresor, BL, Crown Maps, cxxi, 78.1.

[373] Journal of Jabez Fisher, July 21, 1773, Oneida Historical Society MSS; "State of the Guns, Carriages, Mortar Beds Mounted for the Defence of the Garrison of Niagara", Sept. 2, 1774, WLCL/GP, 123.

[374] Bolton to Haldimand, July 15, 1779, BL, Add MSS 21760.

[375] See Return of Ordnance, Jan. 1, 1783, BL, Add MSS 21817 and "Return of Ordnance appropriated for the post of Niagara ...", Jan. 1, 1794, NAC.

[376] Weld, p. 95.

[377] "Return of Ordnance & Military Stores ...", Dec. 31, 1810, BECHS, MSS BOO-11; "Return of Ordnance & Military Stores ...", Dec. 31, 1811, BECHS, MSS AOO-439; Brig. Gen. William Wadsworth to Tompkins, July 6, 1812, *DHCNF*, III, pp. 101-04.

[378] "Plan of the Northern Blockhouse", June 10, 1798, by Maj. John J.U. Rivardi, NARA, RG 77, Dr. 3, Sht. 13.

[379] Col. Solomon Van Renssalaer to Gen. Morgan Lewis, Sept. 11, 1812, *DHCNF*, III, pp. 253-55.

[380] Wadsworth to Tompkins, July 6, 1812, DHCNF, III, pp. 101-04 lists six brass six-pounders. On December 19, 1813, the British captured ten brass and four iron six-pounders in Fort Niagara. Return of Ordnance Captured at Fort Niagara, Jan. 10, 1814, PRO, CO 42/156, p. 343, micro B-129 in the NAC.

[381] Letter to the Philadelphia *Aurora*, Oct. 16, 1812, *DHCNF*, IV, pp. 127-28.

[382] Garrison Orders, Nov. 20, 1812, FNOB, pp. 4-5; Journal of Lt. Col. George McFeely, Nov. 20-21, 1812, CCHS.

[383] Garrison Orders, Dec. 13, 1813, FNOB, pp. 106-09; Burke to Davies, Dec. 15, 1814, *DHCNF*, IX, pp. 297-98.

[384] Extract of a Letter from Kingston, Upper Canada, March 7, 1814, *DHCNF*, IX, pp. 214-15.

[385] Drummond to Prevost, March 15, 1814, *DHCNF*, IX, pp. 238-39.

[386] "Sketch of Fort Niagara", July 6, 1814, by George Williams, NAC, H2/450/Niagara/1814, NMC23032.

[387] Plan, "State of Fort Niagara in Feby 1815", by G. Nicolls, inset on an untitled plan of the mouth of the Niagara River, April 8, 1816, by Nicolls, PRO, MR 127.

[388] A 5 1/2-inch howitzer is shown mounted on the roof of the French Castle in "Sketch of Fort Niagara", July 6, 1814, by George Williams, NAC, H2/450/Niagara/1814, NMC23032. It is likely that this gun was later moved to one of the redoubts.

[389] Fraser to Totten, Sept. 3, 1841, NARA, RG 77, RCE, F164.

[390] "Statement of Ordnance & platforms at Fort Niagara, June 30th, 1864", enclosed in Tardy to Delafield, Oct. 7, 1864, NARA, RG 77, RCE, T3035.

[391] Montgomery to Crosman, June 22, 1867, NARA, RG 92, CCF.

SOURCES

Manuscripts

Archives of Ontario, Toronto, Ontario.
Fort Niagara Order Book, 1812-13 (typed copy of original).
Elizabeth Simcoe Sketchbooks.

American Antiquarian Society, Worcester, Massachusetts
John Bradstreet Papers.

British Library, London, England
Crown Map Collection.
Frederick Haldimand Papers, Add. MSS 21661-21892.

Buffalo and Erie County Historical Society, Buffalo, New York
Fort Niagara Garrison Papers, MSS A00-439.
Manuscript Collection, B00-11.

William L. Clements Library, Ann Arbor, Michigan
Thomas Gage Papers, American Series.
Thomas Gage Papers, Warrants.
Map Collection.

Cumberland County Historical Society, Carlisle, Pennsylvania
Journal of Lt. Col. George McFeely.

Danvers Archival Center, Danvers, Massachusetts
Moses Porter Papers.

Detroit Public Library, Burton Historical Collections, Detroit, Michigan
George Duffield Papers, Correspondence of the Graham and Bethune Families.
John Porteous Papers.

Essex Institute, Salem, Massachusetts
Moses Porter Papers.

Library of Congress, Washington, DC
Alexander Hamilton Papers.

Maryland Historical Society, Baltimore, Maryland
William Winder Papers.

National Archives of Canada, Ottawa Ontario
MG 18, Gaspard-Joseph Chaussegros de Léry. *"Traité de Fortifications divisé en huit livres ..."*, 1714, unpublished manuscript.
RG 8, C Series, Vol. 388.
National Map Collection.

National Archives and Records Administration, Washington, DC
RG 77, Buell Collection of Historical Documents Relating to the the Corps of Engineers.
RG 77, Corps of Engineers Reports, 1812-23 ("Engineers' Book", Entry 221).
RG 77, Letters to Engineers.
RG 77, Records of the Chief of Engineers.
RG 77, Fortification Map File.
RG 92, Records of the Quartermaster General, Consolidated Correspondence File, Fort Niagara, NY.
RG 107, Letters of the Secretary of War.

New York State Office of Parks, Recreation and Historic Preservation, Niagara Region Office, Niagara Falls, New York
Engineering Map Collection.

Niagara Historical Society, Niagara-on-the-Lake, Ontario
Iconography Collection.

Old Fort Niagara Association, Youngstown, New York
Engineer's Journal, 1839-48.
William Wallace Kincaid Papers.
Percy Morgan Papers.
Old Fort Niagara Association Correspondence, 1922-39.
Old Fort Niagara Association Minute Books, 1927-1988.
Oral History Collection, Merle S. Clark (1983-88).
Post Engineer's Record Book, 1905-31.
Post Letter Books.

Oneida Historical Society, Utica, New York
Journal of Jabez Fisher.

Public Record Office, Kew, England
C.O. 42/156 (micro B-129 in National Archives of Canada).
Jeffery Amherst Papers, W.O. 34.
Map Collection.

Samuel E. Weir Collection and Library of Art, Queenston, Ontario.
Iconography Collection.

Printed Sources, Documents and Contemporary Writings

Bethune, Joanna. *The Unpublished Letters and Correspondence of Mrs. Isabella Graham for the Years 1767 to 1814.* New York: John S. Taylor, 1838.

British Army Lists. London: War Office, 1759; 1763; 1768.

The Builder's Practical Directory or Buildings For All Classes ... London: J. Hagger, 1860.

Burton, Clarence M. (ed.). *Journal of J.L. of Quebec, Merchant.* Detroit: Society of Colonial Wars of the State of Michigan, 1911.

Campbell, William W. *The Life and Writings of DeWitt Clinton.* New York: Baker and Scribner, 1849.

Carter, Clarence Edwin (ed.). *The Correspondence of General Thomas Gage With the Secretaries of State, and with the War Office and Treasury, 1763-1775.* 2 vols., New Haven: Yale University Press, 1931.

Cometti, Elizabeth (ed.). *The American Journals of Lt. John Enys.* Syracuse: Syracuse University Press, 1976.

Cruikshank, E.A. (ed.). *The Correspondence of Lieut. Governor John Graves Simcoe.* 5 vols.; Toronto: Ontario Historical Society, 1923-31.

Cruikshank, E.A. (ed.). *Documentary History of the Campaign Upon the Niagara Frontier.* 9 vols., Welland, Ontario, 1902-08.

Cruikshank, E.A. (ed.). *Records of Niagara: A Collection of Contemporary Letters and Documents, 1790-92.* Welland, Ontario: Niagara Historical Society Publication No. 41, 1930.

De Veaux, Samuel. *The Falls of Niagara.* Buffalo: William B. Hayden, 1839.

Fredriksen, John C. (ed.). "Chronicle of Valor: The Journal of a Pennsylvania Officer in the War of 1812", *The Western Pennsylvania Historical Magazine,* LXVII, No. 3, July, 1984, 243-84. Journal of Lt. Col. George McFeely.

Grant, Mr. "Journal From New York to Canada, 1767", *Proceedings of the New York State Historical Association,* XXX, 1932, 181-96 and 305-22.

Hughes, Thomas. *A Journal by Thomas Hughes*. Port Washington, NY: Kennikat Press, 1947.

Hurst, John Thomas. *A Hand-Book of Formulae, Tables, and Memoranda for Architectural Surveyors and Others Engaged in Building*. London: E. & F.N. Spon, 1882.

Izard, Ralph. *An Account of a Journey to Niagara, Montreal and Quebec in 1765*. New York: William Osborn, 1846.

Le Blond, M. *The Military Engineer: or, A Treatise on the Attack and Defence of All Kinds of Fortified Places*. London: J. Nourse, 1759.

Lochée, Lewis. *Elements of Field Fortification.* London: By the Author, 1780.

McElroy, Robert and Riggs, Thomas (eds.). *The Unfortified Boundary: A Diary of the First Survey of the Canadian Boundary Line from St. Regis to the Lake of the Woods by Major Joseph Delafield*. New York: Privately Printed, 1943.

Mahan, D.H. *A Complete Treatise on Field Fortification, With the General Outlines of the Principles Regulating the Arrangement, the Attack, and the Defence of Permanent Works.* New York: Greenwood Press, reprint of 1836 edition.

Melish, John. *Travels in the United States of America in the Years 1806 & 1807 and 1809, 1810 & 1811; Including an Account of Passages Betwixt America and Britain and Travels Through the Various Parts of Great Britain, Ireland and Upper Canada.* 2 vols.; Philadelphia: T. & G. Palmer, 1812.

Mereness, Newton D. (ed.). *Travels in the American Colonies.* New York: The Macmillan Co., 1916. Contains the journal of Lord Adam Gordon.

Muller, John. *A Treatise Containing the Elementary Part of Fortification, Regular and Irregular.* London: J. Nourse, 1774.

Muller, John. *A Treatise Containing the Elementary Part of Fortification, Regular and Irregular.* London: J. Nourse, 1782.

New Century Atlas. Philadelphia, 1908.

O' Callaghan, E.B. (ed.). *Documents Relative to the Colonial History of the State of New York.* 15 vols., Albany: Weed, Parsons & Co., 1856-87.

Outline Description of Military Posts and Reservations in the United States and Alaska and of National Cemeteries. Washington: Government Printing Office, 1904.

Outline Descriptions of the Posts and Stations of Troops in the Geographical Divisions and Departments of the United States. Washington: Government Printing Office, 1872.

Outline Description of U.S. Military Posts and Stations in the Year 1871. Washington: Government Printing Office, 1872.

Scull, G.D. (ed.). "The Montresor Journals", *Collections of the New-York Historical Society for the Year 1881.* New York: The New-York Historical Society, 1882.

Severance, Frank H. (ed.). "Gen. Brown's Inspection Tour Up The Lakes in 1819", *Publications of the Buffalo Historical Society,* XXIV, 1920, pp. 295-323.

Smith, Captain George. *An Universal Military Dictionary.* London: J. Millan, 1779. Reprint by Museum Restoration Service, Ottawa, 1969.

Sullivan, James and Hamilton, Milton W. (eds.). *The Papers of Sir William Johnson.* 14 vols., Albany: University of the State of New York, 1921-65.

Tompkins, Daniel D. *Public Papers of Daniel D. Tompkins, Governor of New York, 1807-1817.* Albany: J.B. Lyon Co., 1902.

Van Vliet, Bvt. Major Stewart. *Outline Descriptions of Posts & Stations of Troops in the Military Division of the Atlantic.* Philadelphia: HQ, Military Division of the Atlantic, October, 1870.

Weld, Isaac Jr. *Travels Through the States of North America and the Provinces of Upper & Lower Canada During the Years 1795, 1796 & 1797.* 2 vols., New York: Augustus M. Kelley, 1970. Reprint of 1807 edition.

Newspapers and Magazines

Buffalo Gazette, Buffalo, New York, 1812-22.

Buffalo News, Buffalo, New York.

Courier-Express, Buffalo, New York.

Daily Cataract, Niagara Falls, New York.

New York Mercury, New York, New York, 1769-71.

Niagara Falls Gazette, Niagara Falls, New York.

Niles Weekly Register, Baltimore, Maryland.

Philadelphia Gazette and Universal Daily Advertiser, Philadelphia, Pennsylvania, 1796.

Waldie's Select Circulating Library, Philadelphia, Pennsylvania, 1832.

Secondary Sources

Babcock, Louis L. *The War of 1812 on the Niagara Frontier.* Buffalo: Buffalo Historical Society, 1927.

Betsch, Maj. W.H. "The Defenses of Oswego", *Proceedings of the New York Historical Association*, XIII, 1934, 108-27.

Brown, George W. (ed.). *Dictionary of Canadian Biography.* 12 vols., Toronto: University of Toronto Press, 1966- .

Cruikshank, E.A. *The Battle of Fort George.* Welland, Ontario: The Niagara Historical Society, 1912.

Cruikshank, E.A. *Drummond's Winter Campaign.* Lundy's Lane, Ontario: Lundy's Lane Historical Society, n.d.

Drescher, Nuala. *Engineers for the Public Good: A History of the Buffalo District, U.S. Army Corps of Engineers.* Buffalo: Buffalo District, U.S. Army Corps of Engineers, n.d.

Dunnigan, Brian Leigh. *Glorious Old Relic: The French Castle and Old Fort Niagara.* Youngstown, NY: Old Fort Niagara Association, 1987.

Dunnigan, Brian Leigh. *History and Development of Old Fort Niagara.* Youngstown, NY: Old Fort Niagara Association, 1985.

Flemming, David. *Fort Mississauga, Ontario, 1814-1972.* Ottawa: Parks Canada, 1982.

Fuld, James J. and Davidson, Mary Wallace. *18th-Century American Secular Music Manuscripts: An Inventory.* Philadelphia: Music Library Association, Inc.

Furness, Gregory and Titus, Timothy. "Master Plan for Crown Point State Historic Site", Waterford, NY: New York State Office of Parks, Recreation and Historic Preservation, December, 1985.

Graymont, Barbara. *The Iroquois in the American Revolution.* Syracuse: Syracuse University Press, 1972.

Hulbert, Archer Butler. *The Niagara River.* New York: G.P. Putnam's Sons, 1908. Reprint retitled *History of the Niagara River.* Harrison, NY: Harbor Hill Books, 1978.

Hultzén, Claud H. *Old Fort Niagara: The Story of an Ancient Gateway to the West.* Youngstown, NY: Old Fort Niagara Association, 1939.

Loker, Donald E. *Lewis Leffman, Ordnance Sergeant, U.S. Army.* Lockport, NY: Niagara County Historical Society, 1974.

McConnell, David. "A Study of the British Military Buildings at Niagara-on-the-Lake, Ontario, 1814-1837", Manuscript Report Series, National Historic Parks and Sites Branch, Parks Canada, No. 191, Ottawa, 1977.

Porter, Peter A. *A Brief History of Old Fort Niagara.* Niagara Falls, NY: By the Author, 1896.

Rifkind, Carol. *A Field Guide to American Architecture.* New York: New American Library, 1980.

Robinson, Willard B. *American Forts; Architectural Form and Function.* Urbana: University of Illinois Press, 1977.

Saunders, Ivan J. "A History of Martello Towers in the Defence of British North America, 1796-1871", *Canadian Historic Sites: Occasional Papers Archaeology and History, No. 15.* Ottawa: National Historic Parks and Sites Branch, Parks Canada, 1976, pp. 5-169.

Scott, Stuart D. "The Patriot Game: New Yorkers and the Canadian Rebellion of 1837-1838", *New York History*, LXVIII, No. 3 (July, 1987), 281-95.

Severance, Frank H. *An Old Frontier of France.* 2 vols.; New York: Dodd, Mead and Company, 1917.

Stevens, Paul L. *A King's Colonel at Niagara, 1774-1776: Lt. Col. John Caldwell and the Beginnings of the American Revolution on the New York Frontier.* Youngstown, NY: Old Fort Niagara Association, 1987.

Stotz, Charles Morse. "Defense in the Wilderness", *The Western Pennsylvania Historical Magazine*, XLI, Nos. 3-4, Autumn, 1958, 57-197.

Strach, Stephen. *The British Occupation of the Niagara Frontier, 1759-1796.* Niagara Falls, Ontario: Lundy's Lane Historical Society, 1976.

Williams, Edward T. *An Interpretation of Old Fort Niagara.* Youngstown, NY: Old Fort Niagara Association, 1929.

Young, Richard J. "Blockhouses in Canada, 1749-1841: A Comparative Report and Catalogue", *Canadian Historic Sites, Occasional Papers in Archaeology and History, No. 23.* Ottawa: National Historic Parks and Sites Branch, Parks Canada,1980, pp. 5-116.

ACKNOWLEDGEMENTS

Unraveling the history and architectural development of Old Fort Niagara's redoubts has been a gradual process, conducted over a period of years. During the course of researching and writing this publication, the author received support, encouragement, inspiration, and sound advice from many institutions and individuals. Special thanks are due the *Architecture, Planning and Design Program* of the *New York State Council on the Arts* which provided partial funding for printing the finished work. In this, as in their other programs designed to encourage the arts in New York, the members of the Council's staff have been uniformly helpful and enthusiastic. Particular thanks to *Buff S. Kavelman* whose job it has been to "shuffle off to Buffalo" to review project proposals in Western New York.

Gathering information on the redoubts has involved nearly a decade of seeking sources on all aspects of the history of Fort Niagara. Staff members of numerous repositories of historical documents have provided guidance, services and tips on potential sources of information. Particular thanks to the *William L. Clements Library*, the *University of Michigan Libraries*, the *National Archives and Records Administration*, the *Local History Department, Niagara Falls Public Library*, and the *Buffalo and Erie County Historical Society*.

Many people have been particularly helpful in ferreting out important information. *John Harriman* has aided in this project as in all of the research conducted by this author in Ann Arbor. *John Larson* and *Betty Phippen*, faithful and enthusiastic Old Fort Niagara Association library workers, have organized clippings and photographs to the point where they are easy to use in research projects of all kinds. *Thomas Ciampa*, *Maurice O'Brien* and *Joseph Thatcher* of the New York State Bureau of Historic Sites have participated in research-gathering trips and provided constant aid with the technical and material culture aspects of research on Old Fort Niagara's buildings and fortifications. Assistance in locating sources has also come from staff members of other institutions, notably *Dennis Carter-Edwards* of the Canadian Park Service, *Scott S. Sheads* of Fort McHenry National Monument and Historic Shrine and *Phil Porter* of the Mackinac Island State Park Commission. *Jim Kimball* of the State University College of New York at Geneseo kindly shared information on his fascinating discovery of John Carroll's Fort Niagara music book. Special thanks also to *Merle S. Clark*, formerly of the 28th U.S. Infantry and now of Pueblo, Colorado, for his voluminous and lively correspondence giving accurate details and very human anecdotes about garrison life at Fort Niagara between 1931 and 1934.

Other colleagues, friends and relatives read copy and made valuable suggestions. Thanks to *Sue Allen*, *Candice C. Dunnigan*, *Dorothy Jane Dunnigan*, and *James P. Dunnigan*. Also to *Dennis Farmer*, Curator of Old Fort Niagara, for his sound advice and his sketches of the redoubts showing how their appearance has changed over the years.

Production of this and the other Old Fort Niagara publications would not have been possible without the dedication of the Publications Committee and especially the tireless activity of its Chairman, *Harry M. DeBan*. Harry's participation has always gone far beyond committee work, for he has designed and laid out every publication since the program was initiated in 1985. Thanks also to *David J. Bertuca* who helped us become at least semi-literate on a new computer system obtained through the efforts of many generous supporters of the Old Fort Niagara Association.

Finally, no acknowledgement would be complete without a "thanks" to all the other members of the Old Fort Niagara Association staff, particularly Assistant Director *Elizabeth M. Diachun*, who patiently survive the author's moods during production of a publication and keep the twentieth century existence of an Old Fort functioning smoothly.

Niagara Region masons repoint the southeast facade of the South Redoubt in the summer of 1986. *OFN 5100/28C.*